SHADOWLAND

I am forgotten, shadow only, gone.

A.P., 'The Prisoner' (trans. Naomi Reiss)

It is said that no one truly knows a nation
until one has been inside its jails.

Nelson Mandela

SHADOWLAND

THE STORY OF GERMANY TOLD BY ITS PRISONERS

SARAH COLVIN

REAKTION BOOKS

For Cary Parker and Christopher Parker-Colvin:
partners in metaphorical crime

Published by
Reaktion Books Ltd
Unit 32, Waterside
44–48 Wharf Road
London N1 7UX, UK
www.reaktionbooks.co.uk

First published 2022

Printed and bound in Great Britain by TJ Books Ltd, Padstow, Cornwall

A catalogue record for this book is available from the British Library

ISBN 978 1 78914 627 1

Contents

Preface

No one knows where I am right now, I realize. People at work, my employer, my customers, my wife, my parents, my friends . . . a whole list of names and faces. When will they start to wonder where I am?[1] I get out of the bus and see grey walls, barbed wire, doors made of steel. They take us to a cell, our names are called. It's a while before they call me. Some of the faces are white, two people are trembling.[2] *It will be one of the hardest days in your life, and you'll never, ever forget those prison gates closing behind you.*[3] I feel terrible and the lump in my throat just gets bigger and bigger. Then it's my turn.

Put your personal things
– clothes too –
on the table.
Undress!
Now?
Here?
Yes!
Come on, I bet you're not usually this shy.[4]

I peel off my jeans, coat, shirt, socks. Hesitate. 'Everything!' I pull down my boxer shorts and put them with the other things. Naked in a room full of monitors and bored prison officers.[5] They take me into another cell. There I have to get undressed and my clothes get searched again. I have to bend over and pull my arse cheeks apart. I have to lift my testicles. I have to pull my toes apart. *Then they give you a package*

Prison cell, Hamburg, 2006.

wrapped in blankets . . . You take it and follow the officer until he opens a cell door, and you have to go inside.[6] The number of my cell is 172, my prison number is 357/9. The officer just unlocks the cell and checks with me that nothing is broken and everything is there. Then he locks the door behind me. My first moment alone in a prison cell.

Foreword

Prisons reflect society and society needs to take a long, sober look in the mirror.
UK prisoner, writing to *Inside Time*, 2017

Prisons are in crisis. The world's prison population is rising faster than its general population; prison has become an industry and in overcrowded, understaffed conditions violence levels are rising. The United States holds more than 2 million of the world's 11 million people in prison, and China holds 1.65 million, or 2.3 million if you also count people held in detention centres.[1] In South America the prison population has almost trebled since 2000.[2] Even in Germany, which is low on the list of the world's most carceral states (taking 171st place out of 223 countries),[3] a 'new punitivity' has led to longer sentences and a sharp rise in the number of people in prison.[4] Keeping people in prison is hugely expensive while its efficacy remains unproven ('Some people just learn to be better criminals in here,' said the prisoner Oliver in 2016).[5]

In the context of the often violent and disturbing stories that follow it is worth remembering that Germany currently locks up far fewer people, in generally better conditions and with better human rights, than (for example) the UK or USA. German nationals in prison in the Federal Republic have the right to vote, for example, unlike people in prison in the United States or UK. The incarceration rate in England and Wales, at 130 per 100,000 in June 2021, approaches double Germany's rate of 69 per 100,000; the USA tops the charts with

638 per 100,000.[6] Recently a prisoner union was founded by people in prison in Germany, focused on issues such as fair pay and pensions. The National Society for the Prevention of Torture (Nationale Stelle zur Verhütung von Folter) visits and reports each year on a sample of institutions across Germany, most recently on conditions during the COVID-19 pandemic.

> *On the one hand there is no one better qualified than a prisoner to report on prison; on the other hand there is no one more partial.*[7]
>
> Hans Kaltenbach, 1957

This is not a systematic history of German prisons. It is the story of Germany told, as far as possible, in the words of people in prison. 'I always say that "prison is the mirror of our society",' wrote Ewald, serving time in North Rhine–Westphalia: 'People society doesn't want to see get locked away. But nobody wants to know how many of those people were made that way by society.'[8] 'Prison is just a magnifying mirror,' agreed the novelist and prisoner Peter Feraru. By that logic people in prison are neither better nor worse than society – like the rest of us, they *are* society.

More normally, people outside encounter the stories of famous or notorious prisoners. This book tells the stories of the 'little people' in prison. Most are or were serving time for crimes committed against a background of unemployment and poverty or the desire to participate in consumer culture. Some of the men were punished for being homosexual, particularly in post-war West Germany, where consensual sex between adult men became legal only in 1969 (it was formally legalized in East Germany in 1968, but the paragraph forbidding gay sex was not enforced after 1957).

Inevitably, some people's stories are missing. I have relied heavily on people's capacity to write their accounts down; but around 20 per cent of the people held in German prisons are illiterate,[9] and not everyone who is literate speaks German or is comfortable writing in German. Not everyone wants or feels able to tell their story. Even though women make up only a small percentage of people in prison, there are a good number of women's voices collected in this book. But there are strikingly few stories about the experience of disabled people, whose presence in prisons is often overlooked, or about what it means to be elderly in prison. Black people, people of colour and white people in prison tell their stories here; however, many of the writers prefer not to use their names (anonymity, pseudonyms and initials are common), and one cannot always know who is speaking.[10] Many describe what the historian Mary Fulbrook calls 'dissonant lives', and I have tried to respect disruption and dissonance in the stories, and not to smooth it over in the interests of telling a 'better' story of my own.[11]

I have focused on the topics and themes that occur most regularly in stories from German prisons across the decades. People in prison have something to say that society outside needs to hear – ideally without demonizing, and without romanticizing. One writer in prison noticed the impulse his readers had to see him 'as an exotic being', or even to admire his criminal status.[12] Valorizing outsider status is a luxury of those who are safely embedded in the mainstream. Prison is a precarious place and houses people who have had precarious lives. Their vision is often of finding a safe space for themselves. 'I hope one day I'll have a wife and children and my own home – maybe even a little car out front. That's my dream,' said Dietmar. 'What I really want, in plain language, is to be boring and middle-class.' Tom shared that dream: 'my hopes for the future are really bourgeois. I want a little house with a garden. With my partner and our kids. Somewhere quiet. A job like the one I'm training for, where I can help other people. I want to give something back.'[13]

But who goes to prison, and why?

I used to think I was poor,
Then I was told
I wasn't poor,
but needy.
Then I was told it was
self-destructive
to think of myself as needy –

I was deprived.
Then I was told that
deprivation had a bad image –
I was underprivileged.
Then I was told that underprivileged was overused –
I was disadvantaged.
Then they said, disadvantaged
meant avoiding responsibility –
I was socially weak.
Then I found out that socially weak was mega-out –
I was precarious.
In Wanne-Eickel I heard I lacked
opportunities to participate.
I must say, I still
don't have a cent in my pocket,
but my vocabulary has been enriched
enormously![14]
Anon., 2017

People are supposed to be incarcerated not because of who or what they *are* but because of things they *do*. It is not quite that straightforward, of course. The criminologist Dario Melossi defines criminality as 'behavior seen as threatening to the dominant group interests'.[15] That complicates the idea that it is only about what we do. It is also about whether it is in the interests of government and society to prosecute what we do as criminal (hence the otherwise inexplicable fact that very powerful people sometimes seem to get away with murder, while our prisons are full of people from socially disempowered backgrounds).

Being a woman is, statistically speaking, an effective way to avoid prison – women make up only between 2 and 9 per cent of the prison population globally.[16] (Before 1989, being a woman in East Germany was less effective as a way of avoiding incarceration, however – proportionally twice as many women went to prison in the communist East as in the West.)[17] In June 2019, 94 per cent of the nearly 65,000 people in German prisons were men. Being trans is an urgent reason to avoid prison, as the disturbing stories of Esmeralda and Michelle reveal later in this book. An online guide has now been published for transgender people in German prisons, with advice on how to stay safe and have their gender identity recognized within the system.[18]

Education matters: in 2013 nearly 60 per cent of men in custody in Germany had either no school-leaving qualification or the most basic one (*Hauptschulabschluss*).[19] But so does your resident status: a survey of the federal states in February 2019 revealed a 50 per cent rate of people without German citizenship in prison in the city-states of Hamburg and Berlin, and one-third in North Rhine–Westphalia (compared to a non-nationals rate of about one in ten people in prison in the UK and one in twenty in the USA).[20] The most frequently represented nationalities among non-German prisoners were Polish, Tunisian, Libyan and Georgian; there are also stateless people in prison. Some commentators explain the overrepresentation of people with a 'migration background' in the criminal justice system by their failure to integrate; others have seen it as a result of trauma in people who came to Germany from a conflict zone. But Thomas Galli, a former prison governor who is now one of Germany's leading critics of incarceration, has swung the spotlight around to point to failings in Germany society and in the criminal justice system.[21]

Not all migration backgrounds are the same, of course: 'The most effective way to avoid prison is to be white and middle class,' as the editors of the Berlin prison newspaper *Lichtblick* summarize the situation. When white middle-class people do find themselves in prison, they regularly express surprise at the way things have gone for them. 'My family background is really unusual for a con,' Jürgen explained. 'My father was always employed . . . My mother was a housewife who looked after her five children very well.' Aneta similarly felt that she 'didn't belong' in prison because she had had a good childhood and education.[22]

Many people in prison are survivors of physical and sexual violence: a team of researchers in England interviewed men categorized as dangerous offenders, and found that they took childhood abuse practically for granted. A few of the men could look back on a relatively problem-free childhood – and described that with puzzlement, as 'something of a mystery'.[23]

A lot has happened to me in my life. It started with my step-grandfather, who sexually assaulted me when I was eight years old.[24]

Stefanie, 2003

In 2018 more than half of the women in prison in Europe had been sexually abused, and nine out of ten had been physically assaulted. 'Almost all women in prison have experienced violence and abuse,' writes Sabine Bomeier, herself a former prisoner.[25] More often than not, women serve short sentences for non-violent offences that are drug- or poverty-related, or both. In Germany, argues Bomeier, some women are effectively forced into petty crime by parsimonious benefit payments – 'especially if their partner insists on having the lion's share of what they get every month for himself. And that's not unusual.' While it is very rare for women to commit violent crimes, when they do, they are harshly judged. 'A real man is expected to hit out from time to time,' Bomeier explains. 'A woman in prison is more likely to be seen as a kind of beast.' When women hit out, culture wallows in fantasies of 'female Rambos behind bars'. In reality, writes Bomeier, women in prison struggle with guilt and shame. They are, in Ann Lloyd's words, 'doubly deviant' and 'doubly damned'.[26]

I don't know how I'll deal with it if one day my children ask me why I abandoned them.[27]

Nancy, 2016

Their guilt is often linked to their children, who are almost always left behind. Prisons struggle, apparently helplessly, to accommodate motherhood – in Germany in 2020 there were only 68 places in secure units for mothers with children (and one father–child unit, in Waldheim prison in Saxony). Some of those units only take babies and toddlers, others permit children up to school age (but never beyond). 'My middle child is fifteen today and I'm not there! Do I even still exist?' worried Karina. When her first grandchild was born, the absence became unbearable. 'I haven't seen her yet, haven't smelled

Saying goodbye in Munich-Stadelheim women's prison.

her. Haven't had her in my arms . . . I can't stand another minute of being cut off like this'.[28]

According to a twenty-first-century report for the European Parliament, prisons are still 'essentially designed, built and run by men for men'.[29] Women's prisons are few and far between, and their geographical scatteredness can mean impossibly long journeys for visiting families. Where specialized facilities for young male offenders are standard, facilities designed for young women and girls are like hen's teeth. Prison is supposed to prepare people to re-enter society and employment, but professional training and education often falls short, especially for women. Women with families who fulfil the conditions for open custody can qualify for the quaintly named 'housewife release' – *Hausfrauenfreigang* – spending their daytime hours at home and returning to prison in the evening.[30]

> *A lot of women think through properly, for the first time, why it is that they're in prison . . . Lots of them come to a sense, for the first time, that what they did wasn't right. And a lot of them are then very sorry for the things they did.*[31]
>
> Katharina, 2010

At some point almost all prisoners in the German criminal justice system will be released, and it is a core aim of the system to encourage people in prison to take responsibility for their actions and feel empathy with their victims. Contemporary Germany has a large and active victim support network, and meetings between perpetrators and victims (using the model of restorative justice) have had positive results for both sides.[32] And still, it is sometimes hard to forgive. Petra, whose young son was sexually abused, admitted that her life became ruled by anger when the abuser was released with a suspended sentence after only three months in prison. 'That situation and this anger I still feel has turned the last year upside down for me. I stopped caring about anything and became apathetic,' she explained. 'I hope my life is going to get better soon and that this anger I feel is gradually going to get less.'[33]

Petra was herself in prison at the time of writing. To recognize how many people in prison are victims as well as perpetrators is not to diminish victims of crime. 'I'm in prison,' wrote Sabine, who participated in the same writing project as Petra, 'and there are too many victims in here. About a quarter of them turned into perpetrators and hurt other people. Others turned on themselves and are being punished for it, again and again. Because they took refuge in drugs and alcohol. Because they couldn't bear to feel any more.'[34]

> *In here everyone has to look after themselves, and use prison as an opportunity . . . to get off drugs, to stop drinking, to sort out a messed-up body or to get mentally more stable . . . to survive this unhealthy prison unscathed.*[35]
>
> Dieter Wurm, 2012

Some people arrive in prison with a physical or psychiatric illness. But there is also evidence that prison makes you sick. Social isolation exacerbates mental illnesses, and poor hygiene and drug abuse allow infectious diseases like hepatitis and HIV to thrive. People in prison are high-risk for tuberculosis: 71 cases were identified in Berlin prisons between 2015 and 2019. Addictive disorders are common and so are sexually transmitted diseases, fungal infections, skin conditions, allergies and heart problems.[36] Officers as well as prisoners are affected by the stress of the environment: German workers average fifteen days of sick leave per year, where prison officers average more than 32 days.[37]

Some people use drugs to alleviate the pain, loneliness, frustration or boredom of prison. In 2016, 5.5 kg (12 lb) of cannabis, 56 g (2 oz) of heroin and 89 g (3 oz) of cocaine were found in Berlin's prisons, and more than a third of people in custody had a substance addiction. In a German prison, a recent prison guidebook advises, 'you can get pretty much everything, drug-wise, that you can get on the street: hashish, of course, but also speed, heroin, cocaine, subutex and a raft of others. Naturally they are more expensive in prison than on the street.'[38] Some institutions have a methadone programme.

I speak of . . .
The prisoner who felt so great that
one morning he was hanging from the window grate.[39]
Gilbert Koester, 1982

The suicide rate 'inside' is far higher than in the general population. In 2018 there were 140 deaths in German prisons, 58 of them by suicide. 'There are three where I know that it worked,' reported Jumbo. 'No one gives a monkey's – they're just cons.' Prison slang even has its own words for suicide: 'sich weghängen' or 'sich wegmachen' (in English prison argot, 'doing the Dutch'). Suicides in prison look to have almost doubled during the COVID-19 pandemic.[40]

Self-harm can land you in what prisoners call the *Bunker*, and the authorities an enhanced security cell (*besonders gesicherter Haftraum* or BGH; in England called a CSU or Care and Separation Unit): a segregated space, often containing no more than a mattress and a WC.[41] Sometimes the light is left on all night; sometimes it is switched on at intervals. Officially the 'lights check' is a safeguarding measure, but the people subjected to repeated blasts of light throughout the night describe it as sleep deprivation or even torture. There is no radio, music or television, and you spend your yard time alone except for a guard. People who have spent longer periods in isolation report nervousness, mood swings and loss of concentration; there can be hallucinations, loss of appetite, sickness and diarrhoea, and apathy. Amnesty International has deplored solitary confinement on numerous occasions.[42]

> *A man in isolation is condemned to waste away . . . held in storage like an object for which there is no further use.*[43]
>
> Ivan Jelinic, 1999

Some solitary cells are clinically clean, but many are not. In 2011 Germany's National Society for the Prevention of Torture criticized a youth prison where the solitary cell was found to be in 'an unhygienic, disgusting condition', its foam mattress covered with dead insects. 'The toilet and the drinking water tap were utterly filthy.' Records showed it was in frequent use. In 2020 the same organization noted that secure isolation cells still only had a mattress on the floor, and no other furniture at all – not even a chair. One state ministry of justice had responded that prisoners wishing to sit down could use the mattress on the floor and lean against the wall.[44]

PREVENTIVE DETENTION

> *We don't know when*
> *We don't know where*
> *We don't know how*
> *We don't know if*
> *We don't know why*
> *We don't know how long*
> *But we think we know that.*[45]
>
> Helmut Pammler, 2008

Preventive detention keeps people in custody indefinitely, if they are still deemed dangerous at the end of their sentence. Germany's use of preventive detention has been criticized by the European Court of Human Rights. It is a legally problematic practice because it detaches incarceration from punishment for a specific crime; for that reason it is not supposed to be punitive, even though detainees are still held in regular prisons. But there is another group of people whose imprisonment is unconnected to crime or punishment: deportation detainees. Deportation detention is used to hold people who have been denied asylum until their deportation can be arranged. They cannot legally be held in regular prisons, and Germany now has a dozen or so specialist detention centres. At the time of writing, the number is growing.

this fearful awareness that the door is closed,
that I've been locked in.[46]

Prisons divide into open institutions (for people not regarded as an urgent danger or as likely to escape) and closed prisons (for everyone else). The benefits of open prisons are widely recognized, but closed institutions are the norm: currently Germany has around 180 prisons, of which only about thirty are either open or have mixed (open and closed) facilities. For people who have never been locked in, it is difficult to imagine being stuck behind a door that has no handle. When Hurricane Katrina hit New Orleans in 2005, around six hundred prisoners were left locked in their cells without food or water while staff abandoned the building. Some were not evacuated for four days, when the floodwaters had reached chest level in the ground-floor cells. In 2018, in Berlin's biggest prison, a man set fire to his cell; a cell neighbour described being locked in as the heat and toxic smoke started to spread. 'I had to stay in my cell for 45 minutes after the fire broke out. They only got us out then. I was panicking. There was smoke rising in my cell and I thought I was going to suffocate.'[47]

For people who are locked in, sounds from outside the cell acquire an almost intolerable importance: 'the door only opens when a bunch of keys rattles; that noise gets burned so deeply into your brain that you react to any high rattling noise with a fiercely beating heart. You're Pavlov's dog,' one anonymous writer observed. 'Every time they woke me, the noises were what broke me,' rapped another. Marianne Herzog, who was held in solitary confinement in the early 1970s, described feeling the effects even post-prison: 'I've only noticed how deeply that enters your soul since I've been outside. It still shakes me when I hear the sound of a cell door being opened on TV.'[48]

Pre-trial and convicted prisoners in Germany are supposed to have single-occupancy cells – but the reality is different. Sharing a cell means using a WC that is often only screened off, and being subject to other people using it ('what's really indescribable is when you're eating and the other guy sits down on the can,' said Rainer). It means sharing your days, nights and the television controls with someone whose tastes and habits might be very different from yours. One man requested solitary confinement for fear that he would 'wipe the walls' with his cellmate, who watched television endlessly while he wanted to read. When nerves are frayed, cells are dangerous places. So are shower rooms, which have no video surveillance. 'We're behaving like animals – we're merciless. It might be because I've been in here for eight months now. No sport, no group activities, just 23 hours a day in the cell,' wrote Jumbo in 2016. 'That gives you an appetite for violence.'[49] In that volatile situation, he remembered, the supervising officers had helpfully provided tip-offs about which inmates had convictions for child abuse.

She never yelled. She never made mock of a prisoner . . . When she was on duty, the corridors were calm. You were the exception, Frau Rudolph.

Prison officers deserve a book of their own.[50] At the time of writing, prisons across Germany are severely understaffed, even though a German study carried out in 2010–11 concluded that the relationship between people in prison and prison officers is key to the climate of a prison.[51] The story of Germany told by its prisoners often features officers acting as they ought not to – administering illicit night-time beatings, passing information about child abusers to volatile residents, discrediting those who complain. Brutal prison guards are central to stories from East Germany. But there are stories of good officers, too. Even in the harsh culture of GDR prisons, some guards chose to help and support their charges. One East German woman, who gave birth in prison and had her baby taken from her, still remembers the guard who secretly brought her news of her daughter and even smuggled in a photograph.[52] In post-war West Germany, the convicted terrorist Marianne Herzog described Frau Rudolph:

> She never yelled. She never made mock of a prisoner.
> She unlocked the door when we rang. She never rattled her
> keys unnecessarily. When she was there, there was justice.
> When she was on duty, the corridors were calm. You were
> the exception, Frau Rudolph.[53]

More recently, in a letter to a prison newspaper, a woman who had just been moved from Aichach prison in Bavaria to Chemnitz in Saxony expressed amazement at the culture change. She was flabbergasted to find that the officers in Chemnitz treated her 'with politeness and respect'. The studied disrespect and chicanerie that she had come to expect in Aichach dropped away. 'Nothing was deliberately forgotten or overlooked,' she wrote in wonderment. 'Embarrassing and humiliating incidents were a thing of the past.' The importance of that was profound. 'Suddenly I was a human being again, with dignity and a meaning.'[54]

One of the more frequent and unsettling stories told is of officers who abuse the fact that their version of events will almost always be believed over a prisoner's. According to the sociologist Howard Becker, there is a 'hierarchy of credibility', where the highest-status group has the right to be believed. Having power, agrees the lawyer Catharine MacKinnon, 'means, among other things, that when someone says, "This is how it is", it is taken as being that way'. Powerlessness, by contrast, 'means when you say "this is how it is", it is not taken as being that way'.[55] For people in prison that has day-to-day consequences.

> he wakes up
> blood testifies
> to their treatment
> the taut swelling bruises
> from the humane system
> a calming cell

in tender shade of green
rounded corners
and a shit-hole in the floor
the prisoner
caused injuries to himself[56]

In this poem by Peter Dittrich, the officers (whose voices we hear at the end) blame the prisoner for his own bruises – and know they will be believed. 'The people out there, on the other side of the wall, never believe a word we say,' agreed a man serving life in the early 1970s. Michelle, a transgender prisoner, never reported her rape in prison in the 2000s, which was coordinated by a duty officer. 'Why would I?' she commented. 'No one would have believed me anyway.'[57] Brigitte and Heinz Kübbeler, who interviewed dozens of people in prison in the early 2000s, remember how some prison officers warned them not to believe everything their interviewees told them. At the same time the interviewees assured them that all prison officers told lies.[58]

FOR MOST READERS of this book, Germany probably feels close enough to home for its systems to seem familiar, but far enough away (perhaps) to make the reading of the stories that follow bearable. Most of us prefer to believe we live in a (more or less) rational modern democracy. But stories from prisons say: *this is not the country you thought it was.*

I'm struggling to believe this kind of thing still happens in Germany.[59]
Karina, 2010

The story as I am telling it begins in 1945, in a defeated country on the edge of social and legal collapse. Orphaned and abandoned children slept in the woods, stealing and scavenging, often laying the foundations for a 'criminal career'. The Allies focused on liberating the Nazi concentration camps and securing Germany's prisons ('the prison guards were old Nazis,' one man reported – 'a real truncheon

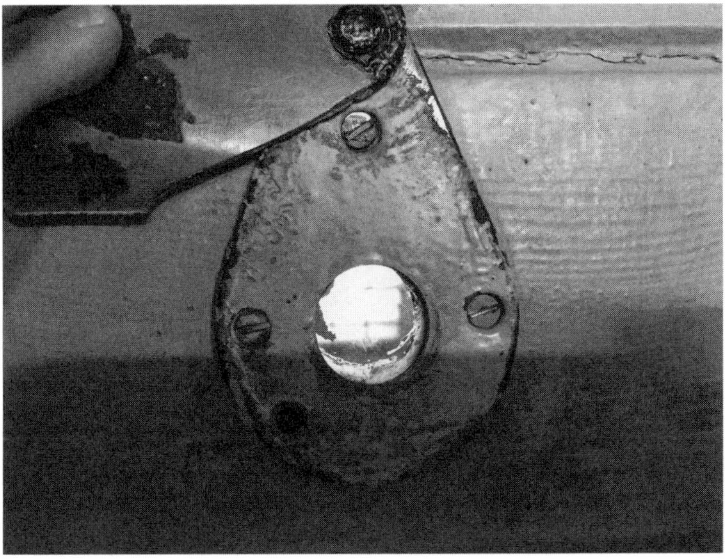

Cell door at Stasi prison.

brigade'). In the eastern zone, Soviet Special Camps were established, where hundreds of thousands froze, starved or died of beatings or tuberculosis. The camps were dissolved with the foundation of the German Democratic Republic (East Germany) in 1949; but its secret police, the Stasi, would have its own interrogation centres and torture facilities within the 'big prison' of a walled-in nation. Meanwhile, in West Germany, a grand prison reform was in planning that would erect, in the words of one prisoner, 'little asbestos walls in Hell'.[60]

Then, in 1990, German unification offered the opportunity for a new start. The Scorpions (and many with them) sang of the wind of change. But how strongly did it actually blow on the inside?

Part I

Unity, Rights and Freedom: West Germany, 1949–68

Human dignity is inviolable.
(Constitution of the Federal Republic of Germany of 1949, §1)

Human dignity goes to the Devil the moment you put on prison clothes.
(Anon., 1971)

1

A New Start?

It was war, and we were poor.
In those days, in Germany, there was nothing to eat.[1]

'Misery all around! Father was smoking blackberry leaves.' A former soldier, writing from prison, described coming home in 1945. 'There was nothing to eat but corn.' Another had fought in the First World War. 'Both of the world wars we lost produced a whole new kind of criminality,' he remembered. 'There was no work to be had.' He had been decommissioned from the army in 1918, but never managed to find a foothold. He spent the rest of his life in and out of prison.[2]

Germany surrendered unconditionally in May 1945, but a guide to dealing with its prisons had already been issued to the Allied troops in March. The *Technical Manual for Legal and Prison Officers after the Surrender of the German Army* instructed unit commanders to take control of any prison installation they came across. Death penalties were to be suspended and corporal punishment stopped.[3] As soon as a prison was secured, its supervision could be turned over either to a temporary director, or to a 'T-Force' unit – trained to take control of sensitive information and institutions. Inmates were assessed and political prisoners were discharged; 'bona fide criminals' were not. In November 1945 the Office of Military Government, United States (OMGUS) issued Directive 19, 'Concerning Principles for Administration of German Prisons.' Drafted after discussions between the four Allied powers, Directive 19 established two key principles:

Berlin, 1945 – the search for food.

first, there must be no arbitrary punishment but 'the exact execution of the sentences imposed'. Second, the aim of prison was 'the rehabilitation and reformation of the offender'.[4] It was reinstating priorities the Nazis had swept from the table.

Myrl E. Alexander was a prison warden in Danbury, Connecticut, when he was sent to administer prisons in the American zone in 1945. For eleven months the man who would later head the entire U.S. prison service was chief of prisons in occupied Germany. In an interview published in 1991, he recalled co-drafting Directive 19. But the rehabilitation of people in prison was not his most pressing concern at the time, he remembered. Nine million refugees from Eastern Europe had sharpened the (already intense) pressure on food and fuel supplies in the post-war chaos, and Alexander found himself struggling to provide the most basic necessities for the prisoners in his charge. Food rations for all Germans had been mandated at seven hundred calories per day, and people outside prison could supplement that by scavenging and growing food. People in prison could not, and were starving. Coal shortages meant prisons hit freezing point in the winter of 1946. That combination of icy temperatures and undernourishment led to a spate of illnesses and deaths, and Alexander decided to make an urgent appeal to the U.S. military authorities. If they did not help, he told them, the American-administered prisons would soon be compared with Nazi concentration camps. His rhetoric worked: 'boom', he recalled, food and fuel arrived.[5]

Alexander's memories are broadly positive. He recollects how, under the guiding hand of the Allies, conditions in German prisons became 'really outstanding' relative to prisons in America.[6] But others found the hand of the occupying forces less benign. August Klemp, who had discovered his father smoking blackberry leaves, had been freed in 1945 by Allied troops from a concentration camp where he was interned for military disobedience. But by 1948 he was back in custody – his erstwhile liberators needed someone to confess to a murder, and Klemp had known the victim. He remembered how U.S. military policemen beat him for an hour and a half. Then they made him stand barefoot on a metal bar for two hours, and beat him again. 'I had no idea what it was about . . . I just knew: if you don't sign they're going to beat you to death.' So he put his name to a confession. Eleven days later he was allowed to see a doctor, who acknowledged his bruises but attributed his loosened teeth to a vitamin deficiency: 'Lots of people have it these days.' In court, the same military policemen swore he made his confession voluntarily. Klemp was in prison for murder from 1949 (when the Federal Republic was founded) until he received a pardon in 1971.[7]

> *Lots of the prison guards were old Nazis, right through the 1950s. A real truncheon brigade.*[8]

Prisons, determined Directive 19, had to be staffed by 'physically fit and unprejudiced persons not suspected of Nazism'. Under Myrl Alexander, the Americans dismissed 90 per cent of prison officers and education staff because of their Nazi connections – but in the French sector, only 10 per cent of staff had to leave. Some were replaced with people who had been sacked by the Americans.[9]

West Germany's post-war Chancellor, Konrad Adenauer, had championed the reintegration into post-war society of ordinary people who had 'gone along' with Hitler, urging the nation to 'make an end of this sniffing around for Nazis'. A tranche of civil servants returned to public positions. By 1965, 60 per cent of West Germany's military officers and two-thirds of its judges were men who had formerly served in the Third Reich.[10] Adenauer's Secretary of State, Hans Globke, had been one of Hitler's senior advisers and co-authored a commentary on the Nuremberg Laws. Globke's history was exposed by the news magazine *Der Spiegel* in 1956, but that did not prevent him, in 1963, from being awarded one of the nation's highest honours: the Order of Merit of the Federal Republic of Germany.

Continuity, rather than change, is the leitmotif in stories from the post-war prison. The young Jürgen Callberg was sentenced to life imprisonment in 1958 for causing the death of a policeman in a car chase. Conditions smacked of the old regime. 'Back then we had to traipse around in wooden clogs, whatever the weather, and keep a distance of at least two metres from the man in front,' he told journalists in the 1970s. 'No one was allowed to talk. In winter it was harsh, with no coats, no gloves, no scarves. We weren't allowed to put our hands in our pockets.' Callberg had been born in 1936 and grew up in the Third Reich. 'German boys don't cry! German boys are hardy and brave,' he remembered being taught. Later he watched American Wild West films featuring hardy, brave men who did not cry: 'those trapper heroes. Hard men who drink hard liquor, and drinking made you hard . . . so I drank.'[11] In Nazi Germany, men's social power depended on tough masculine behaviours – and from Jürgen Callberg's perspective that had not changed in the mid-century USA or the new Federal Republic.

One interviewee remembered the prison chaplain who under Hitler had accompanied prisoners to their executions – 'I didn't trust him.'[12] Another man wrote a radio play in prison, telling the story of the fictional Berger, who as a boy had spent time in a Nazi borstal. On a prison transport between institutions, the now-adult Berger has a flashback to that time, triggered when he recognizes the driver of the transport van. It is the same man who transported him into youth custody in Hitler's Germany. Then an obedient follower of Hitler, the man is now an obedient servant of the Federal Republic. 'I do my duty,' he tells Berger, 'and commit no criminal offences.'[13]

In other areas, too, continuity seemed to prevail.

For homosexuals in Germany – the FRG – the Third Reich still exists!

Overseeing a post-surrender Germany, the Allies left the criminal code (based on the old German Imperial Code of 1871) largely in place. They removed elements introduced by the Nazis, such as the term *Volksschädling* (a dehumanizing word meaning social pest or parasite), and castration as a penalty for sex offenders. But Section 175, which had criminalized homosexuality in men since 1871, remained on West Germany's statute book until 1969 and sent thousands of men to prison because they had consensual sex.[14]

For the gay prisoner E. B. that raised questions about the new Republic.[15] How different was it really from the Nazi state? 'I'm just reading about the cruelty and criminal violence suffered by many thousands of homosexuals in the concentration camps,' he wrote, 'and I ask myself: when a state adopts such macabre laws, stained with the blood and fear of beaten, tortured, mutilated and murdered homosexual people, does it not under current law become guilty by association of those same crimes?'[16] He was writing to the prison campaigner Birgitta Wolf, born Duchess von Rosen in Sweden, who had moved with her German husband to the Black Forest in 1933, where she started a quiet campaign to help people incarcerated under the Nazis. Her aunt, Carin von Kantzow, had until her death in 1931 been married to Hermann Göring, the creator of the Gestapo – the family connection to a senior Nazi left the young Birgitta relatively protected. Still, she took risks – like hiding three Jewish women in

Birgitta Wolf (second from left) with Mary von Rosen, Herman Göring and Eric von Rosen, 1933.

her home near Garmisch-Partenkirchen towards the end of the war.[17] After 1945 she focused her energy on campaigning for prison reform, and regularly took people released from prison into her home. In the course of her life Wolf received thousands of letters from people in prison and former prisoners, and responded to most of them.

Another of her correspondents, E. E., was 51 when he wrote to her. As a gay man he had spent a total of 28 years in prison under two regimes. E. E. grew up in the interwar period, with an alcoholic father who beat his mother. 'You, dear lady,' he told Wolf, 'will be able to see into the depths of my life and ask yourself if it is still a life, and whether I alone am responsible for my cursed deeds'. E. E. had grown up in Weimar Berlin, and the older boys on his street 'soon noticed my inclination', he told Wolf, 'and with promises and threats they got me to give them everything and submit to them. Those were all "normal" boys!' The German capital of the 1920s and early 1930s, as described by Christopher Isherwood in his Berlin stories, had become a place for sexual adventures. E. E. describes a subculture in which he still found protection as 'a pretty boy and a bedtime companion for a lot of actors, Nazi politicians, and "great men" of society'. He first came before a court in 1935, and was able to charm the judge: 'my first juvenile judge, Dr Br., took a fancy to my member – so the trial ended "fairly" for me! In Berlin's legal circles that judge was known as "Madame". I'm not accusing anyone,' he added, 'just trying to show who made me what I am.'[18]

But even powerful subcultures offer only limited protection. Nazism was already suppressing the burgeoning sexual freedom of Weimar Germany. Some powerful men still felt safe – Ernst Röhm, the commander of the SA, was well known to be gay. Then, during the Night of the Long Knives on 30 June 1934, Röhm and other Nazis suspected of homosexuality were murdered by members of the SS and Gestapo. E. E., who describes himself as Röhm's 'lust boy', remembers escaping death only narrowly. He was arrested by the Gestapo, who took him to their headquarters in Berlin's Prinz-Albrecht-Strasse. 'I was made to perform abnormal sexual acts.' His story glosses over the details of what exactly the Gestapo did to him that night: 'They decided I was a *Schweinehund* and should be treated like one. I can't tell you what they made me do for them or the things they did to me.' But he does tell Wolf how, two years later in Spandau prison, a police inspector forced him to masturbate naked, and beat him while he did it. Later he was sent to a concentration camp, where he was

Gestapo headquarters, Prinz-Albrecht-Strasse, Berlin.

yet again sexually abused by officers of the state who identified publicly as heterosexual. From E. E.'s perspective in a post-war Federal Republic, sexual hypocrisy had weathered all the political changes. 'I could name names among my bedfellows of people who are still big players now – lawyers, doctors, actors, and prominent Nazis!'[19]

Where Myrl Alexander had once used the spectre of being compared to the Nazis to shame the U.S. military authorities into sending food and fuel into prisons, E. E. in his letter to Birgitta Wolf shamed the new Federal Republic by pointing to continuity, not change. 'For homosexuals in Germany – the FRG – the Third Reich still exists!'[20]

nobody understands what this is like

'I'm embarrassed to say that I'm homosexually inclined. I can't express how much that makes me suffer,' wrote E. A., 32 years old at the time of writing and a former prisoner. 'I always keep poison in the house because one day it's all going to come crashing down around my ears, and then I'll have what I need – for nobody understands what this is like.'[21] This was, after all, West Germany in the late 1960s, where the rhetoric of homophobia was still publicly acceptable. In 1967 Dietrich Rollmann, a Conservative member of the parliamentary Committee for Prison Reform (Sonderausschuß für die Strafrechtsreform), edited a paperback for the prominent publishing house Fischer that focused on the state of the penal system and the case for reform. Seeking the prisoner's-eye view, he invited a man in penal servitude, Günther Koepping, to contribute an essay. Koepping took the opportunity to complain about gay inmates. Without explicitly using the Nazi terminology of degeneracy and parasitism, he painted a picture of gay men in prison as carriers of a 'perverse sexual infection' and rotten to the core. They had, he declared, been rightly criminalized for indulging their passions, and now posed a permanent threat to other prisoners.[22]

E. E. had issued a robust challenge to the legitimacy of the new Republic in the face of §175, but his story concludes less confidently. 'No law, no prison, not even castration can help us,' he told Wolf. 'The – absolutely – only solution is to renounce the urge voluntarily. But that can only be done in full devotion to Christ. And that has been my path.' Wolf illustrated the tragic outcomes of anti-gay prejudice by publishing the final correspondence she received from E. C., a former prisoner who had written her more than a hundred letters. 'I've tried everything to give my life a decent purpose and to get free of the past, but I haven't succeeded,' he wrote. 'Please forgive me – but the most sensible thing is to put an end to this life that was no longer a life.' On receipt of the letter, Wolf immediately called an ambulance – but it was too late. E. C. had already left his lodging and was later found dead in a hotel room, shot through the mouth: '*He lived three more agonizing hours before death ended his suffering*,' Wolf recorded sadly in an editorial note.[23]

IT WAS NOT Birgitta Wolf's intention to give a voice to people who had committed crimes in the service of the Nazi state. But she read and replied to every letter she received from prison, apparently even to a letter from Gerhard Sommer, the 'hangman of Buchenwald' (as he had requested, she arranged for him to be visited by a Jewish professor).[24] One of her published collection of letters from prison contains a short section called 'Gestapo Crimes', which includes a letter she received from J. A., a low-ranking officer in the Gestapo who had given himself up in May 1945. At the time of writing he had been in prison for 23 years.

J. A.'s story exemplifies what Hannah Arendt in 1963 would call the 'banality of evil'.[25] Born in the first decade of the twentieth century, he chose to become a policeman, and began his professional career in the Weimar Republic. He joined the Nazi Party in 1932 and got a position in the secret police after Hitler's government was elected in 1933. He claims to have seen no reason to abandon his chosen career because of a change in government. 'I was trained as a policeman in a democratic state and I served that state for 4½ years,' he told Wolf, 'so it was my conviction that the orders I was given were right and proper. I had no reason to doubt it in the years between 1928–33, nor during the years of the 3rd Reich.' His career path included promotions within the SS. Following an injury, he was given a desk job in

Caricature of the Gestapo's creator, Hermann Göring.

the Gestapo's Jewish Department (Judenreferat) in 1942 – 'it was one of the less pleasant Departments to work in,' he admitted to Wolf. And still, he claimed, 'my activity was grounded in law and the result of obedience to state authority.' He treads uncomfortably around the mass deaths in Auschwitz. 'My superiors always told me that the Jews in the camps had a very hard life – so the number of deaths that were registered could be seen as normal.' He put it to Wolf that as a 'little man' he had to do as he was told, or else risk consequences not only for himself, but for his wife and children. 'If I had failed to obey orders that would certainly have resulted in prosecution and conviction in a court martial . . . or my immediate execution. Those measures would have had consequences for my family – *Sippenhaft*.'[26] (Nazi *Sippenhaft* involved the families of people accused of crimes against the state being arrested and even executed.)

More than two decades spent in a Federal German prison seemed to have done little to persuade J. A. that his actions as a Gestapo officer were truly culpable. In his letter to Wolf he presents himself as a victim, not a perpetrator. The Federal Republic did not practise *Sippenhaft*, but from J. A.'s perspective his wife and children were being punished with him. They were ineligible for social security, 'because the city of Frankfurt am Main does not allocate monies to support the families of political criminals' – West Germany, he implied, was punishing not only convicted criminals, but their families, just as the Nazi state had.

'There is no doubt at all that J. A. was culpable,' wrote Wolf in an editorial note. But she simultaneously nudged her readers to recognize that Federal Germany might also be culpable, not least of practising class-based justice. '*To date, the superior officer who issued his orders has not been prosecuted; he is living as a free man*,' she noted drily.[27]

BY 1963 WOLF had exchanged around 6,000 letters with people in prison.[28] But her project to raise public awareness and incite debate around reform only really gained ground when, in 1965, a series of fatal incidents dominated the West German headlines. On 30 June 1964 a mentally ill prisoner, Ernst Haase, died in pre-trial custody in Hamburg. He had been brutally beaten by prison officers and left naked and injured in a hot cell known as the 'bell jar', where he died from dehydration and internal bleeding. The case could probably have been hushed up had the secretary who intended to call the mortuary not accidentally dialled the local homicide division.[29] Less than a month later the media reported that another remand prisoner, Anton Wasilenko, had died in Cologne after being beaten by officers and fellow residents.

The public started to take an interest in what was happening in prisons. Dietrich Rollmann, who served on the parliamentary Committee for Prison Reform, published his book on prison (with its essay by the homophobic Koepping) in the wake of the deaths. Its cover blurb referred explicitly to the cases in Hamburg and Cologne.

Birgitta Wolf.

Wolf was another contributor, and may well have nudged Rollmann to include the essays by men serving time. She had been the first to give a public voice to people in prison in post-war West Germany – *The Fourth Caste* (*Die vierte Kaste*), a substantial collection of creative writing by young men in prison (which included the radio play about Berger and his Nazi driver) appeared in 1963. Wolf edited the volume and wrote an introduction making the case for reform. In the ongoing discussions about prison reform, she argued, the knowledge and experience of people in prison were being overlooked. 'There's just one one voice we've forgotten to listen to – the voice of the prisoner himself.' If the Federal Republic *really* wanted to be different from Hitler's Germany, she urged, then everyday Germans needed to know what was happening inside prison walls. 'In the past we made excuses and said that we "didn't know" what was happening. This book is intended to ensure that we can never make those excuses again.'[30]

Wolf was all too aware how careful her correspondents had to be – an incautiously formulated complaint might well lead to solitary confinement, on a bread-and-water diet, as punishment for 'the attempt to spread inappropriate information about issues internal to the institution'. The voices of people in prison had to be 'muted enough that the letter makes it past the censor'. She described prisons in the notoriously conservative state of Bavaria where typewriters were forbidden in the interests of order and security, where young offenders were not allowed to have exercise books to write in, and where anything residents wrote down, including their poems and accounts of their lives, was burned before their eyes on the day of their release.[31] Some developed refined techniques for getting past the censor – Wolf had, for example, loaned a tape recording of one of her speeches on criminal justice to a group of men in Werl prison, with a view to having it broadcast on prison radio. One of them wrote to tell her the broadcast had been forbidden – but his letter was stopped before it left the prison. So he wrote again, formulating differently. 'We listened to the recording of your speech. I have severe doubts, however, that your regressive views – in light of the progressive thinking of prison officials here – will ever be broadcast.' This time the letter was released for posting.[32]

By 1968 she was in possession of more than 7,000 communications from current and released prisoners, and was receiving between three and fifteen letters every day. That year she shared some of those letters, and excerpts from letters, in a second substantial collection. Again she urged her readers to attend to stories and reports from the prison as a means of making good some of the failings of the German past. Contemporary West Germans had to recognize their responsibility, she argued, 'particularly after the experiences of the Third Reich, where we knew too little, because we took so little interest in how prisoners were being treated!' In 1972 a third volume collected poems and creative writing from the period 1954–72: 'voices from the void', she wrote.[33]

Wolf's commitment was to changing attitudes. Her books were not intended to titillate, 'to allow a sensation-seeking public to peer curiously, as if through a suddenly-lit window, into a life that is otherwise hidden from passers-by', but 'to force us all to think, and change our ways of thinking'.[34] That above all would make the young Federal Republic distinctively different from its Nazi predecessor. Post-war West Germany needed to be seen, domestically and on the international stage, as distinct from the brutal dictatorship out of whose ashes it had emerged.

2
The Rubble Children

My brother died in '46, starved to death –
he was two years old . . .
Mum was queueing, was gone to get food, and when she got back he was lying there lifeless in the bed and I said to Mum:
he's gone all quiet.[1]

A young man serving time in the Federal Republic described how his mother had fetched him home in 1945 from the orphanage she had placed him in during the war. 'I had to go begging and hawking for the family so that we had something to eat,' he told Birgitta Wolf. 'If I came home without food my stepfather would beat me with a dog whip.'[2]

In the years that followed Germany's surrender, two-thirds of German children had no fit place to live, and somewhere between a third and a half had no stable family. 'The lowering of moral standards was most conspicuous amongst juveniles, many of whom did not have a normal home or family life,' observed the criminologist Thomas Würtenberger in 1953.[3] Abandoned and lost youngsters, and other children who were trying to escape the dog whip, lived by their wits, stealing and scavenging wherever they could. Children who had been evacuated during the war sometimes took months or even years to find their families again in the post-war chaos – and when they did, they sometimes faced completely new home circumstances. B. C. described making it home, finally, in 1949, only to discover that his mother had married a man twenty years her senior with ten children from a first marriage. 'The household wasn't harmonious,' he told Wolf. 'I ran away a lot.'[4] Convictions for vagrancy and petty theft quickly piled up to build a criminal record that eventually got him a prison sentence. B. G., 33 years old when he wrote to Wolf, described his life as a starving thirteen-year-old.

> I'm hungry, always hungry. I commit my first acts of theft to satisfy the hunger. My sister and I dig sugar beets out of someone's storage mound and at home they get boiled up into syrup . . . And then the hunger, again. I started dealing on the black market so I could at least get bread.[5]

Eventually he ran away from home and in 1948 ended up in Paris, where he found work first in a tomato-processing factory, then with a circus, then in a fairground and finally with a travelling *pâtissier*. But the pleasures of working for an itinerant pastry chef were interrupted when the boy was arrested and imprisoned for vagrancy – the beginning of his criminal career.

B. C., who had run away from an overcrowded household, continued his letter to Wolf with the story of his eventual release from prison in the early 1960s. He decided to start 'a new, law-abiding life' and moved to a town that did not connect him to his past. He met a woman there and fell in love ('she hadn't had much luck in life either'), and they found lodgings together in a farmhouse. A new life seemed to be blossoming for them both. But when the farm changed hands their new landlord rehoused them in 'a room that social services described as not much better than a sty. It was a space in an old corn store. There was no toilet and the only thing protecting us from the wind and weather were bare wooden planks.' Then an accident at work left B. C. incapacitated and unemployed. When his wife became pregnant they started stealing food from local allotments – 'vegetables, potatoes and fruit. Later we went into summerhouses to take household items and appliances, because we needed them – at home we didn't have even the most basic things.' Their son was born in 1963, but it was a harsh winter and the baby died before his first birthday – despite the stolen vegetables, his mother was too malnourished to feed him. 'When my son died,' remembered B. C., 'I had to dig the grave myself, because I didn't have any money for a gravedigger; the Catholic priest and I carried the child to his grave and there wasn't a single flower on it.'[6] At the time of writing he was back in prison, sentenced along with his wife for petty theft and burglary.

MYRL ALEXANDER TELLS the curious story of his visit to a young offenders' institution in Bavaria. He found around a hundred children in their mid- to late teens being held in a dank basement, apparently on the orders of the U.S. military government.

Alexander, who had a lifelong commitment to rehabilitation and the reintegration of young offenders, was shocked enough to pay a visit to military headquarters in Munich and challenge the commanding general. He was told that the young prisoners were 'werewolves': 'kids trained to carry out the Nazi traditions'. But Alexander had spoken with the children and found out something different. 'Their mothers had been killed in bombings and their dads had been on the Eastern Front or elsewhere in the military,' he recalls. 'They were going through the rubble of Munich, Nuremberg or other southern cities, stealing and scrounging for food, and they had gotten picked up and the label of "werewolves" was pinned on them.' Alexander is pleased to remember that, on returning to Command Headquarters in Berlin, he had the decision of the Munich general overruled, and the youngsters moved to work in a forestry nursery near the Austrian border.[7]

Rumours about a surviving Nazi organization called 'Werewolf' circulated in post-war Germany. But Myrl Alexander had met a different phenomenon: the 'wolf children' or *Wolfskinder* who, after losing their families to bombs, illness or displacement, were left to fend for themselves in a hostile environment. Wolf children are more often associated with East Prussia and the Russian zone than with Bavaria, where Alexander found them. Recently, adult survivors have started to tell their stories.[8] But the first published account of life as a wolf child in eastern Germany was given by one of Birgitta Wolf's correspondents, G. C.

There were thousands of kids sleeping in the woods among the old anti-aircraft searchlights, and begging from door to door for bread.

G. C. identified as a gypsy (*Zigeuner*). 'I was 10 years old and alone when the war ended,' he told her. 'My relations were gone with the wind, and who was going to bother about a ragged gypsy kid, a total stranger. I had to make my own way through life like a wild beast. But I wasn't the only one living on the streets,' he explained. 'There were thousands of kids sleeping in the woods among the old anti-aircraft searchlights, begging from door to door for bread.' After six months he joined a gang of about fifteen youngsters, 'lots of them Russians, Poles, or Germans, but all of them kids between about eight and thirteen years old. My life as a hooligan among hooligans started right there.'[9] 'You'll ask me: why did the children organize themselves into gangs?' he continued:

> You see, a child by itself would be mercilessly stripped naked by other gangs, or sometimes even killed – a child by itself counted for nothing, but in the group it was a full member, and was protected by its comrades, and warned of any danger. That's why we hunted in packs through the villages and towns. We plundered Russian army shops – we ambushed young women and sold them to drunken Soviet officers for food, cigarettes (Machorka), and shoes.

All went well for about a year, until the Russian military police caught up with them. 'All those gangs of children stirred up fierce resistance, and there were dead on both sides. You'll think I'm exaggerating, but I'm sorry to say I'm not: many of us had guns.' Adults, he recalled, felt threated, with some justification, for 'as a pack we children showed no mercy to grown-ups. We tyrannized one village until the mayor of that village paid what we called the tribute – things to eat and clothes – and then we moved on, and the village breathed a sigh of relief.' But the adults hit back when they got the chance. G. C. goes on to relate 'a very dirty little story'. Caught by the police in a small town, he was locked in a dark cellar underneath the youth welfare office, where he was beaten unconscious – 'a police chief called Müller hit me with a thick wooden slat till I collapsed'. The next morning, stripped naked except for a pair of ragged trousers, he was taken to the town square, where the village was gathered – 'they ran me barefoot out of town. Müller, the police chief, rode behind me on a bicycle with a whip.'[10] G. C. paints a picture of a society where the older generation's duty of care to the young had crumpled in the chaos.

The story clearly plays in the Russian zone. G. C. claims that in 1946 his group of youngsters was led by the young Werner Gladow (1931–1950), who would go on to lead the notorious Gladow gang in Berlin. Gladow aspired to be the German Al Capone, and he and his gang terrorized the city with armed robberies. He was executed by decapitation in 1950, aged nineteen, in the newly founded German Democratic Republic. But the execution was botched. The first two attempts went awry, while the young Gladow screamed in agony and the public prosecutor fainted.

At sixteen, G. C. was picked up by West German police and put into care in the Federal Republic. But child–adult relations were still a dirty little story, he remembers. 'How did they educate us there? With beatings, with lies and scorn that on occasion was close to being perverse and sadistic.' Writing from prison in the 1960s, he concludes that what he received was a de facto education in crime. The new Republic was 'breeding people with criminal records – where's it going to end?'[11]

> *The beatings I had in my childhood and youth would be enough for a whole city.*[12]

Telling the story of his mid-century childhood, Heinrich Behr – serving life in the Federal Republic – remembered his father as 'an old Nazi'. He 'wanted to turn us boys, my twin brother and me, into hard men. A hard man doesn't cry. He has to be hard and not show his feelings . . . he beat the feelings out of me.' Behr's story is simultaneously of a society in which men like his father were pillars of the community: in his father's case, a respected member of the local town council. Peter Jörnschmidt, another lifer, remembered struggling to read from the blackboard at school, and being taken to an optician by his father – who then thrashed him, because in the professional opinion of the optician, 'all the boy needed was a decent beating, every couple of days, then the problem would solve itself. I was just lazy, he said, and that's why I wasn't doing well at school. My father beat me.'[13]

E. E., who had described his life as Ernst Röhm's 'lust boy' in Nazi Berlin, told Wolf how his father had abused his mother in the interwar years. 'Mother did other people's washing, or delivered newspapers with us and read cards, and then got beaten up by my father in the evenings. It was all lies and chaos.' Like Behr's and Jörnschmidt's, his father was a pillar of post-war masculinity: 'the "decent chap" type, who lived for his work.' E. E. started bedwetting when he was five years old, after the day he saw his mother naked on his bed, being beaten by his father.[14] An even more disturbing story of domestic violence in the post-war Republic is told by H. A., who spent his childhood in 'indescribable fear' of a mentally ill father.

His letter to Wolf begins with his father's abuse of his mother – H. A. remembers him striking her so hard she fell unconscious, and then urinating in her face. It continues with grotesque acts of violence towards the child. In one instance, 'among many', wrote H. A., 'my father pushed my face into my own faeces (I had had an accident in the bed, was just about 3 years old), and then rubbed my face back and forth against the iron railings of the little bed until my forehead, nose, and chin were just a mass of blood smeared with faeces.' Or there was the time when the child witnessed his father trying to burn the corpse of his prematurely born baby sister. 'Because it didn't work (there was a lot of smoke and fumes), my father buried the little corpse in the cellar.' More descriptions of appalling incidents follow: he remembers being four or five years old, 'and my father laid me on my stomach and tied my hands and feet to the bed and lacerated my bottom – which I used to scratch at night until it was raw – with his solder stone (sal ammoniac). The pain made me pass out.' Like most children, he liked eating sugar, but most children are not punished with electric shocks. 'He made me sit on chair with a wet towel on it,' H. A. went on. 'Under the towel there was a contact to an electric apparatus. Another contact was fixed to the sugar bowl (made of metal). I had to put the sugar bowl in my mouth and at that moment my father turned the electricity on.'[15]

H. A. will have been writing around the time of the trial of the SS officer Eichmann in Jerusalem, and he connects events in his mind:

> A particular instance, which only happened once, was like this, and shows that Adolf Eichmann wasn't the first person to make use of a gas chamber . . . As a tiny child, I often watched my mother putting a coin (a 10-pfennig piece) into the slot in the gas meter and turning the little lever. Finding myself alone in the apartment I pushed a one-mark piece, which admittedly was too big, into the slot . . . The damage cost us 16 marks. As a punishment, my father, who had a nervous disorder, put me in a big wooden box where we normally kept my toys, closed the lid and through a slit or hole stuck the gas pipe from the cooker in, and piped coal gas into the box, where I was crouching in fear.[16]

As he remembers it, only his mother's intervention saved him from being gassed to death.

Life was one long beating[17]

A 21-year-old man in prison described the chaotic years after the war when he camped in cellars with his alcoholic mother – and how she would beat him 'with any object that came to hand'. The beatings continued until he was big enough to hit back. His contemporary, Jürgen J., born in 1940, sent a variant on that story to a national writing competition for people in prison. He described his father's death on the Russian front in 1941 and his mother's remarriage in 1949. After that happy event his mother and new stepfather joined forces to thrash him. His stepfather drank, and would then 'rage and smash everything he saw into pieces. When there was nothing left to smash up it was my turn.' The child had nowhere to turn. 'Mother hardly minded at all. She even helped him and would hold me down while he thrashed me with his leather belt. I no longer understood her.'[18]

Jürgen's story continues in a corrective home for children, where – after a brief encounter with a maternal nun who was kindly in the interludes when she was not beating the children – he was assigned a supervisor who inflicted fearsome canings for the smallest infractions of house rules. 'Once I had a bad dream, and wet the bed,' Jürgen remembered:

> His stick came whistling down on me and brought tears to my eyes. 'Such a big boy and still pissing in the bed!' the housemaster yelled. 'I should push your face into the puddle, you damned urchin! Get that sheet taken off and stand in the corridor, so that everyone knows what you are!' So I stood in my wet pyjamas barefoot on the stone floor.

There was, in Jürgen's story, no way of avoiding the beatings – they were administered, like the beatings recommended by the young Peter Jörnschmidt's optician, 'like the daily barley broth'. The result, for the boy, was suppressed fury: 'hate burned inside me.'[19]

Ulrike Meinhof, the Hamburg journalist who in 1970 would co-found the Red Army Faction, had begun to concern herself with children in care from the late 1960s. In January 1968 the left-wing magazine *konkret* published her assessment of the case of 21-year-old Jürgen Bartsch, a former care-home child who had been convicted of murdering four little boys. The Bartsch murders shocked West Germany. But Meinhof's focus was less on the young perpetrator and more on the society that had brutalized him. Rather than describing his appalling crimes, she described the appalling life of institutionalized abuse that had preceded them. What *should* have been shocking West Germany, she argued, was how socially acceptable the systemic abuse of children still was. For the court that convicted Bartsch, 'the care home route is not a catastrophe; for the court corporal punishment is not an issue.' This, she complained, was a court that had assisted in a national whitewash. Bartsch was the scapegoat that would enable German society 'to say nothing in the face of . . . the barbarous treatment of children in its own country, its own families'.[20]

In 1973 Jürgen Roth, an investigative journalist, published a report on West German children's homes. Roth tracked down numerous former care children. He found that beatings were standard in every single care home in the Republic. His sources also reported other kinds of punishments – being slapped in the face with a nappy or pants wet with urine, or having the urine squeezed out into their faces. In a Catholic children's home staffed by nuns, one interviewee reported, 'Sister W. hit children in the face with her fist. She sometimes took a bunch of keys and hit particularly cheeky children on the head with them. She put a hot iron on one child's hands.' On bath days, the same nun pushed the children's heads under the water until they screamed, 'and then she beat them. If children wet the bed they were beaten. Clothes pegs were clipped to their genitals and they had to stand in the corner like that. Or they had to lie down naked on the floor and other children were encouraged to beat them.' A legal case was started against Sister W. in 1972, but had to be dropped because the children's stories were regarded as lacking credibility.[21]

Had she been consulted, Birgitta Wolf could have offered corroboration. She already knew of 'cruel and often enough sadistic' punishments in a Catholic home. Her correspondent, B. E., was 22 years old at the time of writing. He described how children were brutally disciplined 'for any kind of small infringement'. He was himself 'often given beatings to the point where I bled like a stuck pig. I was pretty much beaten to a pulp.' Other children were forced to eat their own vomit, or struck on the head with a heavy bunch of keys ('a popular method in most of the homes', B. E. assured Wolf). The director of the home, who was a priest, had a special desk in his office, full of canes. Children were hit in the face or beaten with a cane on their bottoms or between their fingers. B. E. remembered being pulled out of bed at night and taken downstairs to be beaten or made to kneel on a stone floor. Boys were shamed by being made to dress in girls' clothes and eat in the girls' dining room. Punishments could be incurred for talking during a meal or in the bathroom, throwing stones, wetting the bed or chewing your fingernails, or for 'perversities' such

Children's home in Frankfurt, 1957.

as homosexual activity, masturbation or playing football with your shoes on (playing in bare feet was the inexplicable rule). B. E. himself recalled being beaten so hard by a nun that he was bedridden for a week. He particularly remembered his yearning, as a child in that context, to commit suicide.[22]

The stories are characterized by the children's sense of complete helplessness. There is no adult support and no expectation of being helped by adults if they speak out. When Meinhof made a radio feature about a girls' home in Hesse, one of her young interviewees described the abuse of power by responsible adults as absolutely standard. 'The things they do to you. To start with I answered back and complained. But the grown-ups stick together and they're always right.'[23] Child protection services, explained Wolf's correspondent A. A., 'always want to believe "experienced pedagogues" and dismiss the child's complaint'. Indeed, the more reputable the care home's parent organization (normally a church or foundation), the more likely it was that the complaint would dismissed. 'For ages no one would believe me when I said that choleric thrashers were on the rampage in a home like the Moorburg, sponsored by an organization as famous as xx,' A. A. continued. 'It was only when two boys killed a care worker in a desperate attempt to escape that those things came to light during the trial that followed.' Even Wolf, or her publisher, seems to have felt it safer to anonymize the organization that A. A. had named in his letter (it was in fact Germany's biggest Protestant church, the Lutheran *Landeskirche* in Hanover).[24]

B. E., the child who was 'beaten to a pulp', remembered weeping with fury at his own powerlessness. He concluded that the methods used in care homes were perfectly designed to produce young offenders. Another letter written to Wolf by a young man in prison echoed and supported that claim. The young H. observed how the despotism of adults undermined any sense of right or justice in a child. 'Have you ever seen how a child reacts when it has been beaten since it was small for trivial offences and sometimes even for nothing? Do you imagine that child still believes in law and justice?' The arbitrary brutality of adults destroys any sense of natural justice in a child. And adult brutality could drive children to criminality in an even more direct way: a child in care, explained A. A., would commit crimes just to escape from the care home – 'it would rather be in prison, because the legal rights of prisoners are clearer.'[25]

As the murder of George Floyd in Minneapolis in 2020 and the subsequent rise of the Black Lives Matter movement showed, societies are only ready to hear certain stories at certain times. In Germany, changes to civil law in 2000 made the corporal punishment and psychological injury of children illegal. Soon afterwards stories of abuse rapidly gained popular appeal; in 2015, the director Marc Brummund made his feature film *Sanctuary* (*Freistatt*) about the notorious Moorburg home in Lower Saxony. Accounts of beatings and the maltreatment of children in post-war Germany, both in children's homes and at the hands of their parents, have only really caught the public interest in the new millenium (similarly, the Ryan Report of Ireland's commission into child abuse in Catholic care homes was published only in 2009). A television film called *And Everyone Kept Silent* popularized Peter Wensierski's book *Beatings in the Name of the Lord* (2006). This, the back cover claimed, was 'the suppressed history of children in care'.[26] By that time the accounts published by Wolf and Roth had been in the public sphere for over thirty years.

3
First Calls for Reform

What is happening in prisons is a veiled form of slavery.

Urgent calls for a return to the principle of resocialization started as early as 1946. The First United Nations Congress on the Prevention of Crime and the Treatment of Offenders took place in Geneva in 1955, and agreed the Standard Minimum Rules for the Treatment of Prisoners. Prison labour was discussed at length. The rules decreed that prison work must be useful, and must not constitute a form of punishment but support the prisoner's ability to earn a living after release. Vocational training should be available. Rule 76 recommended 'equitable remuneration of the work of prisoners.' In 1960 a second Congress, held in London, revisited that issue. The General Report of that Congress found the existing remuneration of prison labour 'unsatisfactory. The same must be said concerning the work provided for prisoners.' With a very few exceptions, compensation for prison labour was 'ridiculously small' and the payment people received for their work was determined by factors that had nothing to do with the labour itself. In general, the report concluded, it amounted to 'a veiled form of slavery.'[1]

In 1960, West Germany was not yet part of the UN (it would be admitted, with East Germany, in 1973). In the early 1960s, some West German prisons were paying workers 20 pfennigs per day (the price of a postage stamp). Half of that amount automatically went into a savings account – so a prisoner who wanted to send a letter home needed to work for two days in order to raise the price of a stamp.[2]

In 1966 the Conference of the Federal Justice Ministers suggested raising daily earnings to a minimum of 60 pfennigs and a maximum of DM 1.20, with a possible rate of DM 1.50 for exceptionally productive workers. But in practice a Federal minimum wage for people in prison was impossible to legislate for, because the prison system was (and still is) *Ländersache* – one of the legislative matters devolved to individual states.

Contributing to Dietrich Rollmann's book on contemporary prison problems in 1967, the judge and criminologist Günter Blau assessed the situation. He noted that in the state of Hesse, for example, inmates of Frankfurt's Gustav Radbruch prison (named after the progressive Minister for Justice in the Weimar Republic) were going out to work in the city under almost the same conditions as free workers. But they were not working for the same pay as free workers. People imprisoned in Hesse earned a daily wage of between 40 pfennigs and 1 mark – about one-tenth of what a regular worker might expect. A Federal regulation of 1962 had determined (in the spirit of the UN Congresses) that people in prison should perform 'meaningful and useful work'. But Blau found that work in most Federal German prisons was actually still conceived of as punitive – in particular, people in penal servitude were subject to forced labour that was clearly part of their punishment.[3] Even as Blau's essay went to press, however, conditions were changing.

In 1966 the West German economy had entered its first post-war recession. Economists discussed whether a crisis on a par with the Great Depression of 1931 was imminent.[4] The winter of 1966–7 saw sudden high unemployment. In the first half of the 1960s, Federal German prisons had scarcely been able to meet the demand for labour from a booming industry, but that now changed, and people in prison lost even their minimal earnings in the wake of the economic crisis. Wolf's correspondent D. B. described the desperate situation. 'The prison is rationing everything in order to save money,' he reported. 'A prisoner in Lower Saxony is entitled to 10 grams of soap per day, and that includes washing powder for our underwear, work clothes and bed linen, and scourer for the lavatory, washbasin and washing up.' There were six razor blades per month and chalk for cleaning teeth.

Residents had no chance of buying even the most basic toiletries like toothpaste or additional razor blades from the prison shop, because they had no work, so no money – 'we often discuss with each other how this can go on?'[5]

Everything gets hushed up.

Until the first reform law of 25 June 1969, the Federal Republic retained the historic distinction between prison (*Gefängnis*) – for less serious crimes – and penal servitude (*Zuchthaus*). The latter was imposed with hard labour, and conditions were harsher – dormitories of twelve men or more, and letters home only once a fortnight or even once every three weeks (where people in regular prisons could usually write weekly).[6] Reformers argued that the two-tier system echoed the Nazi's punitive focus on atonement and retribution.[7]

In an essay for Rollmann's book on the penal system, Hans Kaltenbach described his personal experience of penal servitude. He and his cellmates could expect clean bed linen every six weeks at best, he reported. Once a week for precisely four minutes they could take a shower; the only other means of having a wash was a cold water pipe above the lavatory. They were issued with razors three times a week, but there was no hot water to shave with – 'prisoners normally use some of their morning coffee'. To be ill or in pain was disastrous – acute toothache or painful physical symptoms regularly went untreated for days or even weeks, wrote Kaltenbach, because the assumption was made that all prisoners were malingerers. Any resident who reported sick was first assumed to be shamming.[8]

One of Wolf's correspondents, H. G., wrote to her to tell a story no one else would listen to (or perhaps that he did not dare tell anyone else). He had been committed to an unnamed psychiatric unit, a 'so-called safe custody facility'. 'In my room there was just a mattress on the floor. No chair, no table – nothing! The mattress was covered in crusted blood and stank infernally of urine.' But his letter moves quickly from the appalling conditions to the even more appalling brutality of the people responsible for providing care. 'Every evening, cries echo through the building, unimaginable cries! If they don't stop there are injections.' And if they still did not stop, the beatings would start – 'three of the nurses disappear into the sick person's cell, and then the smacking sounds and the patient's shouts tell their own story.' The letter goes on to describe what happened when another patient, N., complained that one of the prisoner functionaries was stealing other people's meat. In response, a nurse held N.'s hands behind his back while the accused functionary hit him in the face 'for about five minutes, till he collapsed unconscious'. H. G. was clearly worried that even Wolf would not believe his story. 'I feel it's important to emphasize that there are witnesses for this!' he assured her.[9]

She was hearing similarly worrying tales from other secure psychiatric facilities, however. F. B. wrote to Wolf from preventive detention, describing his time in a secure psychiatric unit, called 'Block 3', in a room called the dry cell. 'Three weeks I lay there, often totally naked, just 2 blankets, no yard exercise, on the floor . . . Serious murderers with life sentences get jobs there as orderlies – they help with the beatings and "buy" their freedom that way.' He described hot and cold baths and being wrapped in wet blankets, which he accepted as unpleasant forms of 'treatment'. But then he started getting beaten, and one day he was beaten bloody. When he complained to a guard – 'I thought no one got beaten here?' – the guard laughed. 'They don't! It's your own fault if you're crazy enough to bang your head against a wall.' The thrashings continued. 'Sometimes I couldn't see because my eyes were so swollen and bloodied from beatings,' he told Wolf. He began to self-harm. 'I cut my stomach, swallowed things, bit my wrists open and stuck pens in my eyes because I couldn't stand it any longer.' But any act of protest attracted retribution: 'If you misbehave, then that evening the heavy squad comes! They gag you with a towel and tie it behind your head. They put a steel grip around your wrist and pull you 600 metres across the courtyard to Block 3 like an animal being taken to slaughter.'

But over and over again, the story of people in prison is the story of not being believed. In F. B.'s psychiatric unit, officers taunted their charges with that knowledge: 'You're welcome to make a complaint. We have the influence and it will all just rebound on to you – no one's going to believe you.' His final appeal to Wolf echoes the reports of the care-home children who had tried to complain. 'Where does one find help? Where is the special commission to take care of this? Nothing! Everything gets hushed up, false witness is given in court about the prisoner, – the prisoner is lying, is a whinger, a violent criminal, all those familiar catchphrases. Thus the nation's duty to the Constitution is satisfied.'[10]

Birgitta Wolf's disturbance in the face of this story is evident. The letter is followed by another of her rare editorial notes, in which she explains that she hired a lawyer to see whether his account could be corroborated. The lawyer did not succeed. 'But it is striking that similar stories have been emerging from this particular penitentiary for years, over and over again,' Wolf observed.[11]

Human dignity goes to the Devil the moment you put on prison clothes.[12]

'As I said in my last letter, I've lost any faith I had in our constitutional state and I believe that any process of rethinking issues of law and human dignity lies in the very distant future,' D. B. told Wolf. Until they were sentenced, Wolf noted, people in custody had to be hailed using their title and the polite form used to address adults: 'Sie'. But that changed as soon as they were convicted. From then on they were called by their surnames, without a title, and addressed in the 'du' form generally used with children and people for whom one does not need to signal respect.[13]

The opening paragraph of the Federal German constitution pledged to protect human dignity, but prison conditions in the new Federal Republic *still* failed to reflect that constitutional commitment, she complained. In one prison, eighteen men were sharing a cell with one unscreened lavatory, and in a psychiatric unit five patients were squeezed into a two-man cell, their shared toilet just inches from the dining table.[14] Cells designed for a single occupant were holding two or three men, double cells were packed with four. Wolf cited a report written by a man in West Berlin. He was sharing a one-man cell with two other men, with 'one stinking toilet' for their collective use. In another wing of the prison, he reported, residents did not even have the luxury of lavatories – 'just buckets in the corners'. The prison diary of a 21-year-old paints a picture of similarly rudimentary conditions: 'the beds are made of iron, wooden slats, and hardboard . . . An old tin bucket stands in the corner.' August Klemp, the returning soldier who had been forced by US military policemen to confess to a murder, described three men occupying 9 square metres (97 sq. ft): 'there are always two in the way when you're washing or shaving or cleaning up, and there are always four eyes too many on you when you have to use the bucket . . . it stinks like a pigsty!'[15]

> *there are still prisons where 60 men share a dormitory; there are prisons where a stinking bucket is provided for the use of six men – in the same room in which they eat and sleep – and where the so-called coffee is drunk from dog bowls.*[16]

'Everyone wants to get out, and if they can't get out alive they'll do it dead. People swallow spoon handles or have a go at themselves with a razor blade,' Klemp told the journalists who interviewed him. 'I know people who've cut both their arms, top to bottom. They thought that the kind of space an animal needs – eight square metres – well, they thought a prisoner ought to be able to ask for that too.'[17]

A 21-year-old man submitted this complaint to Wuppertal's district court (*Landgericht*) in 1968:

> I was admitted with 20 other men. The prisoners are all herded into a long corridor . . . where they have to strip naked, place their clothing on stools, and take several steps back, stark naked, standing an arm's length from the next man. Then they have to stand there in the cold corridor (in the basement) until their clothing has been searched. Then they are all ordered to raise their arms above their heads, and then to raise their legs and show the soles of their feet, one at a time . . . After that, all the prisoners have to bend over forwards and pull apart their anal opening, so that the officers can see as far as possible into their arses . . . without

> any kind of screen or cover for privacy, without anything, right in front of their fellow prisoners' eyes.[18]

Wolf cited the complaint in a published essay that contrasted the ideals of the West German constitution with the reality of life in prison. She supplemented it with the story, retold in her own words, of what had happened when the same man refused to take off his underpants in front of three prison officers who had left the cell door standing wide open. 'To prevent the custodian, K., from forcibly pulling down his underpants, he had made a knot in his trousers. They tried nonetheless to pull his trousers down by force, and there was a scuffle. The accounts of who dealt the first blow differ,' she reported. 'The prisoner, who is very slight and undernourished, called loudly for help, with the result that the entire building grew rebellious and some prisoners, hearing the smack of the blows on his naked body and his cries, shouted loudly that the guards should leave the boy alone.' Afterwards they did leave him alone, she observed – in an isolation cell, beaten, bleeding and stark naked. Later they took him to another cell, underneath the sick bay.

> It was known as the death cell. Prisoners sentenced to death used to await execution there . . . They left the boy to vegetate in that chamber of horrors for almost three days and nights. The mattress he had to sleep on was soiled with urine and faeces . . . He had to go to the toilet in the dark, using a bucket that smelled even fouler and was even filthier than everything else. Finally he was given 21 days in punitive detention. And all that because he defended himself, first verbally and then physically, when they tried to force him to have his anus inspected with people looking on and the door wide open.

She concluded by citing Article 1 of the new Federal German Constitution. 'Human dignity is inviolable. It is the duty of all state authority to protect it.'[19]

> *Everything gets too narrow, the walls start to close in on you, it all keeps getting narrower – you need to get some air, cause you only have the little hatch, and you get the feeling you're suffocating. That's when guys start to go crazy and smash up the cell.*[20]

Being locked in a small space can cause cabin fever. 'The people it affects don't get medical attention,' one man explained, 'instead they get dragged down into the cellar by the heavy brigade and given one hell of a beating.' When things were quiet, he continued, officers would pass the time by targeting certain inmates – 'prisoners who couldn't adapt to prison life, who were a bit resistant, got dragged out of their cells by force and beaten up in special cells down in the cellar.' Any victim who lodged a complaint would find himself in disciplinary proceedings: 'they were usually given a further term of imprisonment by the magistrate, for resisting state authority.'[21]

Most of Germany's major dailies published the open letter Wolf wrote in 1970 to the Federal Minister for Justice, in which she angrily criticized the practice of solitary confinement. Solitary confinement, she declared, was the most inhuman thing she had seen practised in West Germany's prisons and penitentiaries. People in prison were being isolated for days, weeks or sometimes months for infringements as petty as insulting a prison guard. Wolf described cells in basements, where 'stubborn' prisoners were isolated for weeks at a time, sleeping on bare boards or a concrete block and with only bread and water. Every third day the inmate would be given a mattress and a proper meal. The following day the mattress would be taken away again and they would be back to bare boards and bread and water.[22]

Wolf's correspondent A. B. cut his wrists in a desperate attempt to avoid punitive isolation. Guards dragged him to an empty cell. 'There,' he told her, 'they tore the clothes from my body and tortured and abused me in the most inhuman way. They left me naked in the cell – which only had a canvas mattress and a blanket in it – for three whole days, without dressing the cuts on my wrists.' 'Why are imprisoned people being maltreated in this way?' Wolf objected. 'Isn't physical torture against the law? Why is the government tolerating it? It goes against the Federal German constitution and the UN Commission on Human Rights.'[23]

No one should
lightly
embrace the illusion
that medieval punishments by mutilation
are no longer
practicable;
they exist
now as then –
they have merely been
moved indoors.

A life sentence, for example,
is spiritual mutilation
in slow motion.[24]

Article 102 of the constitution of 1949 had abolished the death penalty in the Federal Republic (East Germany retained it until 1987). Responses from people in prison were complex. 'I'd put it like this: the death penalty has been abolished, but at the same time it's been retained in a far crueller way,' wrote H. F., serving a life sentence, to Birgitta Wolf. Heinrich Behr, who described being beaten by a father who had transitioned smoothly from 'old Nazi' to pillar of the post-war community, now challenged West German society to 'come out and show its colours . . . life sentences are just executions that let you continue living.'[25]

But some who got out argued that life outside was even crueller than prison. A recurring theme in the letters Birgitta Wolf received from people in prison was how impossible it was for them to re-enter society. 'I had to lie constantly to get work and a place to live,' wrote B. C., 'for if word got out that I had a criminal record I'd get shown the door.'[26] Not only did society not want them, they had unlearned any capacity they ever had to survive in it. Wolf noted that, with only one exception, the young men who had contributed poems, prose and plays to the collection *The Fourth Caste* were all either still in prison or back in prison at the time of its publication in 1963.[27]

The worst punishment comes after prison

D. E. was 72 when he wrote to Wolf. He had served in the First World War, but found no work when the war ended, and slid into a 'criminal career'. When he got out of prison in 1929, neither his father nor his brother would take him in. 'I got a place in a shelter for released prisoners,' he explained. 'The director of the home tried really hard to get me a job. He didn't manage to.' So he returned to his home town and found a room there. He even found work – but could not keep it. 'I didn't stay in any job for longer than four weeks – that was how long it took for people to make enquiries.' After five years he was back in prison. Another brief period of unemployment 'outside' in the mid-1930s was followed by prison again at the end of that decade. In the 'rubble times' after 1945 he worked for a time on a building site, but by then he was in his mid-forties and suffering from arthritis. He slid back into crime, and back into prison. When he wrote to Wolf in the early 1960s, he was out of prison and struggling to survive on the margins of Germany's economic miracle – 'So as not to starve I collect old tin cans and live off the things other people throw away.' Society was as unforgiving as ever: 'Who's going to help someone tainted with this kind of stain?' For D. E., prison – however unpleasant the conditions – seemed less cruel than life afterwards. 'The worst punishment comes after prison, and is usually a life sentence,' he concluded his letter, 'that's what I wanted to write and tell you.'[28]

D. H. struggled through Germany's economic miracle in similarly unmiraculous circumstances. On his release from prison, he told Wolf, he had found himself facing a debt to social services of more than 11,000 DM for the housing and maintenance provided for his wife and children. He got a job in a brewery and settled down to start repayments. A letter from social services arrived at his new work address, explaining how exactly the deductions would be made from his earnings. It lost him his job. 'My second job', he continues, 'was in the S. cinema, but I lost that one too after a few days. They didn't want someone with a criminal record.' He managed to get work as an electrician – but lost it again as soon as his prison history emerged. 'My fourth job, in the R. cinema, came to an end in similar circumstances,' he reported. All of his employers had one thing in common: 'they didn't want ex-cons.'

At the time of writing he was back in prison, one eye on his ever-growing debt to social services, and bitterly anticipating a future in which neither he nor his family would ever achieve resocialization 'in this truly caring constitutional state'. In that context, he told Wolf, it seemed realistic to consider whether he 'wouldn't rather stay in prison – at least here they are kind enough to give work and bread to returning prisoners, though sadly not to their families. Deductions from earnings are out of the question here and people are only very, very rarely sacked without notice.'[29]

> *Prison is opium. Once you get used to it you can't live without it.*[30]

W. G. called that effect 'socialization for prison'. His short story 'Humanitas' is the the ironic tale of a recently released prisoner who is requesting re-entry – not into society, but into prison. The magistrate is incredulous:

> 'Now just a moment! Are you saying you want to spend your whole life in prison?'
>
> 'I'd rather – I'm so sorry – I'd rather, yes . . .'
>
> 'You're insane!'
>
> 'I might be. Beforehand, before I got the five years, I wasn't.'
>
> 'Nonsense! The humane, socializing prison system we have now . . .'
>
> 'That's it exactly!'
>
> 'What is?'
>
> 'The socialization! . . . Five years of socialization – that has an effect! . . . I've been socialized – for prison.'[31]

Rudi, the protagonist of W. G.'s radio play *Holiday from Burstadt*, commits a crime in order to get back into prison and to the step-by-step system he understands (an approach to rehabilitation pioneered in England's Pentonville prison, where residents could progress over time, with good behaviour, through a series of ranks or levels that brought privileges and small freedoms).[32] To the police who come to arrest him, he explains: 'Out here I wasn't on Step Three any more, I was on Step Zero, you know, Step Double-Zero.' Rudi thereby fulfils the prediction made by the old lags in W. B.'s short story 'The Fifth Caste', as they gleefully explain the system to an elderly new arrival:

> 'there are lower and higher social strata . . . In here, as a Step Two, you're kinda middle-class . . .'
>
> 'And as a Step Three you enter high society!' the other grinned.
>
> 'And when some guy from Step Three is released, and outside he's in the gutter, in the dirt, Step Zero, you see, then he'll turn a trick to get back inside, where he can be part of high society. He's not going to make it out there, you see?'
>
> The old man didn't understand. He gaped. 'I thought . . . but you said that the progressive system was about socialization . . .?'
>
> 'Sure – socialization for the nick. What did you think?'[33]

P.A.B.'s short story 'The Surprise' adds a dark twist. A prisoner released on Christmas Eve is found hanging from a tree outside the prison gate. It is clearly a suicide, so the question is not whodunnit, but why. The story takes us back in time to a conversation between the dead man and his caseworker. When the man, Unger, responds fearfully to the news of his release, his caseworker offers him platitudes:

> 'With a will to make good you'll be right as rain in six months,' said the caseworker.

'A will to make good?' Unger laughed bitterly. 'I had a will when I arrived here. I've spent nine years in a bell jar . . . Right from the start everyone here focused on breaking my will . . . Prison doesn't teach prisoners to be socialized citizens; it teaches them to be prisoners.'[34]

POST-WAR PRISON REFORM campaigners such as Wolf, Rollmann and Gustav Heinemann (Minister for the Interior in Adenauer's Christian Democratic post-war government, who later joined the Social Democrats) demanded humane and dignified conditions for people in prison. They argued that the criminal justice system could protect society *only* if it could identify the causes of offending behaviour, address those causes and help people reintegrate after prison. That rehabilitative ideal had been articulated by Herbert Jungmann, another of the prisoner contributors to Rollmann's volume of 1967. 'The prisoner expiates his guilt in prison,' he wrote. 'Society needs to communicate to him, through human contact and genuine empathy: you aren't rejected, you too are one of us, and we want you to come back to us. In our eyes you are and remain a human being like us.'

But the ideal clashed with the reality described by Jungmann's co-contributor, Peter Borchert. 'The prison', wrote Borchert, 'is the most perfect desocialization machine imaginable.'[35]

Part II

A Model and Looking Good? West Germany, 1968–89

Incarceration should enable the prisoner to lead a future life of social responsibility, without crime.
(Penal Code of the Federal Republic of Germany of 1976, §2)

They want you to become like them – empty. Don't let it happen. Defend yourself.
(Uschi Keutsch, prisoner in the Federal Republic of Germany, 1982)

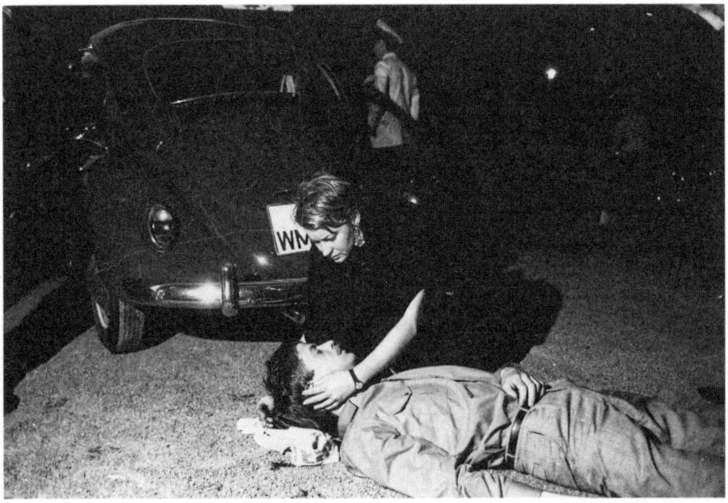

The death of Benno Ohnesorg in Berlin, 1967.

4

The German Model

We want to dare more democracy.
Willy Brandt, 1969

By the late 1960s, political tensions in West Germany were high. In June 1967, a young demonstrator, Benno Ohnesorg, was shot dead by a policeman during a protest against a state visit from the Shah of Iran. The following spring, Rudi Dutschke, the charismatic leader of Germany's student movement, was critically injured by a shot to the head as he wheeled his bicycle along a street in Berlin. His right-wing assassin had been inspired by the murder of Martin Luther King in Memphis, Tennessee, a week before. A few days before Dutschke was shot at, four young activists set fire to department stores in Frankfurt in protest against the Vietnam War. Two of them, Andreas Baader and Gudrun Ensslin, would later co-found the Red Army Faction. They would die in unexplained circumstances in a West German prison before the end of the next decade.

From December 1966, the Chancellor was Kurt Kiesinger, a Christian Democrat and himself a former prisoner – after the war he had been detained for eighteen months by U.S. American forces as a senior member of the Nazi Party, which he had joined in 1933. From 1966 he led the first 'grand coalition' of West Germany's centre-right (Christian Democratic/Christian Social) and centre-left (Social Democratic) parties. The Vice-Chancellor was Willy Brandt – a Social Democrat with a very different history. In 1933, when Kiesinger joined the Nazis, Brandt had joined the left-wing resistance in Norway. He did not return to Germany until 1946. The spectacle of Brandt's co-operation with Kiesinger in government led some on the West German left to reject party politics entirely.

Over the first decades of its existence the post-war Federal Republic shaped the German Model: an economic model that demonstrated the potential of federal decentralization combined with participatory systems of production.[1] Workers co-determined policy and direction (*Mitbestimmung*), national unions led collective bargaining and there was a well-regulated apprenticeship system. When Willy Brandt became Chancellor in 1969, he promised a German model for domestic politics. All citizens, he pledged, would have opportunities to co-determine the developments in state and society – the Federal Republic was going to 'dare more democracy'.[2]

With Gustav Heinemann, whom he had put forward as Minister for Justice in 1966, Brandt presided over the first stages of the reform of criminal law. The Working Group for Penal Reform, which the Nazis had dissolved in 1933, reconvened in 1948. In 1962 a Grand Committee for Criminal Law (Grosse Strafrechtskommission) presented a draft for a new penal code. But the draft failed to shift the focus from retribution to resocialization, neglected to address sexual and morality laws and retained the old two-tier system of prison and penal servitude. A voluntary working group of German and Swiss criminal lawyers responded in 1966 with an alternative draft focused on guiding people from prison back into society. Both the draft and the alternative draft were considered by the Parliamentary Committee for the Reform of Criminal Law (on which Dietrich Rollmann sat). Between the summer of 1969 and the summer of 1974, the Bonn Parliament passed five prison reform acts.[3]

The first act abolished the two-tier system: from 1 April 1970 every Federal German prison was transformed into an 'institution for administering justice' (*Justizvollzugsanstalt* or JVA). Collectively, the reforms decriminalized sexual relations between men over the age of 21, updated family law and liberalized abortion, and guaranteed the right to peaceful demonstration. Continuing that overall move to criminalize and punish less – ergo to reduce the number of people sent to prison in the first place – shorter sentences were replaced

Willy Brandt (left) and Kurt Georg Kiesinger.

with fines and suspended sentences. Within the prison system there was expanded use of day release, home leave and open institutions.[4] The reforms would eventually lead, in 1976–7, to participatory systems in prisons that mirrored the 'German model' outside: prisoner co-determination, or *Gefangenenmitverantwortung*.

In 1972 the Constitutional Court ruled that the principles of the constitutional democracy must also be upheld in correctional institutions.[5] People in prison now had the right to freedom of speech, and the right to protest if their treatment seemed arbitrary or illegitimate. In 1974 Dr Helga Einsele, who had been the governor of Frankfurt's progressive women's prison since 1947, was optimistic that West Germany was 'in a process of transition from a prison system in which prisoners were objects, to a system in which they are subjects'.[6]

The reformers' hopes that people in prison might be treated as 'fellow human beings' were bolstered by the example of Germany's European neighbours. In the progressive Scandinavian system, they observed, 70 per cent of people released from prison did not re-offend – whereas in West Germany, 70 per cent did. Why? Because 'prisoners there are not regarded as dangerous ruffians, but as fellow citizens who have strayed.'[7] In the right kind of world, rehabilitation seemed possible. Hope blossomed for a more inclusive society.

> *Voices from the prison . . . encourage us to tear down, for ever, the walls that separate us from our fellow human beings*[8]

In the grip of that cultural mood, well-known writers started to correspond with people in prison. Ingeborg Drewitz helped found the first newspaper to emerge from a women's prison, campaigned for reform and corresponded in the mid-1970s with a prisoner and poet, Winand Buchacker. Their letters were published in 1979 as *Sentences to Crush Walls.*[9] Meanwhile the novelist Peter Schneider was exchanging letters with Peter-Jürgen Boock, who was awaiting trial as a member of the Red Army Faction. Their correspondence appeared in 1985, in a volume with the title *Rat – Is Dead.* But a short poem by Boock, printed on the book's flyleaf, suggested that even a dead rat can hope:

rat – is dead
hungry rat – is dead
clever hungry rat – is dead
nimble clever hungry rat – is dead
calculating nimble clever hungry rat – is dead
you watch out!
she'll make it[10]

The public had discovered its interest in prisons, and weighty publishing houses such as Piper, Rowohlt, Luchterhand and Claassen (which had published the German translation of Margaret Mitchell's *Gone with the Wind*) started to compete for prisoner writing. Piper brought out a collection of interviews with men serving life sentences, with an afterword by Heinrich Hannover, a high-profile lawyer who would also represent members of the Red Army Faction. German PEN sponsored two collections of prisoner writing edited by its vice-president, Ingeborg Drewitz. Helmut Ortner, a journalist, edited a hefty volume of writing from the prison that promised readers 'a view

Ingeborg Drewitz, 1974.

from the inside'. It was published by a book club in its series of 'basic reads'. He followed it up with a volume of photographs and first-hand accounts, this time offering 'a tour through a hidden world'.[11] In the 1960s, Birgitta Wolf had insisted that writing from prisons was *not* about the revelation of titillating secrets. But now it seemed that keyhole-peeking was allowed, in order (said Ortner) to 'motivate as many readers as possible to engage actively'.[12]

Ordinary Germans' historic failure to offer political resistance seemed somehow to be addressed by writing from the prison. 'Most people know that prisoners write to resist,' commented the prisoner and novelist Peter Feraru. 'Literature by prisoners is viewed almost universally as a literature of resistance,' agreed Sigrid Weigel in the first academic study of prison writing to appear in post-war Germany.[13] That view would become central to the work of another professor of

German literature, Helmut H. Koch. Koch created an archive of prison writing at the University of Münster, and in 1986 co-founded a significant literary prize for people in prison – the Ingeborg Drewitz Prize. He later created an online portal for the 'literature of marginalized groups' (randgruppenliteratur.de), and until 2018 chaired a national working group on prisons (Arbeitskreis kritischer Strafvollzug).

Koch cites an incident at the University of Münster in the later 1970s as his personal turning point. The university pulled its support for a course focused on the contemporary poet Peter-Paul Zahl, because Zahl was in prison, convicted of attempted murder in the suspected context of left-wing terrorism. His 'insignificance in the national canon' was given as a further reason. In response, Koch decided to design and teach his own seminar series on writers in prison, which culminated in the publication of a collection that defined writing in prison as 'survival and resistance'.[14]

> *The opportunity writing offers to change something, both in yourself and in your environment, is huge.*[15]

In the context of a growing focus on resocialization, there was also hope that writing in prison could help in the rehabilitation process.[16] It therefore made sense to encourage and reward it. A national competition launched by the Federal Association for Prisoner Aid attracted 220 entries and produced a volume of twenty winning pieces. Writing in prison is 'more than just a way of passing the time', Ingeborg Drewitz explained in her afterword. It is reflexive, a way of 'thinking through a life from childhood to adulthood'. 'Writing can take you to freedom,' declared Peter Feraru.[17]

That sense of optimism – that change for the better can happen, and that everyone, even someone in prison, can be an agent of change – echoed not only Willy Brandt's hopes for a participatory democracy, but the spirit of 1968. The movements for civil rights, for sexual and racial equality, and against the war in Vietnam all looked, in different ways, to build a freer and better society. From the United States came a new language of social revolution and personal revelation. People in prison could not join the street protests, but they could be part of that new language. German prisoners wrote (in English, borrowing the U.S. activists' terminology) of 'coming out', of 'feelings' and of 'power' to continue the struggle.[18] Some aligned themselves with particular political struggles such as Vietnam:

> They dreamed of cherry blossom
> and a good rice harvest
> but when they awoke,
> exploded out of their dreams,
>
> the blossom was burned
> and the rice harvest eaten
> by the hungry bombers
> who flew over corpses.[19]

Others looked more broadly to the vision of struggle and change. 'in every thinkable and possible way i will try to disrupt & fight your demoralizing system, your conformism, your society – long live the extra-societal disruptive elements in our society!' wrote a woman prisoner in response to solitary confinement. She rejected capital letters (which standard German uses for all nouns) in favour of the lower-case style that left-wing writers hoped might revolutionize language itself.[20]

The mood of the time is captured by a journalist who in 1974 published a critical study of prisons. 'You have to imagine yourself back in those days to understand,' Ulf Stuberger explained when his book was reissued in 2014. 'It was still normal, then, critically to question the methods and policies of the new German state that had succeeded the Nazi dictatorship.'[21] And there was a belief that people in prison might have answers to some of those questions.

> *The treatment of prisoners . . . clearly reveals the extent to which democracy is a coverlet beneath which the old mechanisms of oppression are functioning perfectly.*[22]

Parliament passed a new penal code for the Federal Republic in 1976. It had been drafted, after some controversy, by the Grand

Commission assembled in 1967 by Gustav Heinemann as Minister for Justice: a mix of academics, politicians and practitioners including the distinguished prison governor Helga Einsele. It had put forward its proposals for criminal justice reform in 1971 – ironically the same year in which a nationwide poll revealed that half of West Germans wanted to see the death penalty reintroduced.[23] The proposals for reform became the basis for a government white paper in 1972.

But Brandt's political career was about to hit a wall in the wake of the Guillaume affair. His personal assistant, Günter Guillaume, was arrested as a Stasi agent, and Brandt resigned his Chancellorship in 1974. The new penal code was relegated to the parliamentary back-burner. It was only passed in the spring of 1976, under the new Chancellor Helmut Schmidt, with effect from 1 January 1977. As its primary aim, the new code declared, prison 'must enable the prisoner to lead a future life of social responsibility, without crime'.[24]

Drawing on the United Nations guidelines, the new code set out three key principles: the principle of *alignment*, whereby prison life should resemble life outside as closely as possible; the *anti-prisonization* principle, which looked to limit the effects of institutionalization; and the principle of *integration*, by which the prisoner was to be prepared to rejoin society.[25] The rehabilitative impetus of those principles was to be supported by a tailored programme of treatment. Section 6 of the code decreed that every convicted prisoner should undergo an expert assessment so that a 'prison plan' could be designed to meet their individual needs.

But the new laws said very little about *how* the newly named institutions of justice, using the same staff and buildings, and without additional funds, were to achieve individually tailored resocialization for all. In the context of the global recession that followed the oil crisis of 1973, which caused West Germany's GDP to fall by 1.4 per cent in 1975, Bonn did not see investing in prisons as a priority.

You say: this prison system is individual.
Then you give me a prisoner number
a laundry number

a library number
a toolshed number
an exercise group number.
I am a numbered
individual.[26]

Prisoner voices were already anticipating the gap between the intentions that had driven penal reform and its likely outcomes by late 1976. 'What a great tra-la there's been! And what's actually come of it? Basically zilch!!! Anything they'd have to fork out for has been delayed till the next century,' wrote a group of men in Berlin's Tegel prison. 'The pigs are already running around the place preparing us for the reality that nothing significant is going to change. On 1.1.77 the new law comes into force. It says we're all meant to be resocialized. How's that going to happen in this truncheon-based medieval prison system???'[27]

The new code (§18) declared singly occupied cells the norm. It was not the norm in Tegel, wrote the group, where 'two prisoners are randomly penned in together, in cells that are normally too small even for one'. The men had to take it in turns if they wanted to eat or write at the single small table; an unscreened lavatory meant they had to relieve themselves 'under the eyes and nose of their cellmate'.[28] They were writing to a panel that had convened to discuss prisoner rights in Berlin on 5 November 1976. The prison governor Helga Einsele, the writer Ingeborg Drewitz and the young RAF lawyer Otto Schily (who would later be Minister of the Interior in Gerhard Schröder's cabinet in 1998–2005) were there. Berlin's biggest prison, the letter from Tegel reminded the panel, was designed to hold 385 men but was currently holding 610; five prison reform laws and a new penal code had not made overcrowding a thing of the past.

Eight years later a man in prison in North Rhine–Westphalia would describe the apparently unchanged conditions as 'the tragic reality of the insult that is our allegedly so "modern" penal code'. Under those circumstances, he protested, 'prison is just old-style *detention*: closed for the *new code* because of overcrowding.'[29]

What do you call it, I ask, when you suddenly hate everything and nothing and keep wanting to scream about trivial stuff, or start smashing things up or bawl your eyes out? That's cabin fever, answered Mazze resignedly.[30]

Overcrowding exacerbates the choleric outbursts that residents in German prisons call *Knastkoller* ('prison choler' or cabin fever). In the later twentieth century, cabin fever could still get someone locked in a bare cell with (as August Klemp reported) only 'dry bread, water, coffee substitute, wooden bed with no mattress, one blanket, nothing to read but the Bible'. People in German prisons called the separation unit the 'bunker'; in north Germany, *Kaschott*. Günter Harzen, writing for Wolfenbüttel's prison magazine *Kaschott* in 1973, described the amenities: 'a bucket, a slops pail, a jug of water and a plastic wash basin are there to meet a person's needs. Fortunately,' he added wryly, 'proper food is served only every third day.' On the other two days there was bread and water, and for two out of every three nights the prisoner had to sleep on bare boards – 'every third day you get a mattress, so your bones can remember how good a mattress can feel. The next day the mattress is taken away again, of course.'[31]

Birgitta Wolf had lambasted the practice of giving proper food and a mattress only once every three days as 'unconstitutional' – it was 'mental and physical torture, carefully dosed so that the individual is psychologically broken without showing any visible physical damage'. Even pregnant women and women who had recently given birth or were breastfeeding could be segregated in the bunker, so long as a prison doctor was prepared to sign it off. Post-reform, when the journalist Monika Sperr visited the women's prison in Aichach in 1977, she was shocked to find the same arrangements still in place. In Aichach, being sent 'down the block' still meant 'bread and water like in a medieval dungeon, and warm soup only every third day'. Even people held in regular cells were allowed only one shower a week, she reported. On the other six days they made do with a bucket of warm water in the cell.[32]

What, then, had prison reform actually changed for people inside? 'The contemporary prison', wrote the investigative journalist, Helmut

Ortner, 'does not give anyone locked up in it the shadow of an opportunity to be "socialized". On the contrary: de-socialization is on the agenda.' That, he argued, was the result of a (literally) inbuilt contradiction: the bureaucratic notion that treatment within the system is possible 'is a terminological absurdity. The internal structure of prison means that punishment and treatment are incompatible.'[33] And re-integration still relied not only on what happened in prison, but what happened afterwards.

Ortner published Fred Kreisler's story of 'Life after Prison', which echoed the stories told by Wolf's correspondents in the pre-reform decades. Kreisler had been released after 22 months, during which he worked full-time and amassed savings of 229 DM – less than a month's rent for a one-room apartment. 'That says it all,' wrote Kreisler. Outside prison he found that getting and retaining employment – after less than two years inside – had become practically impossible. 'If you tell them you don't get the job; if you don't tell them and they find out, you're fired.' But in any case a job could be got only if the applicant had a registered abode. It was (and still is) a legal requirement in the Federal Republic that everyone has a registered address. 'I was only looking for a small furnished room,' explained Jürgen J. in his winning entry to a prison writing competition in 1981, 'but I couldn't get anything because I wasn't registered. But how could I register when I didn't have a home address? The same thing with work: no home address means no job . . . I could twist and turn all I liked, I always ended up on the street or back in prison.' His will to reintegrate had, by this time, evaporated: 'I've had enough.'[34] Inside and outside prison seemed to be two sides of a coin, and both showed a society that spat prisoners out, permanently.

PRISON POEM

§1. The prisoner should be enabled
to lead no future life in freedom!
§2. The effects of freedom
must be countered.[35]

Prison work, too, was still an issue. Section 41 of the reformed penal code directed that a person in prison must perform any work task he (*sic*) was allocated, provided that it was appropriate to his physical condition. In the words of one anonymous writer, that meant the obligation 'to be content with miserable starvation wages, and accept the possible loss of any professional skills we already have.'[36] In a poem written for Ingeborg Drewitz, Winand Buchacker conjured up the conditions of quota work in a cell, and put them in ironic dialogue with penal reform:

he squats on the bed,
his back bent.
through his fingers runs the tape,
the curtain tape,
for a housewife in freedom.
though the window light falls slanting
on his endless twitchings
on the caring federal republic
on the criminal justice reform[37]

In the 1980s workers in prisons earned between 1.50 and 5 DM per day, whereas the average daily wage 'outside' was around 133 DM before tax.[38] Around one-third of a resident's earnings was retained in a savings account; the remainder could be used to buy coffee, tobacco and other items from the prison shop: 'we're not supposed to forget how to consume,' commented the imprisoned activist Margit Czenki. And private suppliers made good use of their monopoly. Peter Fritze reflected on the boutique prices ('like on a Berlin high street') charged for instant coffee and cigarettes in the prison shop.[39] In Munich, a writing collective analysed the developing market economy values of the 1980s. Outside, they observed, a person's value is measured by his possessions: 'that's even more true in prison. When you own nothing at all, every little thing takes on huge significance.' The social order in prisons, they reflected, is

> a hierarchical order that revolves primarily around individual ownership. Anyone who earns a lot, relatively speaking, can buy a lot; he can afford increased and demonstrative consumption as a status symbol (and he can even permit others to consume with him – so he has many 'friends') . . . he has significant reserves, so can make profitable business deals.

It was a perfect microcosm of society outside.[40]

> *prison . . . often provides a clearer mirror image than any other area of society of how far humane and democratic consciousness has developed.*[41]

By 1979 Helga Einsele – by then retired as a prison governor, but still a notable figure in the reform movement – was losing hope. 'Nowhere', she observed, 'does one sense a belief that anyone should or could be helped by prison.' The new penal code had produced a watered-down, terminally underfinanced version of the ideas that had once inspired and driven the reform movement. 'I can say nothing about the effectiveness of the reform laws we welcomed with such high hopes,' she wrote in her autobiography: 'the readiness genuinely to invest in this area is as slight as it ever was.'[42]

Writers in prison mocked the discrepancies between theory and praxis. Some compared their conditions with the conditions in which animals were kept – and the animals came off better. 'Transported like livestock? – no way, animals are transported in superior conditions because there's a Society for the Prevention of Cruelty to Animals,' commented Werner Schlegel. Peter Fritze described pacing out a cell: 'just six steps from the window to the door. Even less widthways, not quite 2.8 metres. If someone shut a dog in a place like this the animal protection league would be here in a second.' One anecdote in circulation involved the German Shepherd Dog Association (*Deutsche Schäferhundverband*). That organization, the story ran, was looking to buy a disused prison building to house its canines: 'but a one-man cell doesn't provide enough space for a dog, and that would be regarded as cruelty to animals – so they're planning to knock two rooms into one'.[43] Even feeding someone in prison was reputed to cost less than feeding a dog.

Section 37 of the new penal code determined that work in prison must serve the purpose in particular of providing, acquiring or supporting skills for employment after release. Marianne Herzog, in prison for terrorist activity in the Red Army Faction, noticed that resocialization in women's prisons involved a lot of cleaning work. In Mainz she saw the youngest women inmates used as cleaners for not only the women's wing but the whole prison, 'including the office spaces and some parts of the men's building' – the only resocialization principle in operation was 'the Fairy Liquid principle'.[44] The women were offered no careers advice, sport, television or discussion groups. Men were often not much better off. 'How,' asked Alex in 1980, 'does the would-be progressive law look in practice, in this prison?' Alex tells the story of Darmstadt-Eberstadt, a prison that had twenty apprenticeships and 320 job opportunities – for 530 men. Most of those 'job opportunities' were repetitive tasks for less than 5 DM per day. Many of the men did the work in the same 2 × 4 metre (6½ × 13 ft) cells in which they slept. Eight years on, Manfred would describe another institution where less than half of the men had work of any kind. Those who did were screwing together ballpoint and fountain pens, processing scrap metal ('not just mindless but back-breaking work') or assembling electrical goods. The rest spent the day locked in their cells.[45]

Resocialization, commented the poet and prisoner Peter-Paul Zahl, was a swindle, and prison reform 'the most mendacious story in history'.[46] In the spirit of the German Model, Section 160 of the new code had ruled that people in prison must have co-determination at least in some areas of their lives. But even the new participatory structures seemed meaningless if they were the sum total of change. 'How does prisoner co-determination help to abolish prisons as instruments of violence of the ruling class?' demanded an anonymous collective in 1982. They answered their own question: 'it can't; it's just another instrument to make us acquiesce in the conditions we suffer; to make us wind flowers around the whip'.[47] In her 'ResocIAlization Fairytale' for a prisoner-edited collection in 1982, Uschi Keutsch drew a picture of prison reform as a CIA-style conspiracy to turn people in prison into Stepford Wives. Her protagonist is actively afraid 'of being released with a new set of values: hard work, ambition, punctuality, aspirations, egoism, orderliness, and cleanliness, and the will to strive for fame, wealth, and property. Fear for her life gripped her, and she started to scream.'[48]

5
Terrorist Interventions

It's time!
...
When will you ram the barricades,
When will you rise up, marching together?
Tear the walls down stone by stone,
Crush them, you prisoners, smash them down.[1]

In Germany, 1977 is remembered not as the year the new penal code came into force, but as the year of the German Autumn. It was a season of violence that would culminate in multiple deaths in prison.[2]

In 1968 the student Gudrun Ensslin and her boyfriend Andreas Baader had protested against the war in Vietnam by setting fire to two department stores in Frankfurt. The arsonists were released pending an appeal, and escaped to Paris when their appeal was turned down. In January 1970 they returned secretly to Germany and hid in the Berlin apartment of the left-wing journalist Ulrike Meinhof. Inspired by the Cuban revolution of the 1950s, Meinhof, Baader and Ensslin, and their lawyer Horst Mahler, planned the formation of a West German guerrilla force. But a spoke almost literally hit the wheel when Baader was stopped by police for speeding and failed to remember the details of his false ID. He was recognized, arrested and incarcerated in Tegel prison. Meinhof, an established figure on the Left, pulled strings to persuade the governor of Tegel that she and Baader were co-authoring a book and got permission to meet with him in a library, under guard. During their meeting an armed group, including Ensslin, stormed the library, and Baader and Meinhof jumped through a window to a getaway car. The Red Army Faction (popularly christened the Baader-Meinhof gang) was founded.

The RAF (which seemed blissfully unaware that its acronym coincided with that of the British airforce) set itself the task of offering the resistance the Hitler generation had failed to provide. Federal Germany, the group believed, was colluding in USA-led capitalist imperialism, the natural successor of Nazi politics. 'Its historical bent is fascist, intent on exploitation and subjugation, annihilation, waste, defoliation, the destruction of people and natural resources,' Meinhof would later write from prison. The RAF's 'May bombings' of 1972 killed four U.S. soldiers and caused deep embarrassment to the Bonn government. There was a massive police response and Meinhof, Baader and Ensslin were quickly traced and arrested (Mahler had been apprehended in 1970). They were taken to separate prisons and held in solitary confinement – a practice that would quickly become standard for terrorism suspects. The former RAF member Marianne Herzog, who published her prison memoir to raise awareness of solitary and its effects, tried to describe the indescribable: 23 hours a day completely alone in an isolated cell, one hour in the prison yard, alone with an armed guard. It was, she wrote, 'a slow form of murder'.[3]

Meinhof would commit suicide in prison in 1976. Writing to her lawyer from Cologne Ossendorf (where Anton Wasilenko had died in 1964, sparking the debate on prison reform), she tried to document the effects of solitary:

> the feeling your head's exploding (like the top of your skull is going to tear apart, or burst off) –
>
> the feeling that your spine marrow is being forced up into your brain, –
>
> the feeling your brain's slowly wrinkling, like dried fruit maybe
>
> . . . the feeling you're losing language –
>
> you can no longer identify the meaning of words, only guess –

sentences, grammar, syntax – no longer controllable.
when you're writing: two lines – at the end of the
second you can't remember how the first one began –
the feeling you're burning up inside –
... the clear awareness that you have no chance
of survival.

She described her cell, the window of which was obscured by fine-meshed wire and which had a neon light that burned constantly, day and night.[4] But the permanent silence of her isolation in the prison's 'dead' wing was the unbearable thing. Everything else, she wrote, was 'child's play, nothing – by comparison with the terror of the silence'.[5]

In 1980 Amnesty International wrote a letter to West Germany's Minister for Justice, Hans-Jochen Vogel. Amnesty had concluded a detailed investigation, the letter explained, which revealed that 'the prison conditions of prisoners suspected or convicted of politically motivated crimes in the Federal Republic of Germany are of concern to this organization under its Statute.' There was evidence that prolonged solitary confinement and social isolation impaired people's health. Discussions with experts, said an attached memorandum, 'lead Amnesty International to conclude that it is possible to accommodate security with humane treatment and that the present extreme social isolation of prisoners held in high security conditions is therefore gratuitous'.[6] In the same year, Werner Schlegel wrote of solitary as a kind of death. He had been arrested after throwing molotov cocktails during street protests against the isolation of RAF prisoners (and the death of one of them, Holger Meins) in 1974. He was sent to prison for six years, some of which he spent in isolation. He described that experience in a poem called 'Funeral Song'.

SOLITARY
Is the fear
of never again
living with my

BROTHERS and SISTERS
    in a normal way, together.
SOLITARY
is slow
    unstoppable
        DEATH
            – first your body
            then your soul –
    is silent
        clean
            total
                DESTRUCTION.[7]

Schlegel had been convicted under new anti-terrorist legislation that made forming a terrorist or revolutionary organization a criminal act.[8] In a poem called 'Healthcare', published in 1979, Heinz-Holger Stumme reflected ironically on the new law:

One of my fellow prisoners
must be suffering
from an infectious disease
His door has an extra lock
his window has wire mesh
between him and us there is
an empty cell.
So as not to endanger
his visitors from outside
he changes clothes
before each visit
probably for disinfection purposes.
When he turns his circles
alone in the yard
we have to keep our windows closed.

Today I read in the news
that the illness has a name.

> It's very dangerous.
> They call it
> forming revolutionary cells.[9]

The idea that the West German state regarded terrorism as an infectious disease had also occurred to Ingeborg Drewitz's correspondent Winand Buchacker. 'When I was in Hagen prison I read in the paper that the alleged "anarchist" Lothar Gent had been moved to the same institution,' he told her. Then, one morning,

> I looked out of the window and saw a bearded man, quite alone on a chair, flanked right and left by prison officers. Wait, I thought, that has to be that faint image I saw in the paper, all alone on a chair like that, and under guard . . . But at the same time I said to myself: perhaps he's ill, that man, because we don't have isolation torture in Germany; perhaps the illness is very infectious for other prisoners, and perhaps the prison officers have had immunizations.[10]

Isolation torture has . . . come to replace the death penalty.

Buchacker's faux-naive assertion that 'we don't have isolation torture in Germany' drips with irony. 'A few years from now, history will remember her,' he had written to Drewitz when Meinhof was found dead in her cell on 9 May 1976. 'I'm as sure of that as I'm sure that the new German fascism is going to come back and hit us like a boomerang. The Nazis are back on the advance everywhere.'[11] He remembered the young sex offender whose care-home history Meinhof had lambasted, and who had agreed to be castrated in 1976 and died of the operation – 'Jürgen Bartsch: they just let him die, cold as ice'. The state, observed Buchacker, had failed to prevent the deaths not only of Bartsch but of RAF members in prison – 'Jan Karl [*sic*] Raspe and all the others with unknown names' (he meant Holger Meins, as Jan-Carl Raspe was still alive in 1976). He was not, he assured Drewitz, alone in his conviction that West Germany, by its treatment of the terrorists, was risking its status as a legitimate state – it was a view shared by other prisoners. 'Isolation torture has become the hallmark of justice in Germany; it has come to replace the death penalty.'

He predicted more deaths in German prisons soon.[12]

Terrorists
are caged
because – illegally –
they planted bombs,
and killed people.
Politicians and their henchmen
are free as birds,
because they – legally –
are doing the same.
Where,
please,
is the emergency exit
from this fatherland??[13]

FOR MANY RESIDENTS, part of the experience of prison in the 1970s and '80s was sharing an institution with people who had rejected the legitimacy of the Federal Republic. Writers in prison discussed class justice, the ruling classes and the police state. In Tegel, the editors of the radical prison newspaper *Durchblick* (created to rival the institutionally approved *Lichtblick*) chose the raised fist as its emblem. 'For us the fist is first and foremost a symbol of resistance,' they explained, 'because the so-called "humane" system (prison system) in Berlin is actually so shitty that we *have* to defend ourselves against it every single day! . . . VIOLENCE DEMANDS COUNTER-VIOLENCE and that means RESISTANCE.'[14] 'We think the pigs are swine, especially when we hear about stuff like how Benno Ohnesorg got shot in Berlin,' Jürgen Callberg told the journalists who interviewed him, remembering the young demonstrator shot dead by a policeman during the anti-Shah demonstration of 1967.[15]

Margit Czenki, a member of the Munich Tupamaros, was imprisoned in 1971 for robbing a bank. She described the wake-up call in her prison cell as state oppression – 'wake-up terror'. Prison work was 'forced labour', and her own refusal to work a 'means of struggle'. 'You have to eat the system before it digests you!' declared another woman in prison, attributing the quotation (questionably) to Andreas Baader. Her fear, she added, was that the 'pigs' would 'take away my only weapons in here: paper and pencil'.[16] Prison graffitti reflected the mood: 'the RAF is the solution' – 'kill the police pigs'.[17]

The French philosopher Michel Foucault's famous study of psychological violence in the modern prison, *Discipline and Punish*, appeared in German in 1976.[18] Soon afterwards the prisoner and poet Uschi Keutsch urged her readers to resist the violence that 'goes after your brain' –

> they try violently
> to rule over you
> they want to defeat you
> with their poisoned weapons:
> isolation, humiliation, infantilization,
> repression, sanctions, surveillance,
> communication, contact, and stimulation deprivation.
> they are after your brain
> and your soul and your stomach.
> want to tear out
> your energy, your ideas and dreams,
> sensitivity, feelings, and thoughts.
> they want you to become like them: empty.
> don't let it happen
> defend yourself.[19]

IN 1974 A group of RAF prisoners protested against their solitary confinement by going on hunger strike. Holger Meins, who would soon after die of malnutrition, was force-fed in Wittlich prison and provided a description of the practice for his lawyers' use:

A restraint chair for force-feeding used in Guantánamo Bay.

2 sets of handcuffs around my ankles, a strap about 30 cm wide around my hip, two pieces of leather with 4 straps from the elbow to the wrist on the left arm, another two straps on the right arm – wrist and elbow, and one across the chest. Behind me a policeman or medic with both hands on my forehead, pressing my head firmly against the headrest . . .

The mouth: on the right the doctor on a stool with a small 'crowbar' about 20 cm long, one end curved and pointed, the other curved and flat, like a small frying-pan wrapped in a band-aid. He pushes it between my lips, pulling them apart with his fingers at the same time, and then past my teeth (pretty easy in my case, given I'm missing three teeth) to lever them apart . . . When the jaws are far enough apart, the medic on the left sticks – shoves – the clamp between the teeth . . . The tongue is pulled forward and forced down with forceps, or the doctor uses a finger with a steel sheath on his fingertip.

Force-feeding: A red stomach pipe (not a tube) is used, about the thickness of a middle finger . . . The slightest

> irritation when the pipe is inserted causes gagging and nausea and cramps in the chest and stomach muscles, setting off a chain reaction of extremely intense convulsions throughout the body, causing one to buck against the pipe ... When the pipe is in the stomach, a wider funnel is attached and a standard size jug (about a quarter-litre) is used to gradually force down small amounts of the soup ... They always gave a full jug, even when the gagging was extreme, ignoring it even when my whole body went into cramps that once lasted at least 5 or 6 minutes ...
>
> It is about 3 to 5 minutes before the pipe is taken back out, all depending. (With extreme resistance, I can make it last as long as 20 to 30 minutes, but I'm not strong enough to prevent the force-feeding altogether.)[20]

Just before he died of starvation, Meins wrote that 'you either survive at any price or fight to the death; you're either the problem or the solution, there's nothing in between.' Karlheinz Barwasser, a gay activist and the first prisoner to edit a collection of writing from German prisons, was interviewed in the early 1980s and consciously or unconsciously echoed Meins. 'You can see writing as a big contribution to resistance,' Barwasser asserted, 'you either perish or you make it, there's nothing in between.'

Barwasser described himself as a 'writer for the sake of survival.'[21]

IN SEPTEMBER 1977, RAF activists kidnapped the prominent West German industrialist and former Nazi Hanns Martin Schleyer. Their intention was to force the release of the group's surviving founder members, Andreas Baader, Gudrun Ensslin and Jan-Carl Raspe (Ulrike Meinhof had died in prison the previous year). When the Bonn government remained unbending, Palestinian militants stepped in, and on 13 October hijacked a Lufthansa tourist flight on its way to Mallorca. On the night of 17 October, the aircraft was stormed by German special troops in Mogadishu in Somalia, and all but one of the hijackers were killed. The following morning, the three RAF

The scene in Karlsruhe after Siegfried Buback and his driver were shot dead in 1974.

prisoners were found dead in their Stammheim cells. Ensslin died by hanging; Baader and Raspe were found shot through the head. The autopsy verdict was suicide, though some spoke of murder by the state. The same day, Schleyer was executed by his kidnappers and left in the boot of an abandoned car.

The published correspondence of Winand Buchacker and Ingeborg Drewitz ended two days before Schleyer's abduction, when Buchacker was transferred to an open prison – so we never get his perspective on the concluding events of the German Autumn. But his letter of 8 April 1977 did respond to the assassination of West Germany's Attorney General, Siegfried Buback, by members of the RAF. Buback was a former Nazi Party member, a fierce opponent of communism and the declared enemy of Germany's radical left, and Buchacker told Drewitz about a party held by people in prison to celebrate his passing. The Attorney General, he explained, was 'a swine who has had it coming for years, and for Federal German citizens and for democracy this is a kind of birthday party'.[22] The celebrations of Buback's death in the 'invisible institution' apparently went unnoticed.

But they anticipated a scandal that would explode in society outside a fortnight later, when an anonymous obituarist of Buback (calling himself Mescalero) confessed to feeling 'secret glee' at his assassination, unleashing furious protest and debate.

You're not in Dachau here!

Influential voices in Germany have suggested that the – tiny – RAF was of such immense social and psychological significance for the Federal Republic because its explicit engagement with the Nazi past 'reopened a chapter of the murderous history that preceded its foundation'.[23] In writing from the prison, however, that chapter had never been closed. Marianne Herzog described women she met in prison who were still serving life sentences in the early 1970s and who remembered executions under the Nazis. 'They show me the places where the shootings happened. In Anrath prison. In Frankfurt. In Hamburg.' She found herself wondering which of the officers she encountered had participated in Nazi crimes. 'Did she do that under the Nazis too? Did she take breakfast to the women who were going to be shot in the prison yard afterwards?' When one of the guards yelled at her charges, Herzog shouted back, 'You're not in Dachau here!'[24] The ghost of Hitler walked the corridors of West Germany's prisons persistently after 1945.

For Dieter Bock, writing in Darmstadt-Eberstadt in 1980, entering prison was still overlaid with images of concentration camps. 'You empty your pockets of the personal stuff like keys, money, papers and documents and have them registered, then you take all your clothes off and get given a prison uniform,' he remembered. 'The hostile relationship between the inmate and the prison officer becomes very clear. At that moment images of prison camps or concentration camps came into my head.' In one of his first letters to Drewitz, Winand Buchacker told a similar story. He had visited the concentration camp at Bergen-Belsen in 1972, and stood on the Lüneburg Heath, 'a part of the country I love so much – but what leapt to my mind were the images I'd seen in photos, of the skeletons of the dead stacked up'. The memory of a state that had perpetrated crimes against humanity, combined with the contemporary experience of prison, produced a continuing fearfulness in him. 'Back then I thought it could never happen again, not nowadays. Back then I didn't know what I know now: that it can always happen again, any hour of any day, and nobody hears when you shout that out.'[25] As if to illustrate Buchacker's point, his fellow prisoner Günter Machura told a story about 1970s West Germany, where passers-by stopped to tell homeless people that they belonged in concentration camps.[26] From the prisoners'-eye perspective, the RAF's conviction that Federal Germany was still a Nazi state was consistent with a long-standing anxiety about the continuing legacy of the Hitler era in the criminal justice system.

my own history can't be understood or interpreted without the nazi period

Peter Schneider's correspondent Peter-Jürgen Boock had been one of the group that kidnapped and executed Hanns Martin Schleyer. Two years after the German Autumn he quit the RAF, and was arrested in Hamburg in January 1981. 'the history of the raf, the history of almost all members of the group that i know, and also my own history can't be understood or interpreted without the nazi period and the "guilt of the fathers",' Boock explained to Schneider: 'that's what makes the raf a double challenge for the forefathers.' The 'forefathers', many of whom (like Kiesinger and Schleyer) were former Nazis, now needed scapegoats, he argued, and 'because they insist on being guiltless, and always just "went along with things", we – i – inevitably have to be doubly guilty.'[27] But not all acts of resistance in post-war West Germany were violent.

For me, prison is a continuation of my peaceable act of refusal of this state

The German women's peace movement (*Frauenfriedensbewegung*) emerged in the 1950s in response to the atom bomb dropped on Hiroshima and Nagasaki by the U.S. military in 1945. Out of it came the broader peace movement, which in October 1981 organized the biggest demonstration the Federal Republic had ever seen. It was supported by a new political party, the Greens, which had won its first parliamentary seats in 1979. A key concern of the peace activists was the re-armament of the Federal Republic and the stationing of atomic weapons in West Germany in the context of a developing Cold War. Activists blockaded sites for nuclear weapons – an act for which they could be imprisoned under Section 240 of the penal code ('violent coercion').[28]

Luise Rinser was a novelist who in 1947 had published a memoir of her incarceration under the Nazis, her *Prison Diary*. A biography published in 2011 revealed that she had been economical with the truth about her (lack of) resistance to Nazism.[29] But in the new West Germany she reinvented herself as a prominent opponent of nuclear armament, and won a reputation as a 'Joan of Arc of the German peace movement'.[30] In 1987 she edited Germany's first-ever anthology of writing by women in prison. The title, *Let Me Live: Women in the Joint* (*Laßt mich leben: Frauen im Knast*), struck a self-consciously revolutionary attitude with its use of the argot word for prison, *Knast*. The publisher was Reiner Padligur Verlag, the only German publishing house to have been founded by people in prison.[31] Among the contributors were women who had been arrested at the anti-nuclear blockades, who had chosen to serve prison sentences rather than pay a fine or do community service.

'For me, prison is a continuation of my peaceable act of refusal of this state that is re-arming itself,' wrote Jutta von Ochsenstein. 'In that context I refuse to signal my agreement or pretend that I'm ok with what's happening by giving my money or my labour.' Her fellow activist Andrea Pfeiffer agreed: 'paying a fine, and thereby indirectly co-financing the arms race, or spending the equivalent number of hours doing community service wasn't something I could square with my conscience.' For all their determination, they responded with shock to their lived experience of prison. 'Is it legitimate to cage me and other human beings?' asked Pfeiffer.[32] Kathrin Rodi described how humiliating it felt when prison staff walked into her cell while she was on the lavatory, or rifled through her belongings and read her letters. 'How come it's not a crime to lock people up and treat them like shit?' demanded Maria Braig, less restrainedly. 'The hypocrisy of all of society suddenly becomes really clear in here . . . You should all feel sickened, because you can't keep ignoring the things happening in here and in other places,' she told her readers.[33]

The women of the peace movement were bitterly critical of Germany's choice to invest in war and weaponry while children around the world were starving, and critical of a government that called itself democratic while passing harsh sentences on its citizens for acts of peaceful protest. They questioned the meaning and legitimacy of the prison system. At the same time, unlike the RAF prisoners, they were clear in their view that West Germany was neither a fascist nor a neo-fascist state. 'We're not living in a military dictatorship, and we're no longer living under fascism – we live in a democratic, constitutional state,' wrote Ochsenstein. Even while they rejected Federal German defence policies, they recognized the benefits of parliamentary democracy, and consciously maintained an awareness of activists around the world who were suffering worse fates than theirs for acts of peaceful protest.[34] They thus distanced themselves from the militants who saw their own fates as equivalent to the sufferings of prisoners of conscience under the toughest authoritarian regimes, and insistently presented Federal Germany as a still-fascist state.

Part of the peace activists' concern was that *they* would soon be released, but other, less privileged women, imprisoned on drug- or theft-related charges – 'poor creatures, all of them', worried Braig – would stay in prison. Rodi, for all her feelings of humiliation, knew that she was lucky in comparison with women who would be suffering the conditions of incarceration for years to come – 'I know that I'll be out soon; but what about the others?!' '10 months, 2 years, life . . . how do you bear it?' wondered Ochsenstein.[35]

It was a question that would not go away.

6
'How do you bear it?'

today on an
overcast day in
march a man
in the yard lost
his penis it
slipped
from his trouser leg
and crawled off
with a crowd
of small grey snails
when he saw it
he wept
in perplexity[1]
Ludwig Lugmeier, 1987

Monika Sperr, reporting on the women's prison in Aichach in 1977, listed conditions that were typical: visits were allowed for one hour a month, or half-an-hour each fortnight. The women who had husbands and children sat at long tables opposite their families, with a prison officer supervising.[2] Men's prisons operated in much the same way. In a letter to a prison newspaper, one man explained how he longed feverishly for each visit, sometimes couldn't sleep properly for days before it, 'and then the visit turns out to be a sobering shock: long waiting times, body searches, packed visiting rooms, noise, stress, short visiting times'. Couples and families were 'watched over by prison officers who often have no tact or feeling, and sometimes even subject our wives to their scorn'. The longed-for human contact was spoiled by tensions and strain. And writing home gave lovers no privacy to mend or maintain relationships – letters out and letters in were all read by prison staff. For a married man, the loss of his status as breadwinner increased the pressure, leaving him 'in a vacuum of defenselessness and uncertainty. He knows and feels the danger to his marriage, but his hands are tied.'[3]

'Often the prisoner's wife is the only contact he has to the outside world,' another man explained, 'and that makes him dependent on her. It doesn't matter how his wife tries, she can't stop him feeling conscious of his weakness and reacting with fear.'[4] One woman described how her marriage ended in those circumstances – 'my husband was able to take his own life under the otherwise so watchful eye of the law.' She was left with two children, living on social security – 'and I've discovered that it really matters what kind of a widow you are'. The social exclusion of people in prison is shared by their partners and children, 'in a way that no one thought about when the sentence was passed', commented Alex.[5]

> *What does the state do, under whose particular protection marriage and the family are supposed to be?* NOTHING *– on the contrary, it promotes the disruption and destruction of family ties!!*[6]

Some cherished hopes that the Swedish model of conjugal visits (which had been under discussion in Baden-Württemberg in 1970) would soon be extended across Germany.[7] Writers in prison tried to explain the anxiety that attaches to gender and sexuality inside. 'It's all alive and kicking in here,' Peter-Jürgen Boock told Peter Schneider: 'the macho cult, misogyny, having the stiffest dick, homophobia'. Relationships are bound to collapse, he observed, when men's only access to women is via pornographic images that 'signal only one thing: women are venal and will offer themselves to anyone – cunts, basically'. This was 'a man's world, a world of clichés where only hard language seems to signify . . . so no wonder language starts to shift, and women become cunts, whores, and sluts.'[8] 'Now you say "wank" instead of masturbate and you shit on those emancipated bitches, give them a slap in the teeth if they don't do as they're told,' a writer for a prison newspaper summarized his sexual education inside. Lovers grow apart when one of them is in prison, reflected Harry Graf in his prison diary, 'because they live in such completely different circumstances and at some point they don't even speak the same language any more.'[9]

And there is the humiliation of being caught masturbating when a prison officer enters your cell. Detlef Kruklinski's tragicomic story 'Meat' begins with a man caught in an intimate moment with chunks of tinned goulash. Its protagonist, Franz Flöte, has taken the advice of a cell neighbour and opened a tin of goulash meat to remedy his need to orgasm. But he forgets to tape over the spyhole in his door, and his activities are interrupted by the sudden sound of heavy keys. 'Franz Flöte stared in horror at the door, two open tins of meat in his hands, his penis between them. He gazed into three pairs of eyes that seemed to pierce him.' The comedy does not end well for Franz. Six months are added to his sentence when the officers convince a judge that he is violent and dangerous. Franz becomes impotent.[10]

Women in prison write less anxiously about sex – perhaps because women suffer less social pressure around 'getting some', perhaps because they serve shorter sentences. Luise Rinser published erotically charged poems like Gaby Krücken's:

wild and unbridled
the temptation
the greed for you
raking my fingers through
your chive-yellow hairwisps
biting your rabbit mouth
rubbing your tongue
the tip of mine on your palate
tasting your mouth-smell
your shoulders
slipslipslide
downwards

through your shimmering belly hair
bouncing down below is
the startled
little nose bear – dingdong –
rubbing against my pearl – sliding –
the sound of seashells
the slippery oyster
glistens in her cave.
hey, we're falling in the slime
an octopus sprays
hot ink in
my insatiable
snowflake whirl
a big-talking witch
greedy and sinful
gluttonous and drunk.[11]

Women in prison describe anxiety focused less on sex than on children. During a project they ran with women in German prisons in the late 1970s, the researchers Uta Klein and Gertrud Hardtmann were struck by the guilt and shame the women felt. Women in prison very often see themselves as bad mothers who have failed their children – but prisons are also (still) failing women. Helga Einsele, who created Germany's first mother-and-baby unit in Preungesheim prison, observed that women's criminality was, in the context of the existing system, 'substantially their children's problem'. Statistics from Preungesheim indicated that for every hundred women who went to prison, some 250 to 280 children lost a mother and primary carer. Many of the children were consigned to the care of the state.[12]

My thoughts revolve
around you –
my child!
In going to prison
I took a piece
of your life.

Please try
to forgive me.[13]

And women report less anxiety than men around homosexuality in prison. Because lesbianism had never been illegal, there were no women in West German prisons *because* they were gay; but some women had not known before prison that lesbianism existed. One woman in Rinser's anthology of 1987 admitted to arriving in prison with 'no conception of lesbians or bisexual women'. She describes how struck she was by the calm acceptance of relationships inside: 'how self-evident it was that the lesbian couples sat together in the common room, showing their togetherness, and how open and relaxed they were with everyone else'.[14]

Men's accounts are different. In 1969 the first Criminal Law Reform Act had made sex between men over 21 a legal activity. But the reform law came too late for men who had already built up a criminal record because they were gay. In 1982 Winand Buchacker told their story, in a long, bitter poem called 'the change':

1952 was the his first time in the joint
– for homosexuality –
he was twenty-five and a gentle soul.
he got
two years without parole.

1957 was his second time in the joint
– for homosexuality –
he was thirty and still a gentle soul.
he got
three years and two months without parole.
inside they gave him hell,
the prisoners,
the personnel.

1961 was his third time in the joint
– for homosexuality –

he was thirty-four with a hate-filled soul.
a homosexual judge gave him
two years and six months without parole.
that judge is still free.
they said that he
was a disgusting faggot.
they said
under hitler we'd have gassed you.

1974 was his fifth time in the joint,
– for armed robbery.
he was forty-seven,
disturbed and broken.
the homosexuality law was gone,
but his criminal record was an aggravating factor.
he got
eight years and four months

and is serving it in the former penitentiary,
rheinbach,
with the old familiar guards.[15]

And stigma outlasts laws. 'The homos are different,' Jürgen Callberg told the journalists who interviewed him in the 1970s, 'and they suffer a lot at the hands of other prisoners – they get teased and wound up. They're very sensitive, easily offended, and most people avoid them.'[16]

From different perspectives, both Buchacker and Callberg saw gay men in prison as victims. But others were looking with hope to the shifts in society outside. 'Come out of hiding and fight those who are fighting us,' one writer for a prison newspaper urged. 'It's not against the law to be gay . . . I want to encourage anyone who is openly homo to help another homo have his coming-out.' Marc Wiltzius, an out gay man in prison writing for a collection edited by another out gay prisoner – Karlheinz Barwasser – complained that sex in prison was too often described 'as if it were an endless chain of rape'. Gay men

Gay rights demonstration, Berlin, 1973.

could now live their sexuality inside, he argued. 'Even in prison it's possible to be confidently and openly gay.'[17] But as late as 1987 Peter-Jürgen Boock was unconvinced – 'there's hardly another place where homosexuals are still as hounded, defamed and bullied as they are in prison,' he warned. And again masculine anxiety found its expression in brutal language – gay men were 'cocksuckers, arsefuckers, queer faggots'.[18] If society inside mirrors society outside, then it comes as no surprise that people who disrupt gender roles in prison provoke anxiety and risk violence.

That emerges with brutal clarity in Klaus Mahn's short story 'Esmeralda', published in 1980. Esmeralda is a transgender prisoner who has had hormone treatment, and dreams of having the 'spectacular operation' the German press was just starting to report on. In a men's prison, Esmeralda faces vicious threats from fellow residents and officers. Eventually Esmeralda takes a piece of broken glass and saws off her penis and testicles – over the cell toilet, which becomes the receptacle for discarded masculinity. Bleeding to death, and violently relieved of her masculinity, the protagonist is called 'she' for the first time in the story. She 'dies as she would like to have lived – as Esmeralda.'[19]

'What a bloody mess', says the turnkey,
'not another one!'[20]

Self-harm is disproportionately common in prisons, and takes many forms. During the eight months he spent on remand in Düsseldorf prison hospital, Winand Buchacker was confronted with the desperation of the 'swallowers': people who deliberately ingested dangerous objects such as nails and razor blades. Sometimes the objects could be surgically removed from their stomachs. But one man, Buchacker reported with a kind of fascinated horror, had ingested a mercury thermometer – and refused surgery. 'Can you imagine what that means?' he asked Drewitz, 'and what would happen if it broke inside his stomach?' For all her experience of prisons, Drewitz was shocked: it was the first she had heard of the phenomenon.[21] Outside prison, swallowing is socially invisible. In prison, by contrast, it is highly visible, to staff as well as residents. Three years later, Peter Feraru visualized a story through the eyes of a senior prison nurse. The nurse is advising a young colleague on how to deal with patients who have swallowed bed springs, razor blades or nails. 'Guys like this want to . . . blackmail us, do you see?' she urges, with only a little hesitation to betray that she is choosing her words carefully for a newcomer. 'Remember: never give in.' She explains the clinical procedure:

> We give them sauerkraut. Then off into solitary, with the knife or pencil still in their stomachs. We observe them on camera. If it happens – and sometimes it does – that one of them gets to that critical point where the grim reaper . . . we whisk him off to hospital, pronto, onto the operating table.

The procedures are clear, if harsh. But no one ever seems to ask – observed another writer in prison – *why* swallowers risk their lives in this way.[22] In a poem he wrote for Drewitz, Winand Buchacker tried to explain:

they swallow in permanent panic,
they swallow for freedom
futilely,
they swallow out of fear,
constantly,
individual record: 31 operations.[23]

friday the 13th
said the warder
(who found him)
with a shrug of his shoulders
not without first
– with a shrug of his shoulders –
(dutifully as per the routine)
having ascertained:
THIS ONE'S ALREADY COLD.[24]

Suicide is one of the topics to which writers in prison turn regularly. Those left behind express their sorrow but also, sometimes, a kind of envious irritation at the other's escape. 'It has offended everyone', an anonymous fellow inmate wrote to the departed Lothar S., 'that you have escaped your subjection and now have total freedom.'[25] For Birgitta Wolf's contact R. H. in 1972, suicide was prison's inevitable and logical effect – it was what the institution demanded.

In the cell next door
On the morning of 11 July 71
they found him –
dead –
with a plastic bag over his head
tied round his neck
lying in his bed –
grey,

bloodless.
He had adjusted to the institution –
nothing more
need be said.[26]

Heinrich Behr, a lifer who had experienced a number of prison suicides, described one in particular that stuck in his memory. 'There is one case I'll never forget: a prisoner who had been particularly shamefully tormented kept trying, whenever people from outside visited, to attract attention to his plight by screaming from the window.' One day, a game of handball with a visiting team was due to happen, and staff at the prison were nervous that the man would cause a rumpus. 'So the review officer went to him in his cell and said: you're being moved to another prison. The prisoner replied: if you do that to me, I'll hang myself. The prison officer is supposed to have replied – others heard him say it: go ahead and do that, then at last we'll be rid of you.' Shortly afterwards the man was found dead: he had hanged himself. 'One might assume', Behr concluded, 'that the prison officer would have been disciplined. On the contrary: he was promoted.'[27]

For Behr, this was the story not just of one rogue officer, but of a system. In 1969 the Norwegian sociologist Johan Galtung coined the phrase 'structural violence' to describe suffering that is produced by a systematically uneven distribution of power, and in 1971 Philip Zimbardo concluded from his controversial Stanford prison experiment that systems have the capacity to brutalize even well-meaning individuals.[28] Behr's story points to a belief among people in prison that the system not only produces but *rewards* cruelty.

Against those responsible for the years of solitary confinement and therefore for my suicide . . . I herewith bring a criminal charge of murder

The strangest accounts of suicide are – for obvious reasons – those told in the first person. Harry Graf's fictional short story 'I Got Out' features a narrator who describes his own dead body, hanging at the window. 'My head is a bit twisted, my mouth slightly open, my tongue visible between my teeth, the eyes already a bit clouded,' observes the voice: 'Now I'm free.'[29] But strangest of all is Horst Rakow's non-fictional account of his own suicide in Berlin's Moabit prison in 1976.

Rakow spent four and a half years in solitary confinement, accused of a murder he denied committing. In a manuscript he knew would survive him, he claimed that his prison conditions were a slow form of murder. He described spending all but half an hour of the day in a cell measuring 8 square metres (86 sq. ft) – the remaining time was spent outdoors, alone. In August 1975 Germany's Supreme Court agreed to relax his conditions – he was allowed a full hour outdoors each day and contact with a fellow prisoner twice a week for an hour. But the governor of Moabit inexplicably challenged that decision, and had its implementation delayed for a further month.

In the last months of his life, Rakow was permitted to play table tennis once a week and to have daily contact with a fellow resident. It was both too little and too late. Being socially isolated for four and a half years had made him deeply fearful of the company of others, and contact with people now produced uncontrollable anxiety in him. 'For some time now I have found myself unable to communicate in a relaxed way with other human beings,' he wrote. 'I feel inhibited, clumsy, tense, and stiff. Similarly I can no longer have a coherent conversation. For a while now I have even started to be scared of being in the company of other people. It makes me feel terribly fearful.' On 13 June 1976, after five years in prison, he suffocated himself with a plastic bag. Before he died he wrote a formal complaint against Judge Walter Schwerdtner, who had sentenced him, the State Prosecutor, Pietsch, and the governor of Moabit prison. 'Against those responsible for the years of solitary confinement and therefore for my suicide,' he wrote, 'I herewith bring *a criminal charge of murder*.'[30]

> *Prison is . . . the visible expression of a violence that inheres – often less manifestly – in the contemporary societal system.*[31]

IN 1980 A group of young men in Lübeck's youth prison reported the rape of one of their number by another prisoner. Their complaint, which was written collectively, focused less on the individual act of violence – the rape – and more on the indifference of the system. The responsible officer, Herr Z., not only sent the youngster who had reported abuse straight back on to the wing but incited his cellmates to rape him again. 'I got to cell 604 and hadn't even unpacked when Herr Z. arrived and said the following: "if T. isn't obedient or doesn't wash, you can stick a broom handle in his ass!"' An adult man in prison, Jochen Quentmaier, reported a similar experience in Rheinbach prison two years later. In a letter to a national working group on prisons, Quentmaier indicated that he had been raped at knifepoint by his cellmate. The experience was traumatic in itself, but the focus of his complaint and his bitterest memory was the indifference of the authorities to which he reported it. Rape, he explained, was known about, tolerated and trivialized, not only in Rheinbach but throughout the prison system – sexual violence was widely regarded as 'a workplace accident'.[32]

Stories from the prison accuse the grand reform of merely building, in Peter-Paul Zahl's words, 'little asbestos walls in Hell'. People in prison remained 'a forgotten group on the edge of society', wrote Helmut Koch. To be forgotten is to be profoundly vulnerable: if nobody knows or cares what happens to you, you cannot be safe. In 1999 the distinguished German novelist Martin Walser would argue that the published collections of 'incredibly tough stories' from the prison said 'a lot about the system'.[33]

But they also said something about the relative freedom people in prison in the Federal Republic had to tell their stories of an unsafe system. Prisoners in East Germany were *not* being visited by, or corresponding with, prominent writers such as Walser (or Drewitz or Schneider); they were not publishing critiques of law and society, entering literary competitions or writing for prison newspapers like those that flourished in West Germany from the 1960s.

Not a word was emerging from prisons on the other side of the Berlin Wall.

Part III

Risen from the Ruins: East Germany, 1949–89

Anyone who attacks our antifascist order or disturbs the building of our peaceful society has committed a crime and will be punished for his criminal activities.
(GDR Ministry of Justice, 1951)[1]

it's not me but you, your system, that commits crimes – crimes against humanity. I'm not the criminal – you are.
(Horst Fichter, in Stasi custody, 1952)[2]

7
Bearing Witness

Let us plough and build our nation, learn and work as never yet,
that a free new generation faith in its own strength beget![1]
National anthem of the GDR

In 1946 the Soviet authorities in eastern Germany merged the Communist and Social Democrat parties to create a Socialist Unity Party (Sozialistische Einheitspartei Deutschland, or SED) – soon known simply as 'the Party'. The German Democratic Republic was founded on 7 October 1949. Its national anthem, 'Risen from the Ruins', envisaged a society of free human beings. In fact the GDR held huge numbers of people in prison. It reported much lower crime rates than its Western neighbour, but two-thirds of all crimes were punishable by incarceration.

In 1945 the Soviet Military Administration in the eastern zone had established Special Camps, some on the sites of concentration camps such as Sachsenhausen and Buchenwald. The Special Camps held prominent Nazis and others felt to pose a threat – like the fourteen-year-old Erika Riemann, arrested in 1945 for drawing a moustache on a portrait of Stalin. She spent eight years in Special Camps and East German prisons, surviving rape, near-starvation and, unimaginably, an appendectomy carried out without anaesthetic.[2]

The camps were operated by the Soviet secret police, and survivors remember interrogation methods that defied description – 'they invented terrible games to play with their prisoners,' is all that Wolfgang Löffler, a former internee, would say. 'In the cellar of the Soviet secret service there was no sense of time,' he went on. 'It was always brightly lit with loud music playing. That way you didn't hear the screaming of the people who were being tortured.' Women could expect to be sexually abused.[3] Survivors describe freezing cold, starvation, filth and vermin. Tuberculosis prowled. One in three of the estimated 150,000 men and women held in Special Camps died and thousands more were deported to the USSR for hard labour. Tens of thousands perished during the freezing winter of 1946 that saw Myrl Alexander, in the American zone, appeal urgently to the U.S. authorities to send more fuel and food for his prisons.

In 1948 the Soviet Military Administration declared denazification complete and handed the camps over to the new East German government. Some, including Sachsenhausen and Buchenwald, were closed. Others, such as Bautzen and Torgau, continued to function as penal institutions (and are still in use as Federal German prisons today). Werner Gentz, a seasoned reformer who had driven the Weimar penal reforms and then been removed from the Ministry of Justice by the Nazis, was appointed head of East Germany's department of prisons. He produced guidelines for a socialist penal system, where people in prison would be helped to build a sense of self and community.[4] His vision of a rehabilitative criminal justice was tangibly present in the constitution of the GDR of 1949 (Art. 137), which promised a prison system 'founded on the idea of the education of corrigible individuals through common, productive work.' But Gentz was out of step with the developing power base. In 1950 the Politburo relieved him of his authority over the prison system and transferred it to the Ministry of the Interior and the police. Security considerations, declared a police decree of 1951, must trump the 'false humanitarianism' that had crept in to 'dilute the idea of prison.'[5]

It soon emerged that 3,432 of those held in the Special Camps had been imprisoned without trial. The new East German authorities set about remedying that. Thousands of fast-track court cases took place in Waldheim prison in Saxony over the three months from April to June 1950, and 3,392 sentences were passed – 32 of them death sentences. On a single night in November 1950, 24 executions were carried out in the cellar of Waldheim prison.[6]

Waldheim prison.

In the same year the new Ministry for State Security – Ministerium für Staatssicherheit, more usually called the Stasi – was established.

What can you say of such a time?

Erich Loest was an East German novelist. During the early years of the GDR he was associated with a group of critical political thinkers around Walter Janka (who headed the East Berlin publishing house Aufbau) and Wolfgang Harich, a philosophy professor. In 1957 Loest and others associated with the 'Harich Group' were arrested. Four years after Stalin's death Walter Ulbricht, the GDR's First Secretary, had decided to send a signal. Harich was sentenced to ten years (of which, Loest reports in his autobiography, Harich spent seven in the gruelling conditions of solitary confinement). Walter Janka was sentenced to five years with solitary, and Loest himself to seven and a half years, two and a half of them in solitary confinement. He served his sentence in the Stasi's special facility, Bautzen II – an 'intimate little nick' near the Polish and Czech border just east of Dresden.[7] It neighboured the much bigger 'yellow misery' of Bautzen I, the former Soviet Special Camp that derived its nickname from its yellow bricks.

The prison years fill around one hundred pages of Loest's four-hundred-page autobiography. 'What can you say of such a time?' he writes. 'A year consisted of 365 days, twelve letters, four visits, and two or three stomach ulcers. What can you write about a year like that?' As he was writing his memoir, his daughter reminded him that he had once been someone who liked to tell funny stories – but after Bautzen he was no longer that person: 'funny or grotesque incidents hardly weighed in the balance. Dull fury, apathy, fights about nothing until two men fell on each other's throats – that happened a lot.'[8] In 2013 Loest committed suicide at the age of 87.

The GDR does not 'old political prisoners.

Loest, Janka and Harich were among the estimated 180,000 people sentenced to prison in the GDR for crimes against the state.[9] But any distinction between political and criminal prisoners was officially denied. In an administrative circular of September 1951, the East German Ministry of Justice had declared that

> nobody is imprisoned for his political views. Anybody who attacks our antifascist order or disturbs the building of our peaceful society has committed a crime and will be punished for his criminal activities. That is why prisoners of this kind are not 'political prisoners' but criminal miscreants, and to call them political prisoners is herewith forbidden.[10]

In July 1982 a young East German woman, Petra Koch, and her boyfriend Helmut were arrested by Czechoslovakian border police as they tried to cross into Austria. They had promised each other they would deny everything if they were caught. But when Koch's interrogator started to hit her ('he pulls me up by my handcuffs, and when I'm on my feet he hits me in the face with the palm and then the back of his hand, left, right, left, right'), and hearing Helmut's cries of pain from a neighbouring room, she admitted they had been trying to escape to the West. Both were convicted of illegal border crossing, a crime against the state. Koch remembers a visit from her mother in prison. She tried to tell her mother that murderers in the GDR were treated better than political prisoners; but 'There are no politicals here!' an officer intervened angrily: 'everyone here is a criminal who has broken the law!'[11]

Birgit Schlicke was detained in March 1988, just a year and a half before the Wall fell. Her family had made an application to emigrate West, and she was arrested when the Stasi discovered a letter she had typed to a West German human rights group, describing the bullying tactics used by Stasi officers against the family. She was incarcerated in the women's penitentiary Hoheneck, for the 'treasonable communication of non-secret information'. Schlicke remembers the words of her Stasi interrogator when she described herself as a political prisoner. 'The GDR does not 'old political prisoners. You 'ave committed a crime and you 'ave been sentenced for it. You are no better than any other criminal.'[12] (In their memoirs, former 'politicals' – who tended to be highly educated – delight in recording the regional accents of their less well-educated oppressors.)

In socialist society nobody needs to become a criminal.[13]

The GDR, declared one of its own state publications in 1969, had distinguished itself from the West by fully implementing the humanistic aims of the Allied occupying forces, most particularly the Soviet Union. East German prisons, it explained, now exemplified that humanity.[14]

In legal terms, people who offended against this model republic were not merely 'no better' than any other criminal – they were worse. According to the Penal and Reintegration Law of January 1968, criminality was perpetuated in socialist society by enemies of the state. 'The socialist law of the German Democratic Republic', it declared, 'serves the struggle against crimes that derive from the capitalist era and are nourished by hostile influences and moral degeneracy in the imperialist states.'[15] By that logic it was the fault of enemies of the state that criminality still existed at all. 'You're the worst offenders there are. I'd take any criminal in preference to you,' Erika Riemann was told by one young prison guard in the early years of the GDR. Even in its last years, 'politicals' could expect to encounter ritualized acts of aggression. Mario Mann, who was interviewed in a GDR prison immediately after the fall of the Wall in 1989, had served time for attempting to cross the border illegally (Section 213 in GDR law). 'As soon as you arrived, if you'd been sent down for something political, like 213 for example, you got one in the teeth,' he explained. Officers of the state were 'literally just waiting to smack you in the mouth.'[16]

In a criminal justice system that divided offenders into the corrigible and the incorrigible, politicals were classified as incorrigible.[17] They had failed in their duty to the state, and their primary value to the GDR now was in hard currency. The great hope of most politicals was that they would qualify for *Freikauf*, the system by which West Germany literally bought their release.

we drove across the border. A black Mercedes with four men in black arrived, and I had to show myself. Someone said 'Yes, that's her,' and a briefcase full of money changed hands.

Between 1963 and 1989 East Germany released 33,755 prisoners to the West in exchange for money and goods to the value of around 3 billion DM. 'Two men appeared and told me I was going on a transport. Then they took me to the Stasi in Karl-Marx-Stadt,' remembers Renate Werwigk-Schneider, whose educational work on GDR history has since won her the Order of Merit of the Federal Republic. It was 1968. From Karl-Marx-Stadt she was driven to the West German border at Wartha-Bebra.

> No one said a word. Then a Mercedes arrived with an East Berlin numberplate. The attorneys Vogel (East) and Stange (West) got out. Someone gave me a package with all my papers and a bunch of flowers from my parents. Then we drove across the border.[18]

Wolfgang Vogel was the East German lawyer who brokered transfers to the West for thirty years – a legendary, 'almost mystical' figure, as one memoirist writes. (In 2015, played by Sebastian Koch, he was a protagonist in Spielberg's movie *Bridge of Spies*.)[19] Werwigk-Schneider's story continues on the other side of the border, where a black Mercedes arrived with four men in black. 'I had to show myself. Someone said, "Yes, that's her," and a briefcase full of money – 100,000 DM, apparently – changed hands.' It was an expensive deal. The GDR was keen to recoup the cost of education and training for those who went West, but the going rate was nearer 40,000 DM.[20]

Like political prisoners, exchanges for ransom were not part of the GDR's official story. 'It's an unwritten law that the ransoming of prisoners is a taboo area that no one talks about,' wrote Koch.[21] Those who were selected for *Freikauf* often knew of their prospective release only moments before they were collected from prison – and uncertainty prevailed right up until the moment they were handed over to agents of the West. Elke Lehmann remembers being taken from Hoheneck prison to a Stasi centre in Karl-Marx-Stadt – a normal step on the *Freikauf* journey. She spent three weeks there in happy anticipation of being extradited to the West. But two days before the proposed handover she was fetched from her cell and taken 'to some Major from the Stasi – and he told me to my face, with no preamble: my application to be redomiciled in the Federal Republic had been refused'. She was to return to prison. What, she asked the Major in desperation, had been the point of bringing her to Karl-Marx-Stadt and allowing her to believe that she was about to be released? He answered laconically: 'We just did.' 'At that point,' Lehmann remembers, 'I must have started screaming horrifically.'[22]

THE EAST GERMAN state had no wish to see people in prison record, much less publish, their experience of lived socialism. Other than for the purpose of writing to approved correspondents at home, writing implements and paper were generally forbidden.[23] In West Germany, Birgitta Wolf had declared the connection between people in prison and the public sphere 'paper-thin',[24] but on the other side of the Wall there was no connection at all. No account written by a prisoner of the GDR was published in East Germany during the forty years the state existed. For most, the opportunity to tell their stories would come only after 1990 – though one man who had a lifelong relationship with East German prisons managed to publish sooner.

As a young theology student in the GDR, Ulrich Schacht had been arrested for anti-state agitation in 1973. He was incarcerated in Brandenburg-Görden until 1976, when he was 'bought free' by the West German government. His wife, Carola Schacht, spent nine months in Hoheneck and was released to the West in the same year. In 1984 Ulrich published not his own story, but a collection of eye-witness accounts from the notorious women's prison where his wife had been incarcerated. Originally published in Switzerland, the *Hoheneck Reports* were 'testimonies of human beings in revolt, who dared to determine their own lives – that was their only crime'.[25]

'you bastards! You're taking our children!'

But Ulrich Schacht was also born in Hoheneck prison. His mother, Wendelgard Trampota, had made plans to flee West with her baby's father, a Russian officer, after their application to marry was refused. She was five months pregnant when, in 1950, a Soviet Military Tribunal sentenced her to ten years' hard labour. She gave birth in Hoheneck in March 1951 – slightly prematurely, she told her son in his role as editor of her memoir: 'you must have been in a hurry to shout out your protest to the world.' For fear that baby Ulrich would otherwise be sent to Russia, she declared the father unknown – 'I'd rather look like a whore than have them take away my child, I thought.' But on 6 June 1951 a 'terrible day' came for Trampota and two other women nursing their new babies in Hoheneck. 'Our children were taken from us and driven away in a car. Where to? We didn't know! Powerless in the face of it, I just kept screaming: "you bastards! You're taking our children!"'[26]

Trampota and the other mothers were eventually told that their babies had been taken to a care home, where they could be collected by family members. Ulrich was raised by his grandmother until Wendelgard Trampota was released in an amnesty in 1954. Not every child was so lucky.

Today is Nadja's birthday. A day blacker than any nightmare.

Jutta Giersch, a West German journalist, was pregnant when, in October 1949, she was abducted from West Berlin by the Soviet secret service and taken to its interrogation centre in Potsdam. A Military Tribunal convicted her of anti-Soviet agitation and spying, and sentenced her to 25 years in a labour camp. She was sent to Sachsenhausen and from there to Hoheneck, where she gave birth to her daughter in March 1950. For six weeks she nursed the baby alongside other new mothers in the prison. But one day in April 1950, she recalls, the women were all called to the sick bay, 'for an examination'. When they came back their babies were gone. Giersch remembers the lacerating pain – 'terrible breakdowns, of course' – but also the shock: 'we were uncomprehending with horror that something like that was possible'. Anita Goßler tells a similarly painful story. Sentenced to five years' imprisonment for 'spreading tendentious rumours', she gave birth to her daughter in Leipzig-Meusdorf prison in 1953. She was moved to Hoheneck four months after the birth, where the baby was taken from her. 'It was the worst thing that could have happened to me. I had endless nightmares in which my child was torn from my arms.' When she refused to sign adoption papers she was locked in the water cell: a metal-lined space that could be flooded with water – 'cold water comes and goes, and you start to get horribly chilled,' Goßler remembers. 'The GDR always denied that those water cells, and the dark cells, existed.' But a differently painful moment came after the fall of the Wall. In 1992 Anita Goßler saw her daughter again for the first time. 'Just don't start thinking I'm going to call you Mum,' the young woman greeted her. 'Her socialist education had been effective,' Goßler reflected sadly.[27]

Monika Schneider, apprehended while trying to cross the border West with her family in 1983, immediately lost her four-year-old son Thomas to a children's home. He was not allowed to accompany her to the West when she was 'bought free' two years later. In her short memoir of 2010 she describes her agony at the separation, but also the pain of wondering how her son suffered as an abandoned four-year-old. 'He never wanted to tell me what it was like for him in the home. He told other people that he had been beaten there, and locked in the cellar.' Freya Klier, who lost her fifteen-year-old daughter to a home when the family was arrested at the border in 1988, found one day in every year unbearable: 'Today is Nadja's birthday. A day blacker than any nightmare.'[28]

> *§213. Illegal border crossing. (1) Anyone who illegally crosses the state border of the German Democratic Republic . . . will be punished with imprisonment for up to two years or with a suspended sentence, incarceration or a fine.*
>
> Criminal Code of the GDR, §213.

The GDR operated a forced adoption plan for the children of political undesirables, and parents caught trying to leave illegally could expect never to see their children again.[29] The memoirist Gunhild Gerth remembered Lytte, a fellow prisoner, 'in a terrifying nervous state'. Lytte and her family had been caught heading West in the early 1970s. Her eighteen-year-old son was sentenced to two years in prison; her fourteen-year-old was held in solitary confinement for six weeks. Petra Koch tells the story of Marlies, a new arrival in Hoheneck 'with a dark sense of humour'. It soon emerged that Marlies was dealing with the death of her twenty-year-old daughter, who had been shot in the head during their joint attempt to cross the Hungarian border into Austria. She was also digesting the knowledge that she herself would never be eligible for *Freikauf* – the GDR preferred not to advertise the brutal policing of its borders, so the tragedy of her daughter's death disqualified her from ever being allowed to leave.[30]

The Berlin Wall was built in 1961. Soon the offence of *Republikflucht* (fleeing the Republic) accounted for nearly half of all crimes against the state. Perhaps to avoid the question why anyone would want to flee an ideal socialist state, the offence was from 1968 rebadged 'illegal border crossing'. It was punishable by imprisonment.

In 1976 a young man called Matthias Bath had just matriculated to study law at West Berlin's Free University. A Young Conservative, he saw it as his duty to 'liberate the inhabitants of *Mitteldeutschland*'.[31]

East German workers reinforce the Berlin Wall at the Brandenburg Gate, 18 October 1961.

Together with a fellow Young Conservative who had recently escaped from the GDR – whom he knew only as 'R.' – Bath planned the escape West of an East German couple and their child. A West German Opel driven by Bath was to rendezvous with an East German Skoda near Magdeburg. The Skoda was carrying the family, who would then slide into a specially constructed hiding place in the Opel's boot. Everything went to plan until Bath, in his Opel with the young family hidden in its boot, tried to cross the border at Marienborn. East German border police stopped the car and asked him to open the boot. 'Our journey', he remembers, 'was over.'

What happened to the East German family is unknown. The young Westerner, Bath, was taken into custody and interrogated for several months – in the Stasi's notorious Hohenschönhausen facility, as he later found out. He was eventually tried and sentenced to five years in prison. He remembers his shock at the sight of his cell in Berlin-Rummelsburg in the later 1970s – 3.5 × 4 metres (11 × 13 ft), holding two triple-decker bunks and six men.[32] Bath served forty months of his sentence. Then, one day in July 1979, he was suddenly collected by a group of men in black. They took him to the Stasi headquarters in East Berlin's Magdalenenstrasse. From the Magdalenenstrasse he was driven to the 'mystic' Vogel's legal practice in Reiler Strasse, and from there – this time driven by Vogel's wife in their Mercedes 250 – to the offices of the lawyer's Western counterpart, Stange, in West Berlin. There he met a mysterious couple, subsequently revealed to be the West German spies Hyoon Ya Franke and Volker Franke, who – with him – were to be exchanged that day for a Stasi agent discovered in the West.[33]

Meanwhile André Baganz, a young Black East German, was making his own attempts to escape the GDR. His first try was at the Berlin Wall – but with the lights and guns of the border guards almost upon him, he turned and ran, narrowly escaping arrest or death. Still determined, he tried again, this time in Czechoslovakia, where Petra Koch and her boyfriend had tried to cross over. Baganz made it into some woodlands bordering Bavaria before he too was stopped by a patrol. Miraculously he managed to lie his way out of the situation, and was sent back to the GDR. But during his third attempt, made with a childhood friend, both were apprehended when they took a train to Boizenburg (near the West German border), and arrested on suspicion of trying to leave the Republic.

The two young men managed to confer during a transport between prisons, and decided to attempt a breakout. Two of Baganz's cellmates joined in with the plan to overpower a group of prison guards, take a Kalashnikov from them and cross the border, taking one guard with them as a hostage. Unsurprisingly the plan went wrong, and an officer was fatally wounded when one of the cellmates turned the machine gun on him.

Baganz was later told by his Stasi interrogator that the life sentence he received for his part in the shooting 'could have been worse'.[34] East Germany retained the death penalty until 1987, and the last death sentence is reported to have been carried out in 1981 – the year Baganz and his friends were convicted. Roland Garve, another young East German, who had just qualified as a dentist when he was caught trying to leave the country, remembers treating a twenty-year-old man who was awaiting execution after an attempted breakout. The young man's death sentence was later commuted to life – but, as Garve remembers it, executions by a shot to the back of the neck were still being carried out in the early 1980s.[35]

Baganz's memoir, *Serving Life in Bautzen II*, appeared in 1993. Its original subtitle, *Being Black in the GDR*, disappeared from the second edition; nonetheless it is a story not least about East German racism.[36] André Baganz was born to a white East German mother and her boyfriend from Guinea, who was training as a marine in the GDR. He recalls his mother telling him about her own grandmother's reaction when the baby arrived. 'Child,' she had objected, 'you can't be with a n--! A couple of villages from here there's a Chinese, can't you just take him?' As a boy in the East German provinces, the young André was met with stares and whispering ('it's a n--! What's he doing here?'), as well as direct racist abuse, like being called a 'filthy wog' at bus stops. Eventually he refused to carry a flag along with the other local children for the annual parade in Eisenhüttenstadt, because he had grown tired of the 'audible racist remarks'. He was challenged to a fight when he sat in a café with a white girl, given a beating by his fellow apprentices when he refused to call himself by the n-word, and abused as a 'fucking wog' by his boss. At that point, he remembers, he started fighting back.[37]

In prison Baganz was treated with a certain respect by other inmates, not least because racist fantasies were in circulation that claimed he was a '120-kilo n-- who had killed three policemen' and who regularly tore doors from their hinges. He managed to smuggle an uncensored letter out to his mother and stepfather, explaining how he had come to reject socialism. Their response was uncomprehending (even though they had already been challenged by their other son, a white homosexual anti-communist, to 'wake up'). But they were not alone in their denial. Questioned by the Stasi about why he tried to go West, Baganz mentioned race as a motivating factor. He was immediately told that racial prejudice did not exist in the GDR. 'That kind of thing is forbidden here,' his interrogators assured him – 'even if', adds Baganz the memoirist, 'the youngsters in Eisenhüttenstadt formed gangs to thrash the Algerians and Cubans they called "wogs", for supposedly taking their girls away from them.'[38]

In the 1970s, in an echo of the high-profile events in West Germany in 1964, when two men died after being beaten by prison officers, a prisoner from the Democratic Republic of the Congo (then Zaire) died mysteriously in a separation unit in East Berlin. Matthias Bath tells the story. The man was incarcerated in Berlin-Rummelsburg, like Bath, and like Bath he had been convicted of assisting in an escape to the West. Unlike Bath, he had the misfortune to be Black in a racist system. When he angered his guards by breaking a window they dragged him to the bunker – later that day word spread that he was dead. 'The official cause of death given by the GDR authorities was suicide by hanging,' Bath commented drily.[39] The death never reached the papers, and never became a matter of public interest.

Officially there weren't any Nazis under socialism.

Roland Garve, the young dentist, served two years in Brandenburg-Görden prison after his plans to cross the border were discovered. His first glimpse of a shared cell in the early 1980s revealed the same triple-decker bunks Matthias Bath had seen in the 1970s – the top occupant's head only inches from the ceiling, and at the bottom the 'submarines': mattresses stored beneath the lowest bunk during the day and brought out at night by whomever was unlucky enough to be sleeping on the floor. If they were very unlucky, the available floor space was next to a lavatory crammed in between the towering beds. 'Everyone could watch you going to the toilet,' remembered Garve. The title of his memoir, *Among Murderers*, refers – perhaps surprisingly – to his fellow prisoners. 'I'd been thinking, in my naive way, that there were practically no murderers in the GDR,' he recalls, 'and now I had ended up where they kept the people who weren't supposed to exist.' His response to his prison clothes was to wonder how many murderers had worn them. (Petra Koch and Birgit Schlicke remember their first horrified encounters with Hoheneck rather similarly – 'a den of murderers', writes Koch, while Schlicke recalls feeling 'so afraid of the murderers'.)[40] According to the state-controlled media, violent crime had no place in a socialist society – therefore it did not exist. 'Officially', added Garve, 'there weren't any Nazis under socialism.' And yet he met neo-Nazis in prison, some of them recent converts: 'respectable GDR yes-men turned into hardline neo-Nazis'. In some cells, inmates demanded a Hitler salute as a sign of loyalty – like the existence of murderers, this was a shock for the young Garve, who had 'always thought that extreme right-wing ideas were confined to the heads of a few incorrigible individuals'. One man, serving time for an attempt to escape across the border, shared his dream of a future life in the West, which would involve wearing 'a black uniform with riding tack, jodhpurs and long boots', and carrying a whip 'to thrash communists on demonstrations'.[41]

Were those the lesbian women I'd heard such gruesome rumours about?

Homosexuality, too, was taboo, even in the 1970s.[42] Like their counterparts in the West, women memoirists in particular remember their ignorance and fear of lesbianism. 'Were those the lesbian women I'd heard such gruesome rumours about?' Carola Schacht recalls wondering when she arrived in Hoheneck in 1976. Regina Ebert, arriving in 1979 to a cell shared with 25 other women, was 'genuinely scared – especially of the lesbian women. Before prison I had no idea about that, because people outside never talked about it.' And little seemed to have changed shortly before the fall of the Wall. Birgit Schlicke's naive response to a warning from her Stasi interrogator that she would encounter homosexual women in prison was: 'gross!' She also felt fear: 'I'd never known any lesbians.' In her (reconstructed) *Prison Diary*, sexual relationships between women are presented as part of the peculiar situation of prison – a response to the long-term absence of available men. 'When they are long-termers I can partly understand it,' the *Diary*'s narrating voice muses. 'What I really can't understand is the charm of a lesbian relationship for women on short sentences.'[43]

Like its Western neighbour, East Germany retained the anti-gay paragraph 175 in its lawbooks after 1949; but from 1957 it was not enforced. Homosexual acts between adult men became legal in the new criminal code of the GDR in 1968. Even in the later 1980s, however, gay magazines were not allowed and there could be no political organization of gay men or women.[44] Like Schlicke in Hoheneck, Roland Garve saw homosexuality in Brandenburg-Görden in the early 1980s essentially as a substitute for heterosexuality. 'Lots of the so-called long-termers solved their ongoing sexual problem by getting themselves a so-called "wife"', he remembers. Men who looked feminine 'were called "softies" in prison jargon and treated like fresh meat'. New arrivals who did not know the ropes might be offered money, cigarettes or physical protection, and then coerced into repaying the debt sexually. The violence of prison rape became visible for Garve through his work in the prison hospital, where anal fissures regularly had to be treated.[45]

Gay men in prison who had more loving relationships could expect an aggressive 'look at those bent bastards!', Mario Mann told his interviewer Torsten Heyme just after the fall of the Wall. Prejudice inside reflected prejudice outside: Garve remembers his fellow prisoner Jonas, who had been handed a particularly harsh sentence by a homophobic judge and prosecutor. Jonas described himself as 'totally gay', in contradistinction to those who were merely 'prison gay' ('the ones who made a virtue of necessity and had wives outside'). But the stigma was not just about sex, Mann explained. It was about the closeness between human beings that sex could bring, and the danger such alliances posed to a system built on control.[46]

The 'yellow misery' – Bautzen I.

I was party to so many people's fates in there, so much degradation, and it's too dangerous to write down the truth.

The journalist Torsten Heyme belonged to the Independent Investigating Commission for the Abuse of Office and Corruption, founded in December 1989, just months after the Berlin Wall fell. During that curious year from November 1989 until October 1990, when the post-Wall GDR still existed as an independent nation state, he quickly began interviewing and corresponding with people in prison. After the first free elections made Lothar de Maizière of the East German Christian Democrats head of state for the brief period from April until October 1990 (when the 'two Germanies' would be unified), de Maizière asked the Commission to stop its investigations. But Heyme went on visiting Bautzen I, Brandenburg, Waldheim and Hoheneck, and encouraging people in prison to correspond with him. He found cells measuring 3 × 5 metres (10 × 16 ft) occupied by ten to fifteen people.[47]

Only about 10 per cent of people in prison in the GDR were convicted of crimes against the state,[48] but their memoirs have shaped the story of East German prisons. Heyme's account is unusual, because he met and interviewed people incarcerated for regular criminal offences, whose stories have interested publishers far less. One of his correspondents told the story of his friend and fellow prisoner Mike, who died in prison. 'They had chained him to a door and beaten him – those people made a cripple of him. They beat him pretty well impotent.' Mike died of his injuries, and in 1989 Heyme's correspondent was still afraid of speaking out: 'I was party to so many people's fates in there, so much degradation, and it's too dangerous to write down the truth.'[49] Sometimes it was dangerous even to hear the truth. Lucie Fischer, arriving home from prison in the GDR in 1955, found a family who clearly did not want to know – 'no one in the family ever asked me what it was like for me. My mother just said, "Leave me in peace, I've suffered enough."' Ute Steinhäuser had similar problems after her release in 1979: 'I didn't say much to my friends, because most of them couldn't understand it, or else it really spoiled the mood.' André Baganz remembers trying to tell a prison doctor that his Stasi interrogators had given him drugs or poison – the doctor turned on his heel and left the room hastily.[50] 'Witnesses of utmost abuse do need to share their stories,' writes the human rights expert Nora Strejilevich, 'but "the rest" do not always want to hear.'[51]

Mario Mann challenged his interviewer Heyme to comprehend the hidden realities of the GDR. 'You can't imagine what punishment in prison was like,' he told him. Mann described the segregated solitary cells in Bautzen I, where 'you got sent barefoot to the seg, in winter, and you just had to stand there. It was a standing cell. And, of course, you had handcuffs on and wrist chains.' Or you might be 'hung up to dry': 'I was chained by my arms to the highest bars, so I was dangling about 3 or 4 centimetres above the ground and could just touch the floor with the tip of my toe.' Mann described the pleasure some of his guards took in acts of humiliation and violence, anticipating that he would be disbelieved: 'no one's going to believe it but that's how it was, and it was often! Ask other people, loads of people experienced it. I mean, how do I describe it?'[52] When the unspeakable is spoken, listeners often find it difficult to believe.

I swore to myself that one day I would write down everything I was experiencing and publish it.[53]

Writing down the truth – testimony, or bearing witness – has a visceral importance for survivors. Birgit Schlicke records how her cellmates in Hoheneck, forbidden any kind of writing materials, would memorize one another's contact addresses before they parted, and make mental notes where written notes were impossible. Petra Koch remembers waiting helplessly in a holding cell in Pilsen after her failed attempt to cross the Czechoslovakian border. She had not been told what would happen next. Then she saw that a previous occupant had scratched a note into the cell wall: '*Tuesday plane to GDR*'. Suddenly she had ground beneath her feet again. Others had scratched 'words of hate against the GDR regime', and she herself then used a fingernail 'to scratch my burning hatred into the chalk wall. The satisfaction of that is, in that moment, greater than my fear of being hit with a rubber truncheon. It's like a silent scream.' Matthias Bath described his memoir as a working-through. 'With this report', he wrote, 'I would like to work through my experiences during almost forty months of incarceration in the GDR.'[54] 'Writing down my experiences made it possible for me to work through that extraordinarily difficult time in a kind of self-therapy,' wrote Schlicke; the prospect of bearing witness gave her hope and a moral imperative to survive.[55] Her *Prison Diary* was never a diary proper ('we prisoners were naturally not allowed to keep a record of events') but a memoir in diary form, constructed after her release and published in 2001. She dedicated it to 'all victims of Stalinist injustice in the former GDR.'

8
Stasi Stories

Most people in the GDR knew they could be arrested at any time . . . and that they would then be at the mercy of the Stasi.[1]

When Carola Schacht was taken into Stasi custody she was not told why. She was staying with a friend in Berlin when she was arrested, and went through all the possibilities in her head while she waited for an hour and a half in Stasi headquarters. Eventually a woman came and told her to strip naked. All her clothes and belongings were searched, still without any kind of explanation. When her interrogator finally arrived, he asked her – 'in a friendly tone' – why she thought she had been arrested. 'I really wasn't expecting that question!' she remembered. 'So I just said to him, "I thought you were going to tell me that". But he didn't. For about an hour he kept on asking me why I was there. I didn't know the answer.' Her sense of disorientation was no accident, but part of the Stasi's method. 'You can prepare yourself inwardly and steel yourself when you know what lies ahead. But question marks are nerve-wracking! They undermine your drive to resistance and self-preservation,' wrote Jutta Giersch. Matthias Bath describes the day his parents visited him in Stasi custody, confused and upset. Stasi officers watched them, he remembers, with obvious enjoyment.[2]

The Stasi had seventeen interrogation centres, distinct from the regular facilities for people in pre-trial custody (which were controlled by the *Volkspolizei*) and all geared to achieving admissions of guilt from people accused of crimes against the state. The most notorious

A corridor in Hohenschönhausen.

was Hohenschönhausen, once a Nazi soup kitchen in northeast Berlin. Under the Soviet administration it became Special Camp 3. When, in 1951, it was handed over to the newly established Ministry for State Security (Stasi), the inmates were set to work building a secure unit, complete with interrogation rooms and cells of different kinds, including 'rubber cells' in the basement.[3] Many former prisoners remember the traffic light system in its corridors, designed to prevent any contact or exchange of information between prisoners.

When the light turned red, any prisoner in the corridor had to stand and face the wall until a fellow prisoner had passed.

Hohenschönhausen quickly became one of the Stasi's most feared facilities. Survivors from the 1950s remember being interrogated there by Erich Mielke, deputy head of the Stasi when it was established in 1950 and its head from 1957 until the SED regime fell. 'Mielke amused himself during his "interrogations" by telling me all the different, repulsive ways in which human beings can be liquidated,' remembered Kurt Müller, a communist who had been imprisoned under the Nazis and suffered the same fate again in East Germany. Müller described the delight the Stasi boss took in having the power to hurt: 'he even spoke of having liquidated several people himself.' Walter Janka, arrested for criticizing the Party, also encountered Mielke's brutality; but Janka had met Mielke before, during the Spanish Civil War, and knew how to make the bully collapse. 'With his left hand he grabbed my collar and with his right he made a fist. I was sure I was about to be hit in the face. I got up and said: "Let go of my coat. You know I'm not impressed by threats."' Mielke was deflated: 'quite suddenly he seemed at a loss.'[4]

Interrogations happened at night, and prisoners were 'softened up' for the night-time sessions by being kept awake during the day – they would be roughly woken by their guards if they showed any sign of dozing. Repeat offenders would have their mattresses taken away, or be forced to stand for hours. Another persecuted communist, Fritz Sperling, described nights of torture – 'they kicked my shins, hit me on the head with their fists, and tore out my hair.' His interrogators beat him with their fists and with a steel ruler, and during one session struck him in the chest, just above the heart – in the knowledge that he had already had two heart attacks. For three years he was held in solitary confinement. 'I am convinced that the time I spent in there was intended to drive me insane,' he wrote later. 'In all those years I wasn't given a single book – let alone a newspaper. Other than with my interrogator I didn't speak with a single person.'[5]

Horst Fichter, detained in 1952, remembered 'a small hole, maybe 50 by 50 cm [20 × 20 in.], with a slit in the door for light.' This was one of Hohenschönhausen's 'standing cells' – cupboards too narrow to sit down in, in which victims could be left standing for hours at a time. Fichter was locked in the cell for four hours on two occasions, for offending against discipline. He does not describe his feelings, but Roland Garve remembered his, thirty years later, when he was left in a standing cell for just half an hour, not as a punishment but simply because his Stasi guards needed somewhere to put him until he could be collected. 'I really had to pull myself together so as not to have a massive panic attack; the cell was only about 40 centimetres [16 in.] deep. It felt like being in a coffin,' he recalled. 'Claustrophobia, the fear of suffocating in a small space, is really terrible, particularly when you can't turn around or sit down.'[6]

Elke Lehmann remembers the day she was delivering meals to other women in Hoheneck in the 1970s and opened a door into a cell that seemed to be lined with metal. It had a fresh line of rust running around it, and when she opened the door a swarm of flies flew out, momentarily blocking her view. 'I couldn't see for all the flies.' When her vision cleared she was horrified. 'I saw the girl who was in there – she was wearing these really thin overalls, not even a coat, and she had to sleep on a wooden board that was balanced on two buckets at night.' Lehmann had stumbled upon a water cell – a specially lined dungeon that could be flooded to about hip height. 'It was 'horrible! A dreadful shock! Because I saw it with my own eyes.'[7] (Before seeing water cells with his own eyes, wrote Walter Janka, he had refused to believe that such horror could exist in the post-war socialist state).[8] In Cottbus in the mid-1970s, remembered Mario Mann, prisoners had to enter the water cells in shorts and barefoot – 'then they let water in through a hosepipe; and then you stood there for as long as they felt like leaving you.' Left to stand long enough in hip-high water, the victim would eventually be standing in their own excrement, chilled to the point of hypothermia. Brigitte Ballnow, who survived Hoheneck, told the story of a young woman there who one day called her guards 'Nazi swine'. She was taken to the water cell and kept there for a week – when she came back, Ballnow remembers, she was barely recognizable.[9]

Hoheneck. A massive dark weathered stone building, peppered with countless little barred windows. It stares at us from a thousand eyes.

Hoheneck's 'thousand eyes'.

The former concentration camp Sachsenhausen became Soviet Special Camp 7, which after 1945 held people convicted of crimes against the Soviet administration. When it was finally closed in 1950, around 1,000 women inmates were transferred to Hoheneck, a high-security prison designed to hold half that number. Hoheneck's reputation for brutality and overcrowding would come to vie with the 'yellow misery' of Bautzen.

Hoheneck was a medieval fortress just outside the town of Stollberg in the district of Karl-Marx-Stadt (now Chemnitz). For prisoners, arrival at the hilltop fortress was preceded by a long, cramped journey in the so-called Grotewohl Express, named by its passengers for Otto Grotewohl, the GDR's first prime minister.[10] The sardonically named 'Express' was a goods wagon divided on the inside into narrow compartments with tightly packed seating for the fortunate, and standing room for the rest. Anonymously hitched to a (non-express) passenger train, the wagon would make its circuitous way across the GDR. Hoheneck offered an intimidating aspect to arriving inmates. 'There it is – the fortress Hoheneck. A massive dark weathered stone building, peppered with countless little barred windows. It stares at us from a thousand eyes,' Petra Koch remembered. Anne Niendorf's memory is of stunned disbelief. 'The fortress was a shock! Simply unbelievable.' But Catharina Mäge, arriving in 1976, was startled most of all by 'the faces of the prisoners. They all looked terribly miserable and colourless, no facial expressions, but with deep dark rings under their eyes like consumptives. It was spooky and I couldn't take it in.'[11]

Hoheneck came to be known as the 'springboard to the West'; it held a high proportion of women convicted of offences against the state, most of them hoping to be 'bought free'.[12] They were under the direct control of the Stasi – a shadowy presence personified in the legendary figures of James and Daisy. 'No one ever saw them, and there was no reliable evidence of their existence – and still we were sure of it. Our imagination revolved constantly around the two of them,' remembered Helgard Krumm. 'We wanted to know which window in the office building their desks were behind. Our future depended on them.' Birgit Schlicke felt it too. 'James and Daisy. Two people, a man and a woman, who pull the strings in the prison and seem to decide our fates.'[13]

But Hoheneck also housed women serving long sentences for violent crimes, and over the years they gradually became the majority. They wore uniforms with a broad yellow stripe; life prisoners had a red stripe. 'Politicals' wore a green stripe[14] – even though they did not formally exist in the GDR, the prison system recognized them. They were likely to be allocated high-risk jobs or work in areas where the productivity requirement was known to be unachievable. Regular prisoners were eligible for positions of authority, such as worker-in-charge or cell elder (who wore a silver stripe on her uniform as a mark of rank) – politicals were not. But there were less formal separations, too. Bettina Gilek, who came to Hoheneck in 1979 after trying to escape to the West, remembers two tables in her cell. The 'politicals' sat at one, the 'criminals' at the other. 'Envy and hate ruled,' recalled Renate Werwigk-Schneider.[15] There were 'horror stories', remembered Gunhild Gerth, about the girls' wing in Hoheneck, and the treatment of young politicals there. Adult politicals, too, remember struggling. By the 1970s, Hoheneck held women imprisoned on criminal charges who had been there since the 1950s, 'people who to a large extent were no longer people', Gerth explains. 'After ten, fifteen or twenty years exposed to these vile circumstances, personalities are destroyed', and human frailty in those packed rooms was 'often impossible to bear'. 'It was difficult for me – among forty women like that we were just two politicals,' wrote Anne Niendorf, who arrived in 1972; she and the other political, Ursi, 'stuck together like glue'.[16] Solidarity was between like and like: Elke Lehmann described being 'cut' by her fellows because she formed friendships with women who had criminal convictions. Even in the last years of the GDR, Birgit Schlicke remembers, she felt disapproval of politicals who blurred the boundaries, most of all if they had romantic relationships with women convicted on criminal charges – 'so now I even know politicals who've suddenly discovered their love for a criminal!'[17]

I thought: this can't be true! This can't be the GDR.

For Anne Niendorf, the conditions in Hoheneck came as a visceral shock. 'Once a month we were allowed to shower', she remembered. 'In a kind of cellar. Water came out of some kind of hole in the ceiling and the whole cellar was full of steam. Do you see, the conditions were unbelievable! Indescribable. I thought: this can't be true! This can't be the GDR!' Renate Werwigk-Schneider remembered using a slops bucket in a shared cell. Gerth, who came to Hoheneck in 1973, encountered plumbed toilets, but in a washroom where four basins and two WCs served 48 women – 'unbearable.'[18]

Hoheneck had been designed to hold five hundred women, but until 1975 it held around twice that number. Women slept on the floor and in corridors. Gerth had to sleep in a hallway for a month in freezing drafts, because there was no bunk available in the cell to which she had been assigned. 'I told Lieutenant Schmidt and at the same time asked for another pullover or an extra blanket,' she recalled. 'I'll never forget her answer: "get yourself a girlfriend with hot flushes, then you won't be cold."'[19]

Carola Schacht tells the story of the celebrations in Hoheneck on 7 October 1976, marking the anniversary of the GDR's foundation. While the other women danced and performed, and prison officers shared the decisions of the ninth Party conference, Schacht and her fellow enemies of the state 'sat near the back of the hall and laughed our socks off'.[20] There was a felt physical, mental and moral distinction (where Ariel Dorfman exhorts us not to judge those who find a means of asserting an 'ethical superiority in the face of totalitarianism').[21] The GDR claimed to be a classless society, but (just as in the West) most people with criminal convictions came from underprivileged backgrounds. The 'political' memoirists remember the *differentness* of those other prisoners: 'most of them were tattooed and looked very scruffy.'[22] When it snowed at Christmas, 'the criminals delighted in it like little children,' wrote Petra Koch. Gerth recollects a conversation she had with a criminal prisoner: 'I remember Frau B., our mechanic, asking me once whether I thought she had the right to live free again in society if there was an amnesty? She and her lover had killed her husband. Her relationship with guilt was very different from ours.'[23] Niendorf remembers 'intrigues, meanness and nastiness' that led her to prefer the company of some of her guards to the company of other prisoners'. More normally, prison officers were classed by their political captives with the criminal prisoners. Giersch called her guards 'animals' – 'they came from the underclass, after all,

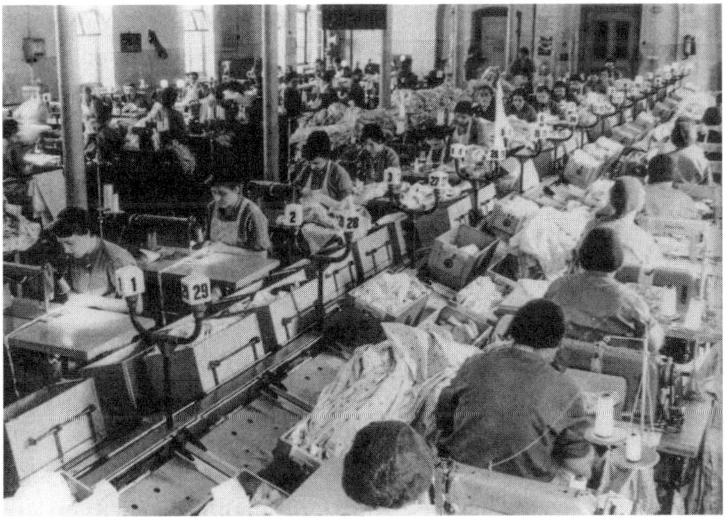

The sewing room in Hoheneck.

lumpen proletariat'. The aversion was mutual. 'For them we are the scum of humanity, enemies of the state, anti-communists, Nazis.'[24]

Give us freedom of thought!

Every person in prison had an education officer, called an *Erzieher* (literally, someone to 'raise' them) – 'like in a children's home', one memoirist comments.[25] The Penal Code of the GDR (Section 2.1) insisted that offenders must become conscious, through work and education, of their responsibility to the socialist state. People in prison were given free access to, and were expected to read, the party newspaper, *Neues Deutschland*. Education officers controlled the letters people in prison wrote and received, determined privileges and punishments, and enforced their attendance at the political education lectures that the attendees called 'infra-red therapy'.[26]

Alexandra Dust-Wiese, who was incarcerated by the Soviet authorities in 1949 for Liberal Democratic activity and moved from Sachsenhausen to Hoheneck with the first group of politicals in 1950, tells a memorable tale of resistance to intellectual control. Soon after their arrival at the fortress, a group of women secretly prepared a performance of Germany's most famous play: Goethe's *Faust*. Dust-Wiese herself played the Devil, Mephistopheles; her fellow prisoner Inge Schulze was Faust. She does not remember who played Faust's lover, Gretchen, but whoever she was, her performance of the young woman who is seduced, commits infanticide in the face of social pressure and is imprisoned under a death sentence was so powerful, and her rendering of the final dungeon scene so moving, that the guards who should have halted the performance not only let it run, but wept and clapped with the residents at the end.

The Hoheneck *Faust* demonstrated theatre's capacity to bring together people separated by politics and society. It also enabled a memorable moment of subversion, in a follow-up performance of Schiller's political history play *Don Carlos*.[27] Because *Faust* had been such a success and was so enjoyed by the guards, the women were given permission to rehearse and perform another play. Dust-Wiese led a prison production of *Don Carlos*, in which she played King

Philip of Spain. In Schiller's drama a young marquis speaks the impassioned line 'Give us freedom of thought!' 'Of course we wanted to speak that "Sire, give us freedom of thought!" line especially loudly,' Dust-Wiese remembers. 'The commandant found out, summoned me to him and said I had to cut it, or the play couldn't be performed at all.' The line was duly cut, but its absence was at least as effective. 'At the moment when Marquis Posa was supposed to say it, the actors kneeled before me, we looked at each other, stood there like dolls and didn't say a word. And everyone started clapping like crazy.'[28]

I wanted never to show my tormentors that they could hurt me.[29]

Wendelgard Trampota tells the story of Reformation Day in Hoheneck in 1951, when word went around to stand up at the end of the church service and sing a famous Lutheran hymn: 'We all stood up, and the guards were already opening the doors – but we didn't leave! Instead there rang out, without organ accompaniment but from a thousand throats, "A mighty fortress is our God".' The guards were too shocked to respond, but the pastor was banned from coming again.[30]

Anneliese Gabel, who came to Hoheneck with the women from Special Camp 3, remembers the sense of solidarity in those early days of the Hoheneck *Faust* and the Reformation Day rebellion – 'we were a community and took care of each other.' Carola Schacht refused to give information to a Stasi officer in return for news about her own release: 'I would rather have served my own sentence to the last day than deliver other people into the hands of the Stasi.' Trampota recalled that one woman even hanged herself rather than provide information that would incriminate others – silence, she had been told, would mean prison for her family.[31] That kind of solidarity made life more difficult for the Stasi. 'In Hoheneck at least it was hard to recruit and place spies. I know that wasn't the case elsewhere,' recalls Jutta Giersch, 'the women imprisoned in Hoheneck stuck together amazingly.' It also made it harder for prison officers to bully the residents. One officer who had been picking on disabled prisoners in the yard was pulled inside by her hair and given 'an incredible beating', remembered Giersch. After that 'no one else got abused in the yard. Our revolt worked as a warning.' A key memory for Petra Koch is the day when she heard a voice yelling at her for turning up her collar against a freezing wind. She turned to see the notoriously choleric guard Sutterer, the 'poison dwarf', who was wearing the collar of her own sheepskin-lined coat firmly turned up. 'I walk towards her, stop right in front of her, look her in her watery unfeeling eyes. They begin to twitch. Without a word I turn my own coat collar down, very slowly, and turn my back on her as I walk away.' The triumph was all the greater for its unexpectedness: 'magically, she doesn't whistle me back.'[32]

But perhaps the most remarkable story is Erica Wallach's. Wallach was arrested in August 1950 and eventually sent to the notorious Soviet labour camp, Workuta. But before that she spent nearly a year in Hohenschönhausen, where she was interrogated six nights a week, from 9 p.m. until the early hours of the morning. When not being interrogated she was held in solitary confinement, under constant surveillance and forbidden any kind of activity or distraction. 'The only object I had been allowed to take with me into the cell was my tiny handkerchief, now worn very thin,' she remembers. 'I pulled threads out of it in a lattice pattern, creating barely visible squares on the handkerchief. From the threads I made white chess figures, and from grey threads pulled from my skirt I made black ones.' She was thus able to play chess against herself, keeping the tiny set out of sight – 'The whole thing was so small that I could easily hide it from the guard's peering eye by putting it behind my knee.' She also made herself a school timetable of 'classes', entirely in her head. 'I kept to my timetable precisely, from the ten minutes of exercise in the morning to writing books and poems – in my head, of course – in the evening.' Everything she had ever learned was revisited and remembered: 'I forced myself to go over every scrap of knowledge I had ever acquired; I went back to school. I had half-hour lessons in French, English, Latin, history, geography, literature, algebra, art history and music.' She addressed the humiliating lack of privacy by dragging her latrine bucket right up to the door, so that her guards' view through their spyhole was only of her face looking up at them: 'by the time they had recovered from the shock and had shouted themselves hoarse, I was done.'[33]

a garlic uprising!

Dust-Wiese wrote of the 'terrible time of hunger' in Hoheneck in 1950, when the starving women sat together exchanging recipes for delicious dishes and laughing. Humour always tends to bubble up where people are disempowered. The women in Hoheneck called their guards 'quails' (*Wachteln*, a play on *Wächter*, meaning 'guard'), and memoirists like to render the officers' regional accents as comic squawking.[34] In Bautzen II, André Baganz remembers, all the guards had nicknames: 'Trixi' was small and thin, while 'Chicken' got his name because of his tendency to 'fluff his feathers' in order to impress. Erich Loest recalls an officer they called First Lieutenant Soulful – 'he came on duty after Eagle Owl, that wiry piece of spite.'[35] Loest also tells a comic-heroic tale of resistance. Prisoners could buy garlic in the prison shop, and after six years in Bautzen Loest got the notion of increasing his intake to four cloves per day. 'My clothes stank, my urine and shit stank, the cell stank. The officers in charge would only open the door a crack to register my presence and then retreat, groaning.' It was, he insists, 'a garlic uprising!'[36]

Garve remembers telling his Stasi interrogator a subversive joke: 'Hey, what's the shortest sentence with "Lenin" in it? *Ich lehn' ihn ab!*' (I reject him). The pun was simple, untranslatable and high-risk. Garve also tells the absurd true story of Norbert, who was officially dead. Norbert had been convicted of murdering three people, and was in possession of a newspaper clipping that reported his death by execution. The public outcry at the murders had been so extreme that reporting his execution seemed politic to those in power; 'but in reality, the prison authorities promoted him to Brigade Leader of the prison's own electric motors workshop,' Garve remembered.[37] The curious joke of Norbert's posthumous existence was very much on the GDR.

A cell in Hohenschönhausen.

We're human beings who have a will of our own again.

The 17 June uprising of 1953 was the high point of civil resistance in East Germany before 1989. In June 1953 an economically pressed Central Committee of the GDR raised the productivity requirement by 10 per cent while simultaneously reducing wages. Workers downed their tools, and on 17 June there was a mass demonstration in Berlin-Mitte, with demands for democracy and free elections. That day and on the days that followed there were strikes and demonstrations involving around a million citizens across the GDR. East German and Soviet troops and tanks moved in against the demonstrators, and the uprising was brutally suppressed. Between fifty and five hundred people are thought to have been killed, and between 8,000 and 10,000 arrested.[38] Former prisoners remember the nervousness of those in power while the unrest lasted. Alexandra Dust-Wiese's father, visiting her in Hoheneck, brought a message from workers in neighbouring Wismut: 'They told me to tell you that they're coming to get you out.' The following morning the officers on wake-up duty were oddly polite, and asked them – please – to get up. 'We just sat and stared at them and said, "Oh God, could you say that again? We're not used to it." They turned bright red and repeated, "Please, would you get up." We were gobsmacked.' But it was a brief moment. The workers of Wismut never made it through, and normality returned – 'The next day we were already being yelled at again.'[39]

A number of survivors remember the Hoheneck hunger strike of 1953. After Stalin's death in March, some Germans serving sentences in Russia were given early release and began to return to East Germany as free citizens. Many of the women in Hoheneck had originally been convicted by the Soviet authorities, and a group approached the prison authorities to request a matching amnesty. It was refused. The hunger strike that followed was an expression of solidarity and community, but it also drew support from outside the prison. 'The population had risen up en masse against the guards,' Giersch recalls. 'They shouted up to us from outside: "Hang on in there!"'[40] But the strike had to be abandoned when the water was turned off (because people who did not wish to eat would also need nothing to drink, they were told). Those, like Erika Riemann, who were identified as ringleaders were punished with solitary confinement. Nonetheless, Riemann remembered, the strike gave them back a sense of themselves:

> We're human beings who have a will of our own again. We can take decisions. We have regained a space in which we

> can act. Our solidarity gives us strength and now for the first time I can feel something that my permanent feeling of helplessness had taken from me.[41]

SITTING ON THE slow train that was taking him to a (yet unknown) prison, Roland Garve remembered books he had read as a child about the Third Reich, and had a vision of himself as an anti-Nazi resistance fighter: 'I would like to have been that kind of hero.' There is clearly pleasure in memories that bear witness not only to human suffering but to the human will to resist. When Garve arrived in Brandenburg-Görden it emerged that his cellmate, Jan, was 'that kind of hero.' Jan had been a tractor driver on a collective farm in Thuringia whose request to emigrate to the West had been refused. In response, he filled his tractor's tyres with water (so they would not burst when shot at) and used old machinery parts to turn the body into a tank. Jan drove by night via the motorway to the border, where he proceeded to try to ram his way through to the West.

> The first barrier was in sight. Westerners in their cars ahead of him frantically veered off the road. Now he was being shot at from a watch tower ahead. At the push of a button a steel gate rolled out across the road in front of him. Jan started to sweat, took off his glasses, ducked deeper to avoid the bullets and put his foot down.

Jan finally lost control of his tractor and rammed a French lorry. He ran towards the lorry in the hope of asylum, but never reached it – he was shot in the leg by border guards. Convicted by an East German court of 'border terrorism', rather than merely illegal border crossing, Jan was regarded by his fellow prisoners as 'a great hero.'[42]

Jan escaped with minor injuries, but not everyone was so lucky. Garve remembered treating men in the prison infirmary who were brought in after failed attempts to cross the border. One was the twenty-year-old Mirko, a disc jockey in love with American music who had tried to escape through Bulgaria into Turkey. He was stopped by Bulgarian border guards with Kalashnikovs, but misunderstood a command one of them gave him. When he stood up, as he thought he had been told to, the young guard opened fire and almost shot off both his legs. After an extended and agonizing journey, during which he was interrogated in Russian, his left leg was amputated in a Bulgarian hospital. Back in East Germany he was sent to Brandenburg-Görden and still hoped to be extradited to the West – but even the legendary Vogel could not help him, Garve remembers. 'His case would have caused a feeding frenzy for the press. Neither the GDR nor Bulgaria wanted to give the West a walking testimonial to the brutal order to shoot.'[43]

My triumph will be to have survived this.[44]

At around the same time, in the Stasi facility Bautzen II, André Baganz was being held in long-term isolation. He demanded to be told why, and eventually decided that a hunger strike was his means of last resort. The decision nearly destroyed him. After nine days of refusing food he was force fed. Guards chained him by his hands and feet to a bed, and a doctor inserted infusion tubes into his thighs, explaining that they could, of course, have been inserted elsewhere – 'but it's particularly painful here'. After half an hour of extraordinary pain he was offered the chance to break off the hunger strike. He refused, and a tube was forcefully inserted through his mouth into his stomach. Baganz tried to resist by not opening his mouth, but the doctor fought back. 'He held my nose. Things got critical for me – I started to wheeze loudly and sucked in air through my clenched teeth. But I knew I couldn't last long.' Yelling in pain and almost choking to death as the tube was pushed twice into his stomach, he capitulated.

Psychological agony followed quickly on his escape from physical agony. 'The anger and frustration at my helplessness drove tears into my eyes. I felt endlessly small. These people had shown me what a pathetic creature I was, and that they could do whatever they wanted with me . . . The feeling hit me like a wave. I sat and sobbed like a little child.'[45] Nonetheless he continued to do stretches, press-ups, leaps and knee-bends in the cell, and used the books and newspapers he was allowed access to in order to build up his knowledge as much as he possibly could. Like Erica Wallach nearly forty years before, Baganz focused on resistance as survival.

9
The Big Prison

The big prison is the GDR.[1]

Karl Heinz Lange was first put in care in 1952, when he was nine years old. He was moved from a youth home to a prison in 1965. When Torsten Heyme interviewed him – still in prison – in 1990, he asked him how he felt about having effectively 'missed' socialism in the GDR. But Lange disagreed with the premise of the question. 'I experienced it in the children's homes. And I experienced it in here too: the eternal submissiveness; that was just like outside,' he responded. If anything, he had seen the realities of the GDR all the more clearly in prison. 'You just experienced the hierarchy better in here: power for the few and powerlessness for the rest.' Day-to-day social arrangements mirrored life outside: 'if a prisoner was somebody, outside, or had relatives who were somebody, those prisoners always got special treatment. And prisoners who worked with the Stasi got all kinds of advantages and special arrangements.'[2]

There was never a second when you did not feel watched, Birgit Schlicke remembered bitterly, 'whether you were on the toilet or washing yourself during menstruation.'[3] Foucault could not have known it, but even before he famously revisited Jeremy Bentham's panoptical vision of the prison in *Discipline and Punish* (1975), East German prisoners were experiencing prison as a reflection of the panoptical or all-seeing state. Panoptical control is as much *felt* as it is real: inmates in Hohenschönhausen would eagerly demonstrate their loyalty even without an education officer present to see them, remembered Hans Eberhard Zahn – 'it worked perfectly well without one.' The prison, he reflected, 'was already quite clearly a little GDR'. Hoheneck, too, was a perfect microcosm, as Petra Koch discovered – prisoner functionaries helped enforce the oppressive system just as the willing citizens outside did. She described a woman serving time in Hoheneck who used her life sentence to gain influence: 'she was the extended arm of the state.'[4] Women interviewed there in 1990, soon after the fall of the Wall, described how they had been encouraged to spy on fellow residents with promises of privileges and special deals, and how people in prison were also used by the Stasi to spy on prison officers. The Stasi, observes Anne Niendorf, was 'a state within a state', and, like the state, its officers had absolute power. 'They can do whatever they like.'[5]

Home – reformatory – prison. I was raised and educated by the state.

Torsten Heyme visited and interviewed people with criminal convictions who outlined a 'career development' similar to that described by people in prison in the West. 'Most people don't become offenders from one day to the next – a development like that happens in stages,' one interviewee told him. A children's home is followed by a juvenile reformatory – 'and then the first crime'. After that comes 'borstal, youth prison . . . then you're beyond help'. Mario Mann, described exactly that path: being in a children's home until he was fourteen, then in different juvenile reformatories until he was eighteen – 'from that point it was bang, bang, bang: one prison or penitentiary after the other'. Robert Goldstein put it even more succinctly: 'Home – reformatory – prison. I was raised and educated by the state.'[6]

Like their counterparts in the West, people in East German prisons had also often experienced violent childhoods. Goldstein was put in a home in 1976, when he was eight, to protect him from his father – 'he was always thrashing me.' In the home there were more thrashings – and 'then they sent me home to my father to see how that went, and so I got thrashed again.' Axel Wiesner, serving ten years for stabbing a man, described his abuse by a father who expressed his

A guard tower at the border between East and West Germany.

dominance at home by raping his two daughters and making his son masturbate and fellate him.[7] Steffen Seidel was placed in a children's home where his education officer used a high-heeled shoe to hit him on the head. His carers responded to bedwetting by making him strip naked and run the gauntlet of a double row of other children, who were afterwards encouraged to give him a brutal scrubbing under the shower. He ran away multiple times. Captured and brought back, he was sent to the office of the director, Frau Ulich, who beat him with a glass fibre rod and locked him in a dark room for the rest of the day. 'No one ever asked why I kept running away.' At fourteen he was transferred to the youth prison in Wriezen – a dark, brutal place, he remembered, 'anything but an educational institution.'[8]

Juvenile reformatories, called *Jugendwerkhöfe*, were a particular feature of the criminal justice landscape in the GDR. Steffi Weiß, aged sixteen, tried to wrest the steering wheel from a taxi driver who was taking her to the notorious reformatory in Torgau. She was subsequently convicted of attempted murder. Asked by Heyme in 1990 whether anyone had listened to her story during the investigation and trial, she responded simply: 'they took no notice.'[9] Seidel described the reformatory in Wriezen, whose guiding principle was sharp discipline. Individual infringements and failings were met with collective punishments – the whole group would be hauled out of bed at night and the children made to march in their nightshirts before being sent back to their dormitory via the 'gauntlet' of a double row of officers. 'They were standing there with rubber truncheons in their hands, and you had to pass through whether you wanted to or not. If they felt like it, or if someone was moving too slowly, they'd hit out.' Like Steffi Weiß's, Seidel's experience was that East German society outside preferred not to know. 'I've told a lot of people, but no one could imagine things like that happening; they made out I was crazy, but there are witnesses. Lots of youngsters who were there with me can confirm it.' Indeed, Mario Mann recalled a very similar game in Torgau called 'fire brigade', played on the stairs: 'You have to run up and down the steps basically till you go numb – and on every step there's a screw.' Each 'screw' was holding a rubber truncheon, 'and of course he's gonna hit you with it if he feels like it . . . that's education.'[10]

The education went on and on. Steffen Seidel described to Heyme his first meeting with his education officer in Bautzen. 'I decide what the house rules and the rules for your behaviour are here,' the man explained. 'And I have unlimited means with which to enforce those criteria.' Then, Seidel recalled, 'he slowly laid a rubber truncheon, handcuffs, foot restraints and a wrist chain on the table'. Seidel remembered Bautzen not just as yellow misery but as 'hell' – 'unforgettable and terrible.'[11]

useless for anything beyond sweeping the yard

After prison, the socialist world of work was hardly more welcoming for ex-prisoners than the capitalist world of work in the West. One professionally trained painter and decorator told Heyme how he had been given to understand on his release that his home district currently had no need of painter-decorators: 'paradoxical information, given the building programme for new housing that was underway'. The message seemed clear:

> everyone who comes out of prison is worthless; useless for anything beyond sweeping the yard. The prejudices start before you've even put a foot outside. I went through it a couple of times. The result was that I didn't care about all that reintegration stuff because I knew I was always coming back in.[12]

Mann, too, was sceptical of a system in which education for socialist society was based on brutal constraint plus 'infra-red therapy'. 'None of it helps you get back in the swing of things afterwards, so you don't end up back in the nick. In here they just tried to pump us full of red ideas: we were always having "current affairs conversations", reading the Party newpapers, that kind of stuff.'[13]

The women Heyme spoke with described pathways that were both similar to and different from the men's. For them, care homes were less often the path into prison; more often they described violent childhoods with parents who beat them, followed by marriages to violent husbands. Speaking with Heyme, Anke told the story of a husband who beat her up and left; her father then tried to take her eldest son from her because she was a 'whore'. Doren got a divorce from a violent alcoholic husband – but could not get him to move out of the house because no one was willing to intervene. 'The divorce never got taken seriously. I had lacerations from my eyes to the top of my skull,' she told Heyme. 'I'd shut myself in the living room with the children – and he smashed the door down on top of us, frame and all.' Real, existing socialism was deaf to her stories of abuse. When her father finally went with her to complain, her former husband was given a warning, but allowed to continue living with her – 'I started drinking a lot.' Sylvia Stark told the story of an alcoholic husband who beat her, attacked her with a razor blade and locked her in the house, while the police declined to interfere in a family matter.[14]

'Why weren't there women's refuges?' demanded Doren. The answer, at least in part, was that the GDR would not acknowledge domestic abuse by providing safe spaces for women. She felt utterly without recourse: 'you get divorced and are still living in the same apartment and you're not left alone, he keeps on hassling you, hitting you. You go to the police and nothing happens!' she remembered. 'I went everywhere, even to the youth advice centre – answer: we can't do anything for you.'[15]

LIKE ITS WEST German counterpart, East German criminal law made an explicit commitment to young people and the family.[16] And as in the West, that commitment was not reflected in visiting arrangements for people in custody. People imprisoned in the 'alleviated' system could receive visits monthly – those in general custody were permitted visits of one hour once every two months, remembers Garve. Anne Niendorf and Gunhild Gerth, imprisoned in Hoheneck a decade earlier, remembered visits being allowed only four times a year, on each occasion for half an hour. In Bautzen II in the late 1950s and early '60s, Loest recalled, four visits per year were the norm, plus one letter a month. Gerth could receive and write one letter each month, so she had to choose whether to write to her husband or her children, who were living with an aunt. In Hoheneck in 1990, Doren told Heyme, they were allowed to write three letters home a month – 'lots of families fell apart because of that.'[17]

Anke's and Doren's stories suggest that the women were serving life because, in running away from domestic abuse, they had left a young child alone in the home, and the child died. That would put them among the 'child murderers' who were widely regarded, as Birgit Schlicke remembers, as 'the scum of the prison' (simultaneously she recalled that 'among all the criminals I spoke to there wasn't a single woman who hadn't been damaged by her milieu'). Like so many women in prison in the West, Doren described her surviving children with painful longing and guilt: 'we're in here – and that's our fault – but in our thoughts we're still with them.'[18]

It's not possible that something like this exists in the GDR.

Prisons in East Germany were under the control of the Ministry of the Interior and were the direct responsibility of the police (Volkspolizei). Like the police, prison staff had military ranks such as Sergeant, Lieutenant, Captain, Major or Colonel.[19] Gunhild Gerth remembers Hoheneck in the 1970s, when prisoners were sent outside for fifteen minutes each day to march 'cell by cell, each the same distance from the next, in rows of four, hands on your side seams. One time in winter I pushed my hands up into my sleeves and they made me step out of line and stand with my face to the wall.' Cellmates were members of the same work detail or 'commando'. 'If you made contact with another commando you'd get sent to the bunker. In II.6 wing they once nailed all the windows shut – punishment because the prisoners looked out of them.' In theory, 21 days in punitive solitary was the maximum; but in fact, remembers Gerth, the punishment could be extended by releasing the unlucky woman for a single day and then starting again.[20]

In the 1950s even menstruating could land you in the bunker – the only sanitary padding the women had were their foot-rags, but the penalty for being caught without foot-rags on your feet was three days in punitive isolation. During the Hoheneck hunger strike of 1953, Erika Riemann suffered a fearsome blow to the head that caused her to lose her sense of taste and smell. Punished for her part in the strike with solitary confinement, she tried to commit suicide. But her attempt to hang herself with a rag rope failed – and as a penalty for her suicide attempt she suffered another 21 days in solitary, in chains.[21] Wendelgard Trampota was locked in a 'dark cell' for three weeks after she was caught making a carnival costume for a cellmate. The cell had no windows, a crude bed with a straw mattress, two blankets and a shelf. There was nothing to do except exist. Two out of three days she was given only barley coffee and dry bread – 'every third day there was a hot meal.' In Stasi custody twenty years later, Bettina Gilek also found herself in solitary with only dry bread to eat, 'three slices three times a day. There was a stool in the cell, which was screwed to the floor, and the walls were painted a dark colour; it was unbearably

Punishment cell, Bautzen II.

hot during the day and unbearably cold at night.' She was allowed no reading materials or distractions of any kind. A bucket in the cell replaced a toilet. Gilek had tried to make contact with other prisoners via the time-honoured method of knocking on the wall. 'After that I hardly dared knock again.'[22]

Anke, interviewed by Torsten Heyme when the Wall fell, described a 2 × 2 metre (6½ × 6½ ft) separation unit whose fold-out bed was locked away at four in the morning. It was unlocked again at 9.30 p.m. – 'if you were lucky'. The heating was regulated from outside, and was set so that the space was cold: 'but you weren't allowed a pullover, warm tights, anything at all'.[23]

Even in the last days of the GDR, prisoners classed as suicide risks or violent would be chained by their hands and feet to the floor, remembered Schlicke. Their screams would echo through the stairwell. 'Horrible! When it gets too loud, a couple of screws from the hard squad race down to the cellar. Keys . . . a couple of dull truncheon thuds . . . then quiet.' Matthias Bath described the 'awful feeling' of waking in the night to hear a man chained to the floor begging to be released so that he could go to the toilet. 'Maybe an hour later someone will finally come and say "prisoner, that's all well and good, but I need to go too and I'm going to go first," and then laughs and disappears for the next few hours.' The awful feeling peaked when it became clear that the man in the next cell was now 'lying weeping in his own excrement'.[24]

'I often said to myself: it's not possible that something like this exists in the GDR' – the communist politician and former anti-Nazi activist Fritz Sperling was in denial of Hohenschönhausen even while he was imprisoned there. 'I sometimes said to myself: what you're experiencing is bound to be something you're dreaming because of the experiences you had under fascism.'[25] Thirty years on, newly arrived in prison, Roland Garve was told stories by the old lags – until the 1970s, they told him, 'they used methods like shutting people in the dark, making them stand barefoot in water with the window open, denying them food or administering whippings.' Garve remembers nearly fainting with shock – for him, as for Sperling, this was not an East Germany he recognized, and he barely knew how to credit it. 'What he said sounded to my ears like Western propaganda.' But his disbelief, too, was eventually replaced by bitter experience. One fellow prisoner told him about the 'socialist methods' that were still popular with the officers – making a man who had fallen prey to cabin fever lie down on a steel concrete surface, for example, and chaining him there by his hands and feet for days. Exactly this would happen soon after to Garve's cellmate Thomas, who flipped out during a three-week period in solitary and was chained by his hands and feet to a concrete block for eighteen hours 'to calm him'.[26]

Later he witnessed a choreographed attack by prison officers on another friend, Andi, who had somehow aroused their antipathy. 'As we were marching back inside at the end of the exercise hour, Andi got filtered out of the crowd at the entrance,' Garve recalls.

> Suddenly the stunted little head warder who was walking in front of Andi stopped, making sure that Andi walked into him. 'He's attacking me!' he shouted. With a hurling movement he pulled his victim to the ground and started beating him with his truncheon. That was the signal for his colleagues to join in. Andi had no chance of getting away and made no attempt to fight back. He crooked one arm over his head and the other across his back, trying to protect his head and kidneys from the blows. It was no good. They'd obviously been waiting for a chance to practise their 'targeted' educational techniques on him.[27]

You're already dead, man!

Garve tells an unsettling story of prisoner-on-prisoner violence. The story of Lessing is a premonition of the notorious Heibach affair of 2006, when a young man in prison in unified Germany would be tortured and then hanged by his cellmates.[28] Young Lessing was the resident scapegoat in Garve's six-man cell, whose dominant occupant was called Hinrichs. One day Hinrichs found that he was missing a couple of grams of tobacco and a few cigarette papers. It was obvious who would be blamed. The cell had put their young scapegoat on trial before, and once again Lessing was placed in the dock. Predictably, they found him guilty, and moved to the familiar next step in the process – Lessing's punishment. His cellmates fell upon him: 'the beating he got made the wooden screen in front of the toilet collapse.' But then the violence spun out of control. Hinrichs held out a rope to the young man:

> 'on you go, hang yourself, ya murdering swine! It's the most sensible thing you can do, ya nonce!' Lessing looked around with big troubled eyes.
>
> 'Two years ago we cut down someone like you, and you know how he stared as a corpse?! Hey? Just like you now. You're already dead, man!'
>
> 'I don't wanna be dead!' Tears ran down Lessing's cheeks. Like a little child looking for its mother he gazed around for help.

Luckily for Lessing, the prison's inflexible timetable intervened in the unfolding events. 'Thank goodness they called us to the exercise hour,' Garve concludes.[29]

See how concerned we are about you? All this effort we're making to help you.

By the 1970s the GDR was the second-strongest industrial state in the Eastern bloc. In 1971 Erich Honecker succeeded Walter Ulbricht, who had been head of state for 21 years. In 1972, West Germany's Chancellor, Willy Brandt, recognized the GDR as a distinct state, and in September 1973 both Germanies were admitted into the United Nations. Both participated in the Conference on Security and Co-operation in Europe which began in July that year, and both signed the international Helsinki Accords that concluded the Conference in 1975. 'After that the cells in Hohenschönhausen got running water, the toilets had lids and the walls were painted in a lighter colour,' Sigrid Paul remembers.[30] The Stasi moved away from physical violence during interrogations, and towards question sessions held in the daytime, rather than during the night. Water cells fell into disuse and the GDR's new Penal Code of 5 May 1977 brought some day-to-day improvements for people in prison, including better pay for prison labour, better food, longer and freer daily periods outdoors and more frequent visiting hours.[31]

Ellen Thiemann recalls no physical abuse in Hohenschönhausen in 1973. She does, however, remember 'sleep deprivation, psychiatric drugs and sedatives, solitary confinement and bullying' – methods which 'quickly turned a healthy, fun-loving woman into a wreck'.[32] Those 'invisible' methods would become the new normal, as Waltraud Krüger discovered when, in 1980, she made an application to leave the GDR. The new Penal Code of 1968 had got tougher on crimes against the state – even a request to emigrate could now be criminalized under Section 124. Krüger was detained by the Stasi and taken not to an interrogation centre, but to a secure hospital. 'The doctor told me that the Stasi and the district lawyer were of the opinion that something was psychologically wrong with me,' she remembers. 'Every morning, lunchtime, and evening they gave me injections.' Her 'treatment' culminated in a bizarre interview with her Stasi interrogator, during which he explained to her that seeking to leave East Germany was 'not normal behaviour'. That she had been hospitalized and medicated *proved* her mental unfitness to make a decision to leave. But it also exemplified the loving kindness of the state she had mistakenly tried to reject: 'See how concerned we are about you? All this effort we're making to help you – no one would make this kind of effort in the Federal Republic!'[33]

mean fighting dogs, owned by the Stasi

The United Nations Standard Minimum Rules for the Treatment of Prisoners of 1955 had stipulated that 'no prisoner shall be employed in the service of the institution, in any disciplinary capacity'.[34] The arrangements in Bautzen II flew in the face of that stipulation, Erich Loest remembers. Bautzen II held not only those considered a particular threat to socialism, but socialism's supporters, gone astray: those who needed special protection because they had spied for the Stasi in other prisons, and former Stasi officers. 'At the top of the pile,' Loest explains,

> were the prisoner functionaries, almost all of them former Stasi officers. They had a wing to themselves and were allowed wrist watches and to go up and watch television in the common room every evening – they could move

> around the building freely and take a shower as often as they liked. When they handed out food they made sure they got the best bits.

They also 'told their masters everything they did or didn't want to know'. As usual, the situation inside prison mirrored power relations outside. 'After months of humble anxiety on remand they had got their eagle-eyed gaze and confident voices back – they had subordinates again,' observed Loest.[35]

Loest was writing of the 1960s, before East Germany was admitted into the United Nations. But even after it joined the UN in 1973 the GDR operated a system where prisoners were appointed to and rewarded for positions of disciplinary responsibility. In theory, prisoner functionaries were forbidden to use physical violence – but Steffen Seidel describes the 'yellow misery' in the 1980s, where prisoner operatives called *Hausarbeiter* were given truncheons and encouraged to use them. They were, remembered Seidel, 'mean fighting dogs, owned by the Stasi'.[36] Roland Garve recalls the situation in Brandenburg-Görden in the early 1980s, where prisoners called orderlies maintained the smooth running of the prison and wore an armband with the letter O. At the next level up were brigade leaders – 'the Nazis called them Kapos' – whose armbands bore the letter B. At the top of the heap were the shift leaders, a small but powerful group who wore the letter S. Garve remembers a particular shift leader who liked to advertise his power: 'he lorded it behind his desk like a Stasi officer. He would take a luxurious drag on his extra-long filter cigarette as he gazed at us. In front of him was a porcelain cup of steaming, freshly brewed tea.'[37]

Hoheneck, too, operated a system uncomfortably close to the *Kapo* system that had operated in concentration camps. Schlicke encountered Ulla Jürss there, a former Nazi guard in Ravensbrück. In Hoheneck she was serving a life sentence – and wielding authority again, as a work supervisor.[38]

I thought I was in a concentration camp.

Held in solitary confinement in Hohenschönhausen, Hans-Eberhard Zahn found himself remembering a famous picture of Carl von Ossietzky, 'humiliated in a Nazi concentration camp and looking into the arrogant face of an SS man. There was no escaping the thought: SS and Stasi henchmen were made of the same stuff.' Alexandra Dust-Wiese characterized a Stasi officer who interrogated her as a 'Gestapo man'. Hoheneck had been a Nazi prison, and even after 1945, writes Ulrich Schacht, 'it did *not* stop being a place where brutal and subtle human rights abuses were happening.'[39] Anne Niendorf remembers arriving at Hoheneck to 'gaunt, pale faces. Concentration camp – that was really my first thought.' And Birgit Schlicke's response a decade later was the same: 'I thought I was in a concentration camp.' (Curiously, she later formed a close friendship with a notorious former concentration camp guard, Erika Bergmann, whom she called 'Granny'.)[40]

At least I know I'm innocent.[41]

Many former political prisoners of the GDR have now been formally rehabilitated by the government of the Federal Republic. Looking back, the memoirists understand themselves as innocent victims of a guilty state. For Lucie Fischer, the thought that she was 'guilty of nothing' sustained her throughout her time in Hoheneck. Petra Koch recalled looking out of a prison bus in Prague and meeting the stares of passers-by without 'any kind of shame . . . I'm not a criminal.' Bettina Gilek passed through the railway station at Karl-Marx-Stadt on her way to Hoheneck: 'the people on the station goggled at us, of course. But I know that I didn't feel any shame. I was even proud, in a way – I looked at those people and thought: you must be able to see that I haven't done anything wrong.' Nine years later Birgit Schlicke experienced the town similarly as she she moved through the station handcuffed to a fellow political, Ramona. 'The people at the station were staring over at us,' she remembers. 'I looked back at them without fear or shame. *Surely they can see that Ramona and I aren't criminals!!*'[42]

Yet the division between political and criminal prisoners in the GDR is often oversimplified. André Baganz remained in prison when the Wall fell because he had not only committed an offence against the state (when he tried to escape from the GDR), but was also serving a criminal sentence for his involvement in the death of a policeman. Mario Mann, too, served time for both political and criminal offences. Anger with the state that had bullied, brutalized and tortured them affected people in prison across that divide. Baganz dreamt of killing his captors: 'my hatred had reached a level where I no longer recognized the communists' right to life, and saw it as a heroic act to rid the world of them'. Fantasies of violence, Garve remembers, 'were a vent for our feelings and sometimes provided a kind of satisfaction, as if we could have caused the GDR pain with our talk'. For Mario Mann, interviewed by Torsten Heyme, the outcome of his time in prison was 'just hate' for the socialist state. 'What have twenty years in secure institutions made of you or given you?' Heyme asked Steffen Seidel. 'Hatred, mistrust, and a certain brutality in my dealings with other human beings,' Seidel replied. Standing in front of the Hoheneck fortress on the day of her release, Schlicke remembers, she felt fury grip her: 'the fury I'd been suppressing for so long. I turned towards the gate of the prison and shouted something like "you bunch of criminals."'[43]

The big breakout

In the summer of 1989, a wave of people arrested in the attempt to cross the border began to arrive in prisons. By the autumn they were joined by another wave of people, this time arrested during the mass demonstrations for change.[44] Mikhail Gorbachev had been elected General Secretary of the Soviet Communist Party in 1985, and had initiated processes of reform in the eastern bloc that would eventually open borders. East Germans responded to glasnost with hopes for political reform in the GDR, and with peaceful demonstrations demanding it. On 18 October 1989, amid a general sense of crisis, Erich Honecker was replaced as head of state by Egon Krenz. Krenz immediately promised to reform the travel laws and on 27 October announced an amnesty for all those convicted of attempting an illegal border crossing or participating in demonstrations.

But people in prison were making their own demands, and at the end of November a labour and hunger strike was declared in prisons across East Germany. The strikers demanded their immediate release from prison and the reform of the criminal justice system. When Krenz resigned on the morning of 6 December 1989, the new leadership under Manfred Gerlach was facing a mass prison breakout. Gerlach quickly announced a general amnesty for all prisoners convicted of crimes against the state, provided they had been sentenced to less than three years. André Baganz was not eligible and was released only in May 1991. But he remembers a press conference in Bautzen the day after Krenz's resignation, when those officers who had not already fled were held to account for their practices. The fearsome 'Trixi' – 'formerly law and order incarnate' – was now 'a little heap of misery', while the governor of the prison struggled vainly to assert that there had been no 'solitary confinement' in Bautzen; merely 'solitary accommodation'.[45]

BAUTZEN II, LIKE Hohenschönhausen, has now become what Pierre Nora calls a site of memory (*lieu de mémoire*).[46] The former Bautzen I is still operating as a prison in the unified Federal Republic. Hoheneck, too, continued to operate as a carceral facility after unification – it was closed only in 2001, when state of Saxony sold the buildings to a company that planned to transform it into a recreational complex. But victim organizations intervened. The site was finally bought back by the city of Stollberg in 2004 and is now, like Hohenschönhausen and Bautzen II, a memorial site of the former GDR.

In 1992 one of the earliest post-Wall publications on East German prisons collected experiences nearly half a century old from 35 men and women who had been interned there in the immediate post-war period, from 1945 to 1956. The volume was edited by the 'Bautzen Committee', an organization of former inmates and their relatives that set out to research and memorialize 'the suffering of the many innocent victims'. Together with the German War Graves Commission and with the help of the army, the Committee organized a search for the remains of people who had died in Bautzen I and II, many of whom had been buried in unmarked graves on a hill outside the prison. There is now a cemetery, with a chapel to commemorate the dead who could not be located.[47] Silke Klewin and Klaus-Dieter Müller, both leading figures in the memorialization of GDR state brutality, have written with reference to the prison strikes of 1989 that 'places of incarceration can also be places of self-assertion and resistance'. Writing, too, can be a place of self-assertion, and, parallel to the carceral sites of memory, memoirs of former inmates can be read as sites of resistance.

Part IV

Wind of Change: Germany after 1989

The prison system was asleep when democratization happened
(*Der Lichtblick*, 2015)[1]

10

Wind of Change or *Plus ça Change?*

Prisoners are necessary so that the masses can look down on someone.[1]

The Berlin Wall fell symbolically, and was physically torn down in places, during the night of 9 November 1989. Eight months later, ten former West German terrorists were discovered to have been living and working under the special protection of the East German state. 'What a perverse situation,' commented the Western news magazine *Spiegel* in gloomy delight.[2] Most turned king's evidence in return for lighter sentencing. But Inge Viett, who had begun her new life in the East in 1982, refused to testify, preferring to face a probable life sentence. In letters written from remand in 1990, she links her own fate with the fate of the GDR. 'My situation is painfully bound up with what's happening here,' she reflected: 'the liquidation of a society as a historical subject'.[3]

Viett had been a key figure in the 2 June Movement and later in the Red Army Faction. In the mid-1970s she was twice imprisoned for suspected terrorist activity and twice escaped custody in West Berlin. In 1978, when the 2 June Movement dissolved to become part of the RAF, she was responsible for liaising with the Stasi around shared interests in destabilizing the West German regime. In 1981 she was almost apprehended in Paris. She shot at Francis Violleau, the policeman who gave chase – he was paralysed, and spent the next nineteen years until his death in a wheelchair. In the aftermath of the shooting, Viett took the decision to withdraw from militant activity.

She used her Stasi connections, which she had already leveraged to place other 'retired' West German terrorists in the GDR, to acquire a new East German identity. For the next years she lived and worked in Dresden as Eva-Maria Sommer. But that identity was blown when an East German friend visited the West and saw one of the many 'wanted' posters of terrorists with a photograph of 'Eva-Maria' on it. The Stasi quickly moved her to Magdeburg, where she became Eva Schnell.

Viett saw the East German protesters who precipitated the peaceful revolution and the fall of the Wall as ignorants who had abandoned their historical responsibility to the socialist project. East Germany, for her, was a society where people had been able to live 'free from any kind of threat to their existence. They loved to moan and groan about the things that malfunctioned and the goods they couldn't get hold of, but they never had existential worries.'[4] She refused to testify against the Stasi officers with whom she had worked. Her refusal had less to do with protecting the secret police than with preserving her own anti-capitalist integrity, she explained in a letter to Gisela Steineckert, a writer who had been an establishment figure in the GDR – 'it would mean losing my own lifelong struggle against the notion that people can be bought or sold, against consumer attitudes to human relationships.' She sent a similar letter to another star of the East German literary establishment, Christa Wolf. 'To avoid a life sentence I'm supposed to participate in a deal based on betrayal and venality,' she responded to Wolf's critique of her stance. 'Be subordinate, and make yourself useful . . . that's the rhythm of capitalist relations, capitalist modes of functioning. I've dedicated my life to resisting that rhythm, and now I'm supposed to roll over?' For her the Stasi was not merely an apparatus of the state, but a set of complex human individuals, 'people I had many-layered and difficult relationships with.'[5]

'My dear,' she wrote to her girlfriend in Magdeburg about the rapid processes of social and political change, 'our own government and the Federal Republic are behaving like escapees from a political madhouse – I don't know how else to talk about this brutal destruction of the GDR's identity.' East German citizens, she warned, were transfixed like rabbits in the headlights by the promise of the Deutschmark and by fear of unemployment – and strategists in the West were 'using that mercilessly, and aren't going to let go until everything that has even a glimmer of socialism about it has been eliminated'. East Germany was being violated by a rapacious market that was already eating its children: 'I'm sure you too have read that the suicide rate in the GDR has leapt over the last few months.'[6]

Viett's post-Wall hopes were tied to the Party of Democratic Socialism (PDS), the successor party to the Socialist Unity Party (SED) that had led the German Democratic Republic for forty years. The PDS emerged towards the end of 1989 in response to a surging thirst for democracy in East Germany. But, to her deep disappointment, it lost no time in distancing itself from the Western terrorists the GDR had sheltered. In a letter to the party leader, Gregor Gysi, Viett (signing herself with her East German name, E. M. Schnell) sought to address what she saw as his party's misunderstanding of left-wing militancy in the West. 'The genesis of left-wing terrorism in the Federal Republic was linked to the domestic and international processes of capitalist society in the post-war order,' she explained; it had moral legitimacy because it demanded 'the emancipation of human beings from their dehumanized, alienated, profoundly marketized status in those processes'.[7] Gysi's response, if he sent one, is unknown.

Momentum for further and lasting change was gathering, and it seemed nothing now could prevent a 'national orgy of unification'.[8] The treaty joining the two Germanies was signed on 31 August 1990 and came into effect on 3 October. The five eastern states of Brandenburg, Mecklenburg–West Pomerania, Saxony, Saxony-Anhalt and Thuringia (which in the GDR had been fourteen administrative districts) became part of the Federal Republic. Those new federal states (*neue Bundesländer*) were subject to the Federal German lawbooks, penal code and criminal justice system. Judges and prosecutors who had worked in the GDR could apply to be reinstated – but only if they were willing to face questions about their party membership and about their participation in political trials. Some preferred to take early retirement.[9]

A shake-up of the German terrorities was in process the likes of which had not been seen since the end of the Second World War. But was it mirrored on the inside?

This kind of imprisonment ought to be a thing of the past.

Over more than twenty years, until it dissolved itself in 2018, Germany's Critical Working Group on Prisons (*Arbeitskreis kritischer Strafvollzug*) received and responded to letters that documented both the conditions in custody and the distress of those who encountered them. 'In here, the constitution and human rights have the status of used toilet paper,' a man in Naumburg prison told the Working Group in 1996, describing cells 1 metre (3 ft) long and 3.5 metres (11 ft) wide. 'But with a cheery "what do I care about the law" the prison is using the cells not just as places to sleep; it's grotesque how some people are banged up for 21 hours a day minimum.' A year later a letter arrived from a man in Waldheim prison in Saxony. Held in a segregation unit, he had resorted to drinking his own urine, because his desperate requests for water were persistently ignored. 'This kind of imprisonment ought to be a thing of the past,' he concludes.[10]

Abuse and injustice in prisons are widely believed to happen only in the past, or in countries other than one's own. When, in 2020, a widely read German broadsheet interviewed Manuel Matzke, speaker for the German Prisoners' Union (*Gefangenen-Gewerkschaft/Bundesweite Organisation* or GG/BO), about a high-profile case of alleged rape in a prison cell, the journalist remarked that the details emerging in court were 'like something from an American Hollywood film.' 'It happens in German prisons too, I'm afraid,' Matzke contradicted drily.[11]

In penal theory, the *principle of less eligibility* says that, in any given economic circumstances, people in prison must live in conditions 'worse than the living standard of the lowest stratum of the working class.'[12] 'In pre-trial detention there were four of us in a two-man cell,' complained a group of men in custody in 2008. 'Pre-trial. In the country of human dignity.' Halfway through the next decade, in 2015, a contributor to Tegel's prison newspaper *Lichtblick* still found conditions on remand 'too hardcore for central Europe.' Post-remand, reported other Tegel residents, the prison's Complex II 'definitively does not provide the kind of conditions for inmates that would correspond to legal requirements in central Europe, in Germany in the year 2017.'[13] Corinna, who took part in a writing project in prison, described how odd it felt to face basic privations in twenty-first-century Germany: 'running water, a daily shower or a hot bath. In the twenty-first century, in the middle of North Rhine–Westphalia, normal kinds of things suddenly turn into unattainable luxuries.' 'What's really indescribable is when you're eating and the other guy sits down on the loo,' explained Rainer, struggling to communicate to Brigitte and Dieter Kübbeler, a couple who in 2003 conducted interviews with people in prison across Germany, the experience of sharing 7 square metres (75 sq. ft) in Rheinbach prison. Katharina described the later 2000s: 'the worst thing for me was going to the toilet. Because everyone in my cell had a perfect view of it from their bed.' And the complexities do not end there, as Sigrud explained: 'you at least try not to take a shit while someone else is eating or drinking. But still there's the thought in the back of your mind that . . . the door could just open and a male screw could be standing there.'[14]

People in prison in East and West Germany in the decades that followed the founding of the two German states in 1949 had expressed shock at the conditions they were held in. But a national report for the unified Federal Republic in 2020 noted that there were still shared cells that had no wall or partition dividing the washing facilities and WC from the main living space. Some of those were no bigger than 8 square metres (86 sq. ft), including the toilet area.[15]

I am a nothing.[16]

'You will completely lose any kind of self-determination,' warns Dirk Glebe, author of the *Prison Handbook* (2011). 'Prisoners are objects,' agrees Hubertus Becker. 'They cannot decide when they go to bed, when they get up, what clothes to wear, what work they do for what pay, or when, where, or what they eat.' New arrivals discover that they have to shower at set times on certain days of the week, and eat food and wear clothes they have not chosen or bought themselves.[17] They are subject to a timetable which typically includes a wake-up call around 6 a.m., lock-in for the night around 9 p.m. (although sometimes as early as 4.30 p.m., particularly at weekends) and one hour outdoors in the yard. For Becker that constitutes a kind of dying:

'Being in prison means the end of a thousand things that make human beings love life. Imprisonment is a process of getting used to things ending, to death.'[18]

People arriving into custody give up their wallet, house keys, watch, mobile phone – all the markers of adult identity and socio-economic status. 'In modern Western culture, material possessions are so large a part of the individual's conception of himself that to be stripped of them is to be attacked at the deepest layers of personality,' wrote the sociologist Gresham Sykes in his well-known study *The Society of Captives*. Not only our creature comforts such as hot showers and private bathrooms but our clothes, bank cards, mobile phone, house and car keys say that we are *somebody*. They are status markers, and their absence says we are nobody. The German prisoner, poet and novelist Peter-Paul Zahl coined the term 'nobodification' to describe the fate of people in prison.[19] Custody is not just about being less comfortable, but about losing the things that say you *are someone*. In the 1980s Peter Fritze had complained about conditions in the newly reformed prison ('if someone shut a dog in a place like this the animal protection league would be here in a second'), and in 2015 an anonymous writer was still feeling the irony: 'we constantly watch programmes about zoos in my cell, on the little TV. The similarity is remarkable. But the animals have bigger cages and more variety in their lives.'[20]

Rosemarie Müller tells the first-person story of a woman in prison who wants her own mug. 'The other prisoners here have their own mugs. I want one too, and it's taken two and a half months because my request keeps coming back rejected. What's going on here?' Mug ownership might seem trivial to someone who has keys and a mobile phone, a hot shower and privacy. But for this woman it encapsulates her identity and humanity, and her fear of losing herself. 'Who am I, in here? Do the lawmakers really intend prison to be this inhuman?'[21]

> *Even in prison I'm trying to retain some dignity. According to the Constitution my dignity is inviolable. I wish that some notice would be taken of that.*[22]

'I am a numbered individual', the poet U. K. wrote in the late 1970s. In 2008 Hubertus Becker, a former prisoner and a jury member for the Drewitz Prize for Prisoner Literature, observed the still-dehumanizing moment of entering custody: 'the prisoner is supplied with a number. He is stripped naked. Only now does he step inside the world of the prison.'[23] Katharina, who took part in a prison writing project, described entering that numbers-driven world:

> you're handed a package . . . with 1 bedsheet, 1 duvet cover, 2 blankets, 1 pink nightie, 1 tooth mug, 1 toothbrush, 1 comb, 1 small piece of soap, 1 cup, 1 jug, 1 each of bowl and plate, 1 breadbin, spoon, fork, teaspoon, 1 small glass bowl and 1 knife that doesn't cut, and a plastic bowl to wash in – as your basic kit. Then additionally 2 handtowels, 2 flannels, 2 handkerchiefs. For clothes you get 3 pairs of underpants (second world war), 2 vests, 2 pairs of socks, 1 bra that doesn't fit, 1 pullover, 1 cardigan, 1 pair of jeans, 1 pair of slippers.[24]

Carrying that precisedly calculated bundle, the new arrival then follows a prison officer through the corridors to her cell. The law stipulates single occupancy unless there is a danger of self-harm – but more than a quarter of people in German prisons still find themselves in shared cells.[25] 'If you're lucky,' commented Katharina, 'you end up with women you get on with. But winning the lottery is more likely.' She remembered her first sight of a dirty four-woman cell with a toilet in full public view, a broken window (in midwinter), insufficient blankets and rats: 'I just thought: it can't be true that there are prison conditions like this in Germany.'[26]

'I'm struggling to believe this kind of thing still happens in Germany,' agreed Karina. She had seen a young mother who did not speak German have her baby taken away and put into care – the mother was awaiting trial and the remand unit had no mother-and-baby facilities. The woman would later receive a 'not guilty' verdict, but nothing could change the fact that she had been separated from her newborn. 'Incomprehensible, cruel, and a violation of human dignity!' declared Karina.[27]

More broadly, noted Dieter Wurm in the prison newspaper *Lichtblick*, people who are not familiar with German language and culture are negatively impacted in criminal justice contexts.[28] Often that is true even for people from other countries who do speak German. Marco Lobito, an Italian remand prisoner in Bavaria, wrote to the Critical Working Group in 1996, noting that it was 'completely normal for foreigners to get "you wog" and other insults hurled at them.' 'I hope you will believe what I'm going to describe in this letter,' he opens. 'When I was arrested, a policeman deliberately rammed his knee into the small of my back . . . He also said I should piss off back to Calabria. Then he pushed his fingers into my eyes and tortured me that way until my whole face was covered in blood.' He showed his bleeding eyes to another policeman, who accused him of lying. 'He simply claimed I had fallen. Not even the judge who issued the warrant for my arrest commented on my injured face.' Lobito felt betrayed: 'How can you believe in justice when the state just tramples on human rights?'[29]

Naim Kilig, a Kurdish detainee in North Rhine–Westphalia in the same year, similarly described the betrayal of his key beliefs about Germany as a country of human rights. 'I was violently abducted, just as it happens in Turkey,' he told the Critical Working Group. His German guards had received a tip-off that Kurdish inmates were planning a demonstration. They floored, gagged and cuffed him, he reported, before forcibly transporting him, still gagged and cuffed, to an isolation cell in a different prison: 'I was treated, physically and psychologically, in a manner akin to torture.'[30]

As so often, the society of captives reflects the community at large. Anton, whose family came to Germany from the Russian Urals in 1993, wrote an autobiographical sketch for a project with young men in prison. He describes feeling glad about his family's move to Germany at first, 'because I'd heard so many positive things about the country.' But they were the only Russians in a small village, 'and I found out almost immediately what racial hatred is . . . I quickly learned what *Kanake* [a violently derogatory term for someone seen as racially 'other'] means.' At secondary school he met other Russian boys with similar experiences and discovered gang identity; this was a turning point in his story of becoming criminalized.[31]

Feeling culturally excluded within the nation is part of the story of Germany told by its prisoners. So, too, is being physically excluded from the nation. Hassan, aged thirty, described waiting to be sent 'back' to Turkey after serving his sentence. '[It was] hard, because I've lived in Germany for thirty years,' he explained to the Kübbelers. 'I don't have any kind of relationship with Turkey. I've no idea what I'm going to do there.' Metin Günes, from a Kurdish migrant family, faced a similar fate after losing his appeal. His lawyer had omitted to mention to the judge that the entire family lived in Germany. 'My siblings came over to me and were sad. I comforted them and promised to take my case to the European Court of Human Rights.' All this, writes Günes, took place inside the 'cruel court in the pretty city of Düsseldorf . . . situated right on the corner of the Königsallee – a wonderful contrast! Within me Adorno's words rang out: "The other side of civilization is barbarism!"'[32] His command of German and familiarity with German culture and thought clearly eclipses that of many Germans whose right to remain is not in doubt.

My dignity has been crushed and I cannot bear it.

Like their predecessors in the post-war decades, people in prison in the early twenty-first century refer bitterly to Germany's constitutional promise that human dignity is inviolable. In a letter to the Critical Working Group in 2012, a man held in Celle prison described what happened when he objected verbally to a body search. In response to his protest,

> two officers took me into a room . . . one of them pushed me repeatedly and when I sat down on a chair to take off my shoes, as they asked me to, he thrust me back on to the floor. The maltreatment and the humiliation of it made me cry. I was made to undress in front of about seven officers.

They locked him naked in a cell and left him for five hours. Back in his own cell, he was punished with two weeks' confinement to the cell and a week without television. Citing the surveillance video as proof, he made a complaint via his solicitor, but the prison's response was that its surveillance videos were routinely wiped after five days. The authorities quickly turned the tables on him: 'The public prosecutor's office dropped my complaint and raised a case against me for making a false accusation,' the letter-writer went on. 'In January 2013, six officers from the prison bore witness against me in Celle district court, portraying me as a liar. . . . *My dignity has been crushed and I cannot bear it.*'[33]

In 2016 Christian Vinke, writing from Tegel prison, warned in a letter to the in-house newspaper *Lichtblick* that people in prison were still not believed, which made it practically impossible to prove that an officer had used arbitrary or illegimate measures: 'it will be claimed that the prisoner has a tendency to make accusations that have no basis in fact.' Complaints against a particular officer in Tegel, a group of 27 residents had reported to the Critical Working Group in 2012, were met by that officer 'with a malicious grin, and the response that the complainant should go ahead and bring a court action against him.'[34] 'A prisoner who is attacked by screws theoretically has the right to self-defence,' observes *Pathways through Prison* (2016), a guidebook co-written by people in prison, former prisoners and others including medics and lawyers. 'But any prisoner who actually hits back knows that they will come off worst, both physically and in the legal process that follows.'[35] *Pathways* is available free to people in prison, but in some prisons it has been banned.

Has justice become a question of geography?

Before the arrival of COVID-19 in Germany in early 2020, the most significant ructions in the post-unification criminal justice landscape happened in 2006, in the shape of a Federal legislative reform that shifted responsibility for penal law from central government to the individual states. Certain issues, such as the protection of the human rights of people in prison, remained a Federal (and European) matter. But states could now develop their own penal codes for adult offenders, and were *required* to have specialist laws regulating the detention of young people.

Broadly speaking, the more politically conservative a state, the more quickly it jumped at the chance to create its own legislation for prisons.[36] Bavaria, the conservative southern German state that the prison activist Birgitta Wolf had complained about in the 1960s and the journalist Ulf Stuberger in the 1970s, was the first to pass a state-specific penal code, in 2007. It was followed by Baden-Württemberg. Hamburg introduced a new code in 2009 and Hesse in 2010; Lower Saxony and North Rhine–Westphalia developed independent legislation in 2014 and 2015 respectively. The remaining ten states collaborated to develop a joint legislative model (*Musterentwurf*),[37] and codes based on that model were passed in Brandenburg, Mecklenburg–West Pomerania, Rhineland-Palatinate, the Saarland and Saxony in 2013; in Bremen and Thuringia in 2014; in Saxony-Anhalt in 2015; and finally in Schleswig-Holstein and Berlin in 2016. Political orientation influenced not only the speed with which state-specific laws were passed, but their flavour. Baden-Württemberg and Bavaria, both with a strong tradition of centre-right rule, reversed the priorities that had driven the reform laws of 1976 and put public safety ahead of resocialization as prison's aim. Rather than being primarily a source of support for people intended to rejoin the community (as it had been in the mind of the reformers), prison became primarily a place to contain people felt to threaten that community.[38]

Prison is supposed to teach offenders to obey the rules.
So why can't there be rules for how prisons work that apply to everyone?[39]

One could argue that putting public safety first, and the resocialization of people in prison second, only formalized what had long been the de facto approach. But it also made a difference to the real lives of people in prison. A research study undertaken in Germany in 2010–11 showed that there was far less violence in open prisons,[40] but legislation in Bavaria, Lower Saxony and Hamburg nonetheless declared closed prisons the norm. A person's experience of prison came to depend heavily on which state they were incarcerated in. In 2015 in Thuringia and Bavaria only about 5 per cent of people in prison were serving time in open prisons compared to 22 per cent in North Rhine–Westphalia and 25 per cent in Berlin. In 2012 people imprisoned in Bremen were granted day release more than ten times as often as their fellows in Saxony-Anhalt. And in 2017 people in prison in Bavaria and Baden-Württemberg were entitled to just one visiting hour per month, where Berlin permitted up to two hours and Brandenburg four. 'Has justice become a question of geography?' asked Jürgen Reissig in the prison newspaper *Lichtblick*.[41]

BY THE 2010S Ulf Stuberger, a journalist who had begun investigating German prisons in the 1970s, was observing a culture shift – the public was no longer very interested in the people formerly called 'marginalized', now 'the precariat'. In the new millenium, prison was catching public attention primarily in the context of calls for harsher punishments, or in fictional television series such as the hugely successful *Behind Bars* (*Hinter Gittern*). 'I have to laugh when I think of the series *Behind Bars*,' wrote a woman in prison in the 2000s. 'None of it even comes close to the reality of life in prison.'[42]

Publishers, too, were less interested in writing from the prison than they had been in the 1980s. Reimund Neufeld started facilitating writing groups for women in prison in 2006, but struggled to find a publisher for the texts. 'Who wants to hear these stories?' he recalls being asked, 'what's the point of them?' One of the women involved in Neufeld's writing groups, Claudia Franck, went on to co-organize the 16 Bars Project with him. 'We want to give prisoners and ex-prisoners a voice,' they explained. 'We want to initiate an active and honest dialogue between prisoners and society.'[43] But the dialogue is (and perhaps always has been) between prisons and particular segments of society. Writing from contemporary prisons tends to be published only by specialist presses with sociopolitical or religious agendas.

At the same time, however, new technologies are enabling stories from the prison to be heard. Germany's most established prisoner newspaper, *Der Lichtblick*, has existed since 1968 and is edited by inmates of Berlin's Tegel prison – it proudly claims to be independent and uncensored[44] (though it has also been called 'officially-unofficially censored'), and these days it is available online to readers outside prison.[45] By its own account it reaches more than 40,000 readers in Germany and beyond. Dirk Glebe's *Prison Handbook* for those entering prison is available via Books on Demand, and Friedrich Peters's *Prison Diary* of 2014 is printed and distributed by Amazon.[46]

> *in the 1990s the system of punishment is no longer being profoundly questioned or held up for discussion . . . But prisons are part of society and concern all of us.*[47]

IN LATE MAY and early June 1990 riots were reported in Hamburg's notorious Fuhlsbüttel prison. 'Santa Fu' is a high-security facility and stands on the site of a former concentration camp. Residents were protesting against the conditions in which they were held and the continued neglect of the rights of people in prison, as defined in German law – things were felt to have got much worse since the appointment of a new Senator for Justice for the city-state, Wolfgang Curilla. Frank Niemeyer experienced the revolt on the ground. Later named as a ringleader and transferred into solitary confinement in Nuremberg, he wrote a detailed description of the riot from the prisoner's-eye perspective.

Niemeyer's account begins on 28 May 1990, when two men climbed on to the prison roof, watched by around a hundred others in the yard. Soon there were two hundred men in the yard. They tore the yard door off its hinges for ease of access and brought mattresses and blankets outside. A podium was improvised and speeches were held. Men lit fires and the prison chaplain brought out canisters of hot coffee. 'This is my first night under the stars in twelve years,' one man whispered. The following night news came that a sympathy protest had started in Mannheim prison in southern Germany. On 30 May Senator Curilla tried to start a conversation with the men on the roof, who refused to speak with him. The media had gathered – 'we saw the North German TV crew as a kind of life insurance – our protection against violence,' wrote Niemeyer. The protesters were told that their food would be stopped if the riot continued. But help arrived in the form of the Hamburg anarchist community, who threw first fireworks, then food and a megaphone over the prison walls into the yard. 'The sky above us turned dark with fruit, cans, chocolate,' remembered Niemeyer. On 31 May a group of prisoners, including Niemeyer, met and negotiated with the Senator they nicknamed Gurilla on issues such the charges levied by the state of Hamburg on people in prison, and the situation of immigrants threatened with deportation. The negotiations became lengthy, but no significant assurances were given or commitments made. Eventually the negotiating group announced via loudspeaker across the prison that it had not been able to achieve any concrete outcomes. 'The night began that would become headlines.'

the situation in the prison was like a civil war.

It was the night of 31 May to 1 June 1990. During that night cell windows were ripped out and glass bottles filled with water hurled into the central area. An iron door was torn from its hinges. 'It's no exaggeration to say that the situation in the prison was like a civil war,' Niemeyer recalled. In the morning around a hundred police and prison officers in riot gear stormed the prison, via its chapel, and enforced a lockdown. Unlucky men who did not get back inside their cells in time could be heard screaming as they were beaten with truncheons: 'greetings from Senator Gurilla.' People watched from their cells as one of the men on the roof refused to come down, instead throwing stones at the advancing police and brandishing an iron bar. Eventually he was overpowered. 'I saw Martin lying on the ground,' remembers Niemeyer, 'and the pigs hitting him again and again, even though he wasn't even moving. Then they took him to the bus where the others were, but they had to carry him because of his injuries.'[48]

Surviving your time in prison is a constant fear and worry.

Niemeyer tells the story of two men in 'Santa Fu' who did not survive to experience the riot. One had been treated for a kidney problem for three years, even though the postmortem would reveal that he had lung cancer. Another man died from a heroin overdose;

Protest in Rummelsburg prison, September 1990.

if he had been offered therapy rather than locked in a cell, Niemeyer comments bitterly, that man, too, might have lived.[49] Nearly twenty years on, little seemed to have changed: in 2017 an anonymous correspondent in *Der Lichtblick* promised a story in the series of 'dramatic, shady, senseless and absurd tales from the prison hospital'. His story began with intense abdominal pain. He threw up the oral painkillers that were handed out to him – but it was a Saturday, and he could not be examined by a doctor in the prison before Monday. He spent three days in acute pain before he finally saw the doctor, who established that he had a inflamed gallbladder. He was immediately admitted to hospital and operated on. The moral of the story, for its writer, is 'how limited my possibilities for action are and how helplessly we are at the mercy of the prison system . . . Surviving your time in prison is a constant fear and worry.'[50]

the punitive character of prison trumps healthcare, wellbeing and treatment.[51]

In a high-profile case in 2014, Constantin M., a 21-year-old Romanian man, died in what can only have been agony in Herford prison in North Rhine–Westphalia. He was serving a seven-month sentence and had spent time in a prison hospital. Doctors had suggested that he really needed to be in a secure psychiatric unit; instead he was kept in semi-isolation and often had restraints on his hands and feet.[52] One night, about four months before his release date, he was found dead in his cell. The autopsy found pieces of plastic in his intestine and a litre of pus in his stomach. Charges of negligence against the prison's director and doctor were later dropped. In the same year another prisoner with immigrant status, the 33-year-old Rasmane Koala, was found dead in his isolation cell in Bruchsal prison in Baden-Württemberg. His body was skin and bones; it was reported that he had been on hunger strike. In Germany, the state ministry of justice must be informed if a prisoner does not eat for more than a week, but apparently no report had been made. Again, the charges both against the governor and the prison doctor were eventually dropped, though the doctor was sentenced to pay a fine.[53]

You often hear that prison doctors don't see the sick patient, but only ever the offender.[54]

'Prison doctors in particular tend to assume that it is prisoners' own fault when they are ill, or that they are shamming,' commented the law professor Christine Graebsch in 2020.[55] 'If they weren't clearly on the edge of death they were automatically in danger of being written off as a malingerer,' Frank Niemeyer had written of Santa Fu in the 1990s, and a letter from a women's prison registered no change in 2017: 'If you don't assert yourself you'll be called a malingerer, given wrong treatment or none at all.' 'You really do need to make an effort if you want to be taken seriously,' warns *Pathways through Prison.*[56] A letter from Chemnitz women's prison registered amazement: the writer had discovered after her transfer there that women reporting sick in Chemnitz were simply allowed to see a doctor.[57]

When COVID-19 arrived in German prisons in early 2020, then, it arrived into a system already beset with problems of medical care. The first case of COVID-19 in the general population in Germany was confirmed on 27 January 2020, near Munich. The first deaths from the virus in the general population were recorded on 9 March. Soon afterwards, first reports began to emerge from German prisons, collected and published via the Prisoners' Union and its solidarity organizations.

On 16 March 2020 a letter from a unnamed man in Berlin described fear. 'At a time when the coronavirus is spreading like wildfire, no drastic protective measures are in evidence,' it begins. 'Conditions here are catastrophic: there are no soap or antibacterial gel dispensers and we're given barely any cleaning materials. The staff are reporting sick, which means that prisoners are being banged up earlier.' Three men had apparently reported with symptoms of COVID-19 but were sent back to their cells without seeing a doctor, and told to stay there and not stir up a panic. They were not tested for the virus. 'You can see the fear in the faces of the officers as well as the prisoners.'[58]

Towards the end of March, a group of men in Tegel prison reported that new arrivals were not even having their temperature taken. Even the prison officers were making complaints, they reported. With 120 men outdoors during yard time, social distancing was hardly possible. Manuel Matzke, the spokesperson for the Prisoners' Union, was receiving hundreds of letters and phone calls from people in prison. 'People are afraid,' he told the news magazine *Focus*. 'They feel insecure and vulnerable to the virus.' Too few single cells meant that many people in prison were sharing despite the distancing rules. Marvin D., imprisoned in North Rhine–Westphalia, noted that where three prisoners were sharing a cell, it was simply not possible to mantain the 2-metre distancing rule.[59] 'Social distancing just isn't possible in prison', commented Matzke.[60]

> *In the current situation, no-one who isn't dangerous should be in prison.*[61]

When COVID-19 struck, most German prisons were at or beyond capacity, with individual states reporting 'hopelessly overcrowded' conditions.[62] On 31 March 2019 there were 65,796 people in prison in Germany, occupying around 90 per cent of the national capacity. Given the unevenness in numbers between institutions, a 90 per cent occupancy rate in practice means overcrowding, and a widespread first response to COVID-19 across the Federal states was to try to reduce the numbers of people in prison. Prison sentences that had been imposed because someone would or could not pay a fine (for a driving offence, for example) were suspended or delayed. Some states postponed convictions for young offenders. People convicted of non-violent crimes had their entry dates into prison delayed. From across the country there were reports of a spate of sudden releases. By the next census date, 31 March 2020, Germany held just 46,054 prisoners. 'People here are talking about lightning releases,' wrote a prisoner group in Tegel in March 2020. 'They have nowhere to live, nothing at all, they've been put out on the street in the cold.'[63]

For those still inside, one critical issue was lack of information – 'prisoners are being told nothing.' Another was the anxiety about a generally poor quality of care: 'you can step on a nail and they'll still give you ibu[profen].'[64] On 17 March a letter was sent from a prison near Rostock. 'What's going on here is creepy!' it began. 'Here in Bützow we have a case of COVID-19, a social worker. So yesterday morning (16.03) all the cells were unlocked by staff wearing hazmat suits. After that we were banged up for the whole day.' New arrivals were now going through quarantine: 'the women's wing is now the quarantine for arriving prisoners. The women moved into the men's G wing yesterday.' Clear plastic dividing walls prevented physical contact between residents and their visitors. Day release was cancelled, no one was being transferred and the prison shop had closed, the writer reported. Two other prisons in the same federal state (Mecklenburg–West Pomerania) were taking similar measures.[65]

Operating in prison buildings where corridors were narrow and the cells small, many governors must have felt helpless, particularly in the face of a widespread squeeze on protective equipment. One of the few reponses available to them was to lock down the institution, thus isolating prisoners even more radically from the world outside – from family, friends and all external sources of mental, physical and resocialization support. On 27 March a report appeared via the now-suspended Twitter account of prisoners in Luckau-Duben in Brandenburg. Its author, Christine Schwenke, was 67 years old and had been in prison since May 2015. Continuing education had been suspended, she reported, and so had religious services. The Catholic priest who otherwise visited, the social worker and the prison's psychologist were all absent, and the women had been told that visits were suspended indefinitely. 'None of the staff are asking about the women's justified, significant concerns about their children and family.'[66] Two days later the education facilities were closed, and only prisoners working in the laundry and canteen still went to work.

Marvin D., meanwhile, had been transferred to Bochum-Krümmede, where the conditions were similary austere. 'It was like this,' he explained:

> One hour yard time in the mornings. Showers twice a week. Otherwise strict solitary confinement for 23 hours a day . . . Lunch was normally at 11am. Tea arrived at the same time. And from then on you were banged up for the night. No-one came by again until breakfast. Not even the regular checks to see you were alive. If the officers permitted it you you could use the phone for 5 minutes about every two weeks. There were no visits, no Skype or any other kind of contact to the outside.

From Bochum he was moved to Aachen prison, where he found better arrangements in place: Skype calls for 30 minutes every month, and some opportunities to have social contact.[67]

Interviewed by a Berlin magazine in April 2020, Manuel Matzke criticized local failures in communication. People in prison and their families knew far too little about the emerging plans and policies, he complained. At that time there was no information, for example, about what happened if a prisoner in Berlin tested postive. Italy had already seen riots in the wake of the suspension of visiting, and the situation in German prisons was 'explosive'. 'There are people who haven't seen their children in six weeks . . . People outside are are stressed by the limitations on their lives right now – but the mental burden prisoners are experiencing is much greater.'[68]

By October two prisoners in an open prison in Bremen and two staff members at the same prison had tested positive. Two guards tested positive in Werl, and three prisoners, a staff member and a doctor in Untermassfeld in Thuringia. Further cases were reported in both Thuringia and Bavaria. In early 2021 a prisoner in Bielefeld sounded the alarm: the prison had five cases of COVID-19. The infected men were in quarantine, but men who had been in contact with them, the writer reported, were still at work despite showing symptoms. 'The prison officers don't take the symptoms seriously, and threaten anyone who refuses to go to work with disciplinary measures.'[69] On 12 January 2021 Bavaria was reporting 175 positive tests among prison staff and 81 positive tests among residents. Sixty had recovered, ten had been released and there were eleven current cases. There had been no deaths of staff or prisoners, although one person with a medical history who had tested positive while in prison died two and half months after being released.[70] Tegel's prison newspaper *Lichtblick* devoted its first issue of 2021 to the pandemic. Contributors reported nine cases of COVID-19 in Tegel and Moabit prisons, and that, just prior to the outbreaks in December 2020, prisoners had been transferred from Moabit to Tegel without any kind of medical examination, even though two men held in Moabit had already shown signs of the virus: 'reports suggest that, despite having cold symptoms, the men were only superficially examined and were treated with German prisons' favourite panacea, Ibuprofen.' Some 540 Tegel residents then spent Christmas isolated and in quarantine – 'a huge psychological and mental burden'.[71] Significant disadvantages were suffered by people approaching release, who would normally have spent preparatory time in the community and had opportunities to attend job interviews and look for accommodation.[72]

But *Lichtblick* also reported on some exemplary responses to the pandemic. In its response to the magazine's nationwide questionnaire, the Bavarian Ministry of Justice reported its decision to introduce generous phone-call allowances to compensate for the suspension of visiting, and financial support for those who struggled to afford the call charges. People in prison whose work was suspended received some pay nonetheless, so they could still buy items in the prison shop. In other states, too, where work shifts had to be suspended, payment was still made at a full or reduced rate. Even before the arrival of COVID-19, some federal states had introduced multimedia systems that allowed people in custody to Skype and send emails to their families from their cells. Some residents had in-cell landlines (though others still had to stand in corridors, with very little privacy, in the traditional way).[73]

At the time of writing, in August 2021, there have been no recorded deaths from COVID-19 in German prisons,[74] compared with 91,637 deaths reported by the Robert Koch Institute for the general population. The suicide rate in prisons almost doubled during the first year of the pandemic, however: in 2020 there were 77 recorded deaths by suicide, compared with 43 in the preceding year.[75] By the third wave of the pandemic, in May 2021, some prisons had spent a total of five months in total lockdown,[76] and it is striking that the massive increase in self-harm coincided with a time where some people were banged up 23 hours a day, when visits from families and friends were repeatedly suspended, alongside day release, religious services, group sport, communal eating, legal advice and drug and mental health support, and access to coffee and tobacco via the prison shop, or indeed via visiting family and friends.

On a positive note, some prison governors in Germany see the measures that have been taken to reduce prisoner numbers as an opportunity, and are keen not to return to overcrowded conditions. There might even be improvements in healthcare: since 2019 Baden-Württemberg has been trialling so-called tele-medicine in all seventeen of its prisons, with allegedly positive responses from residents. In May 2020 North Rhine–Westphalia announced that it would introduce tele-medicine in seven institutions in the first instance, and the state of Saxony, too, has made interested noises.[77]

11

Death in Siegburg and Other Stories

There's a lot of violence in here.[1]

In Hamburg's 'Santa Fu', Reiner spent a total of six years in solitary confinement, including one two-year stretch. In solitary, *Pathways through Prison* explains, 'the prisoner experiences the absolute power of the state in the very fibres of their being.' For Reiner, it brought home to him his profound vulnerability:

> you can yell all you like and they just laugh at you. You have no-one to lobby for you, you're nothing, done for. That's powerlessness. They can do anything they want with you. They can attack you at any time, beat you up, anything. You just keep thinking about that.[2]

'Life in prison is constant hope and worry – a time of insecurity, when fear and anxiety are your constant companions,' wrote a contributor to *Lichtblick* in 2013. 'The loss of security, control, and autonomy constricts your throat, grips your heart and crushes your soul.'[3]

'I often think of suicide,' wrote Karina, while Katharina told the story of a woman who hanged herself, unnoticed, in the middle of a working day. 'Prison is a cruel thing,' she reflected. 'The people inside are supposed to be under observation, at least you'd think so.'[4] German prison officers 'count the live pigs' (*Lebendschweine zählen*) in routine daily checks – but prison suicide remains, in Harald Dreßler's words, just reality. 'A week ago a friend of mine hanged himself, and when I asked a prison officer why he said: it's just reality, Herr D.'[5]

since this morning
it's gone quiet

he was twenty-two[6]

In a prizewinning poem, Dieter Wurm tracked a 'criminal career' from its familiar beginnings to its logical end.

First he hung round in his mother who didn't want him.
Then he hung round a home unliked and managed.
Then he hung round the street aimless, lonely, and alone.
Then he hung round rent boys and had to take it.
Then he hung round his buddies steel in his fist, robbed and stole, hit and got hit.
Then he hung round in the nick again and again; as always, he had no way out.
Then he hung round my wing, and in my cell, stone-walling us all.
No-one could take that for long, so in the end he hung around alone,
Till one morning he was hanging from the bars on his window.[7]

In his report on the Santa Fu revolt in 1990, Frank Niemeyer counted three recent suicides, two of them in solitary confinement.[8] Suicides happen particularly where there is overcrowding, and the risk level is especially high for young men. Most happen soon after a person is incarcerated – many of the people who die are therefore on remand, in pre-trial detention.[9] 'I've been in prison for a year and during that time I've been aware of four suicide attempts, two of them successful,' wrote Stefan Adler in 2018. 'On our wing things have got so bad that the suicides – which are sometimes happening monthly – are no longer being reported, to stop them from becoming public knowledge,' claimed a prisoner liaison group in Tegel in 2017. A similar account emerged in the same year from Aichach prison in Bavaria. 'The suicide rate gets covered up,' wrote a woman held there. 'No one hears about it. Neither the public nor the inmates.'[10]

Between 2017 and 2020 almost half of the recorded suicides in German prisons were of people who were not German citizens. That coincides with rising numbers of people in prison who do not have German citizenship (in 2019, half of the people in prison in the city-states of Hamburg and Berlin were not German citizens, and one-third of those in North Rhine–Westphalia). There are also reports of 'dozens' of suicides of people held in detention pending deportation, though the government does not keep records on this.[11]

an african man
burned to a flake and a stain
on a fireproof mattress on the tiled floor of cell no. 5
shackles on arms and feet – nose bone fractured
Suicide! officials say
obstinate in their refusal to investigate
the possibility and much more
plausible explanation
of him gotten struck
by lightening[12]

Not all verdicts of suicide in custody are uncontested; and here again, people without German citizenship are particularly affected. In 2005 the body of Oury Jalloh, an asylum seeker from Sierra Leone, was recovered from a burnt-out police cell in Saxony-Anhalt. Local police claimed he committed suicide, tearing a hole in the fireproof cover of his mattress and setting fire to it with a lighter they had apparently missed when searching him. The case was reopened in 2013, when an independent fire test suggested that Jalloh could not have set fire to the mattress himself, and that it could not have burned up as completely as it did unless a flammable liquid had been poured into it. In 2019 a medical report, commissioned by the group Initiative in Remembrance of Oury Jalloh, established that his body sustained significant physical injuries *before* it burnt. But the regional court in Naumburg in Saxony-Anhalt ruled against accepting the report.[13]

Similar uncertainties surround the alleged suicide of Amed Ahmad, a 26-year-old Syrian man, in September 2018. Ahmad died from his injuries after in a fire in his cell. He had been wrongfully arrested by police who were searching for a man with a somewhat similar name, and held for two months in Kleve prison in North Rhine–Westphalia. It emerged after his death that he had protested about the mistaken identity, but had been ignored. It also seemed that he had used the call button in his cell when the fire broke out. At the time of writing the case has still not been satisfactorily explained. An Initiative Amed Ahmad has been founded, which links itself explicitly to the Initiative for Oury Jalloh. 'The racist stigmatization, criminalization, and pathologizing of Amed Ahmad when he was arrested is partly to blame for his death,' a spokesperson for the group has said.[14]

A third case is strikingly and tragically similar. In July 2020 an Algerian man, Ferhat Mayouf, burned to death in pre-trial custody in Berlin's Moabit prison. A number of men held in neighbouring cells reported that he had cried for help, but that prison staff had unlocked his door only after the cries had stopped. The authorities maintained that it was suicide, and that there had been no cries for help.[15]

On 30 July 2021 the organization Death in Custody reported 185 deaths at the hands of police or in custody of Black people, people of colour and people affected by racism in Germany since 1990, including nine deaths in cell fires.[16]

For a Nazi in uniform it's a comfortable atmosphere.

'You find them in every prison yard,' wrote Hubertus Becker in 2015 of the neo-Nazi scene: from the shaven-headed 'morons' who identified with Germany's far-right NPD to the militants who were calling for an end to democracy ('Adolf Hitler is my ideal and I'm fighting for a new dictatorship').[17] But he also notes with concern that, in recent years, far-right leanings have been in evidence among prison officers. He relates some 'brownecdotes': the story, for example, of his cellmate in Weiterstadt who requested kosher meals. 'I'm Jewish,' he told the officer. 'Then be glad you're still here,' was the response, 'some Jews weren't so lucky!' Another story goes back to the winter of 2012, in Rohrbach prison, where Becker pointed out to a guard that another prisoner had trampled a swastika into the snow. 'I can only see footprints,' smiled the officer, and walked away. 'Prison seems to be their natural habitat', Becker reflected. 'For a Nazi in uniform it's a comfortable atmosphere. It encourages him to crack down. His tendency to sadism is compatible with the business of taking revenge on criminals.' Becker tells a final anecdote from Weiterstadt prison in Hesse in 2011, where an African man complained that another inmate was calling him the n-word. The officer receiving the complaint, Becker recalls, did a crude impression of a chimpanzee and asked, 'do you want him to call you monkey?' 'The dignity of prisoners, especially from Africa, Russia, Turkey or the former Yugoslavia, isn't looking good,' Becker concluded.[18]

> *No person shall be favoured or disfavoured because of sex, parentage, race, language, homeland and origin, faith, or religious or political opinions.*
>
> Constitution of the Federal Republic of Germany, Art. 3

Ten years on, the dignity – and safety – of Black people and people of colour in prison is still not looking good. In 2020 Dresden's public prosecutor raised a case against six prison officers, who in 2018 are alleged to have physically abused North African men in their custody, and to have used WhatsApp to joke about the abuse. A senior official apparently used racist terminology in the chat, and referred reverentially to the house that was Hitler's birthplace in the Austrian town of Braunau. The news magazine *Focus* printed some of the messages that were exchanged. 'Don't overdo it, at least not visibly,' one read. Another shared advice to 'leave no marks.' The accused officers explained the chat as a kind of pub joke. The injuries sustained by the men in custody had, they maintained, been incurred while officers were pursuing their duty of care. At the time of writing it is unclear whether the case will come to trial. Rebecca Stange, the governor of Dresden prison, has described the events as 'a one-off occurrence'.[19]

But there are indications of a broader problem. An officer employed in Leipzig prison was accused of involvement in a radical right-wing attack, and another in Berlin's youth prison apparently displayed tattoos inspired by the far-right band Kahlkopf (Skinhead), including an SS rune – again, a local government spokesperson described it as a one-off case. Despite objections from the prison officers' union, Berlin has very recently introduced a reporting system for 'anti-democratic tendencies' among prison officers.[20]

> *The prisoner's statement was contradicted by the screws' statements, and that always means the prisoner is lying.*

'It's almost self-evident that prison officers can attack you with impunity,' wrote an anonymous contributor to a prison newspaper in the 1970s or early '80s. 'During my time in prison I've too often experienced how prisoners get beaten up by guards,' wrote Frank Niemeyer in his account of the Santa Fu riot of 1990. 'Normally several of them came into the cell together . . . Afterwards the story was always that the prisoner attacked them and hit out wildly. The prisoner's statement was contradicted by the screws' statements, and that always means the prisoner is lying.'[21] Similar stories recur through the decades.

> He woke up and felt the blood pulsing through his veins
> like it would make his body burst . . . Broken crockery,
> splintering wood, and again and again the cry: NO, NO,
> PLEASE STOP.
>
> He shot up like lightning, sitting straight up in his bed . . .
> He forced himself not to breathe, so as to hear better . . .
> A dull thud followed. Dull like a body falling to the
> ground. And screams: NO, PLEASE STOP, PLEASE . . .
> the truncheons were thwacking.[22]

Herm Klingstedt's short story was among the prizewinning entries to the Ingeborg Drewitz competition for writing from prison in 1999. It is presented as a work of fiction. A similar story, by Ralf-Axel Simon, won a prize in 2008. 'The trampling herd is getting closer,' reports its nervous narrator – 'A short pause before the key is pushed into the lock'. On this occasion – relief – it is the lock in somebody else's door. Then there are more noises, 'like a dog whimpering, punctuated by furious shouts: "this is for running the girl over the second time, after she was dead!" – "yell all you like, no-one's listening to you!" "push his head down, push it down!"'[23]

> *at night my fellow prisoners kick the doors in fury, some scream and cry, others set fire to their cells, some destroy things because they are being destroyed, and some of them even die.*[24]

A STUDY OF 48 prisons by Lower Saxony's Institute for Criminological Research in 2011–12 revealed that one in six adult men had experienced

Berlin Tegel prison, gate 2.

serious physical violence in the preceding four weeks. In women's prisons the rate was a little lower, but in youth prisons it was significantly higher.[25] Not all people in prison experience direct violence. But in a system where there is understaffing, and where the stress levels for both residents and staff are high, people in prison are always disproportionately at risk. Accounts describe how confinement, coupled with the frustration of what Peter-Paul Zahl calls nobodification, foments violence: Jumbo tells the story of attacking a suspected paedophile in the shower room – 'my built-up fury about the shitty prison conditions adds energy to my hate of child-fuckers.'[26]

Since 1989 at least four people have been tortured to death by fellow residents in German prisons. Instances of torture not leading to death include a case in 2006 in Oslebshausen near Bremen, where cellmates pulled six toenails off their victim. In 2012 in Hamlin's Young Offender Institution, four inmates systematically abused and tortured a fifteen-year-old over a period of two and a half weeks. They hung him upside-down, beat him with a broom handle, a belt and a piece of cable, and tied him up and left him under a cold shower. One was accused of urinating on him. The incident was hushed up. In Bernau prison, near Bavaria's famous nature resort Chiemsee, two people in prison were murdered by other prisoners in 2019–20.[27] Anecdotal evidence suggests there are countless instances of unrecorded torture.

For me it was living in a permanent state of fear.

'There's a lot of violence in prison', Rainer told the Kübbelers, echoed by Dietmar: 'there's a lot of violence in here.'[28] 'For me it was living in a permanent state of fear,' Tom described his year in prison to the 16 Bars Project. 'Because you never knew what was going to happen in the yard. Or when the wrong kind of person was in your cell. Or if you went around the corner and someone had their eye on you and there wasn't a guard around. There are no friendships.' And there is no safe place, as Katharina would discover. 'At night I was so afraid of what my cellmates might do to me that I could hardly sleep. And I had no idea how to protect myself. I didn't want to speak to an officer – and anyway I didn't think any of them would be interested.'

Her solution was to throw herself down the stairs on her way to the showers, in the hope of being hospitalized.[29]

Violence, sometimes even violent death, is the fate particularly of nonces (in German, *Sittiche*; prisoners known or suspected to have molested children). Dirk Glebe advises readers of his *Prison Handbook* to take great care *not* to be thought a nonce: 'always have your enforcement sheet or – even better – your court decision to hand, to prove the contrary.' Even in youth prisons, where nonces are rare, certain residents – notably any new arrival who shows fear – are forced into the role of victim. These are the so-called 'vicks' or 'fish', who become the focus of others' pent-up aggression. 'There are always people on the look-out for victims,' Martin explained to the Kübbelers. 'There's an internal hierarchy,' agrees Katharina. 'The aggressive ones, who signal that they're out to get everyone, have the power.'[30]

Gay men are another high-risk group ('gays often get treated like "immigrants" or "nonces",' warns *Pathways through Prison*). 'I don't know anyone here who can deal with gays,' asserted Bilal, a young man in youth custody in the 2000s. 'One of the hairdressers is gay,' added another young man, Christian. 'He touched one of our orderlies from behind and tickled his neck, and the guy jumped up and yelled, hey, you fucking queer, don't touch me. Touch me again and I'll bash you, fucking poof.'[31] Writing from a men's prison in 2015, Ralf Wegner described his own exclusion as a gay man. 'Every move you make in here is watched and (mis)interpreted by other prisoners,' he explained. 'I get endless condescending and painful remarks and comments, lines get crossed and rumours get spread.'[32]

> *My upper half all woman, and the rest of me – biologically – still a man; that was just the absolute burn-out syndrome for the mills of justice.*[33]

Transgender people in prison are also targets of violence. Michelle had undergone hormone treatment, but her genitals were still male. '"They used to burn things like you at the stake!" was among the nicer things people said to me,' she remembers. Her story begins when, despite identifying as a woman, she was sent to a men's prison, where her arrival was awaited eagerly. The duty officer responded to an instruction for special protection by allocating three other residents to accompany her into the shower room (a space without closed circuit television, so a popular location for violence) – 'it was obvious that they'd talked about this and planned it beforehand.' Michelle faced the inevitability of gang rape. '"Ok, let's get it over with," I said as coolly as I could; I certainly wasn't going to do them the favour of showing my fear'. She never reported it – 'no-one would have believed me anyway.' Writing (finally) from a women's prison, she ended her story with a fantasy of revenge. 'These days I'd slice open the prison officer without blinking an eye, and my shower companions with him.' For her, that reflects what prison taught her: 'You learn a certain tendency to violence in prison – you have to be able to help yourself.'[34]

The boy hasn't spoken a word since.

Interviewed in the young offenders section of Cologne prison in 2007, Fred told the story of a boy on his wing who was raped. No one had done anything to help. 'The boy hasn't spoken a word since.' Oliver K., who was sent as a young man to an adult high-security prison, found himself sharing a cell with two long-serving inmates. 'At first I felt protected,' he remembers: 'but I soon had to deal with the price of protection. Oral sex was the price.' If he refused, his 'protectors' took away his tobacco, forced him to scrub the cell toilet endlessly or became violent.[35] In a high-profile case in 2018, a 35-year-old man alleged that his cellmate had raped him repeatedly. The case went to court, but the defendant was acquitted for lack of evidence against him. 'There are a lot of unreported cases,' commented Manuel Matzke. 'When the cell door is closed, no one checks to see what's happening inside.' And the system prefers it that way, in his view: 'Anything that happens behind the walls of silence is meant to stay there. As little information as possible is meant to reach the outside.'[36]

Sometimes, however, it does reach the outside. In 2006 Germany was shocked by the headline news that Hermann Heibach, a young prisoner in Siegburg, just north of Bonn, had been raped, tortured for eight hours and then hanged by his three cellmates.

Heibach was twenty when he was sentenced to eighty hours of social service for forcing a kiosk owner at knifepoint to give him alcohol and cigarettes. The age of criminal responsibility in Germany is fourteen, and if an offence is committed by someone over eighteen but not yet 21, the courts have discretion to apply juvenile law. Heibach failed to report for his social service, so he was sent to the youth prison in Siegburg on a six-month sentence. There he was quickly identified as a 'fish'. Over the course of one of the notoriously boring Saturdays in the institution, his cellmates tortured and then murdered him. They beat him with chunks of soap tied in towels, kicked him and made him drink water mixed with salt and chilli powder and then eat his own vomit. They fed him urine mixed with spit from the toilet brush holder in the cell. Then they forced him to perform oral sex on them, and raped him with a hand-brush. He managed to push the alarm bell, but when the duty officer arrived at the cell door, his cellmates were able to fob the man off. After taking a break to watch a football game on television, they discussed what to do next and decided to hang him. After several unsuccessful attempts with cables that broke, they finally managed to hang their victim with a torn-up sheet. One of them later said that they were curious: they had never seen someone die.[37]

The media responded to the Heibach case as if violence in prisons were an unheard-of thing. 'Their crime shocked Germany,' reported the biggest national daily, *Bild-Zeitung*. 'The entire country was shocked by the brutal events of autumn 2006,' echoed the news magazine *Stern*.[38] But Klaus Jünschke, a former member of the Red Army Faction who himself spent sixteen years inside, has refused to treat stories about brutality in prisons as shocking – because, he argues, it is so clearly systemic. Jünschke is now a political and social commentator with a particular interest in youth justice. The events in Siegburg, he argued, actually revealed an unpalatable normality. The media might paint the satisfying picture of a nation in shock, but for Jünschke the violence in Siegburg was not shocking but historic and structural, fed by institutional neglect and general indifference.[39]

this consuming hate, which only prison can give rise to.[40]

Angela and her girlfriend Sandra both took part in Reimund Neufeld's writing project for women in prison. Together they wrote a disturbing fantasy of what it would be like to inflict violence on another woman.

> Seeing the blood, slicing her open, pulling out her entrails, letting her suffocate on her own entrails, hearing bones cracking, crunching, feeling how the knife slides into her skin to tear the entrails out – her intestine coiling through – between my fingers – blood and other stuff running down my arm, feeling warm blood on my body, slamming her head against the wall and hearing her skull crack, feeling her skin splitting open with every blow – and blood, lots of blood – making my heart beat faster, it's so satisfying . . . so satisfying to push my knee into her throat, harder and harder, and her eyes are radiating pure fear, and that's making me even crazier, yes! – her body switches off – so I wait until she comes to again . . .

In one sense, the imagined victimization of another person seems to bring them back into being as *somebody*. In another, the piece seems to document the effects of the brutalization of the imagination. These kinds of fantasies are 'normal in a place like this,' argued Angela. 'I'm neither sick, nor crazy – it's this place that makes me think of things I never thought about before.' They are 'thoughts everyone carries in them – everyone!' But it is prison that triggers their emergence. 'I've become much harder,' she observed. 'I just feel permanent rage and hate . . . In these eleven months I've cried maybe once or twice – from rage. It's always just rage.'[41]

What hopes for resocialization are there in the violent prison?

12 The Desocialization Machine – Remixed

'You have to be punished,' my father used to say when he thrashed me, because he wanted to bring me up to be a respectable person. 'You have to be punished,' society says now, and locks people up in prisons . . .
The problem with this kind of punishment is that the child is damaged for its entire life, and the prisoner is released sick in body and mind. The question arises: who is the perpetrator and who the victim?[1]

'A lot has happened to me in my life,' nineteen-year-old Stefanie told the Kübbelers. 'It started with my step-grandfather, who sexually abused me when I was eight years old.' When her mother remarried she was physically abused by her stepfather – 'he really beat me to a pulp.' She was later sent to prison for killing a man who had been beating and raping her for years.[2]

Fifty-seven per cent of women in German and European prisons have suffered sexual violence, and 91 per cent physical violence.[3] 'Almost all women in prison have experienced violence and abuse,' writes Sabine Bomeier, a former prisoner. In 2004 a journalist, Katrin Panier, conducted interviews with seventeen women who were or had been imprisoned – thirteen of them spoke of severe domestic violence, including sexual abuse. For some women, prison becomes a safe space relative to domestic life outside – 'I'd rather be in prison than at home with my husband,' said Sonja. Even after a divorce Sonja's ex refused to leave the family home, drank and was violent.[4]

Eleven of the 37 pieces written by women in prison for Neufeld's collection describe domestic violence. Marta, a Polish woman held in North Rhine–Westphalia, described her parents' fights, writing as if to her remembering self. 'Do you remember the eternal battles? . . . Did you see the blood that she saw, that came from the cuts on her mother's hands?' Marta herself was raped when she was ten years old. 'Do you remember the day when the disgusting, horrible, vile, unscrupulous pastor took away her joy in life, forever? . . . Can you still hear her cry for help?' Marta found herself unable to write autobiographically in the first person.[5]

Manuela was raped for the first time when she was seven. 'My mother used to finance her alcoholism in the pubs that way.' Like Marta's, home was anything but a safe space. 'I was raped again when I was nine. It was my grandfather. I let it happen for a couple of weeks, until my lower abdomen started really hurting again.' While their mother was spending time in hospital after a suicide attempt, Manuela and her sister took the opportunity to move out. 'We lived with a friend . . . He hit me regularly and abused me a few times.'[6] Aged thirteen, she found herself locked in a flat with a man who was refusing to let her out. In the story her thirteen-year-old self is drunk and seems about to be raped again. But her story cuts off: there is no ending, no closure, no moment of reflection – the narrative just stops. Like Marta, Manuela seems ultimately unable to tolerate her experience in the first person.

> *There's violence in prison, I wouldn't argue with that . . . But there's violence outside too. And the ways of dealing with it here are the same as out there.*[7]

Men in prison are also affected. Martin told the Kübbelers about being sexually exploited in childhood by his father as well as by the local curate, who had recruited him as an altar boy. Ralph described a stepmother who 'abused me sexually with a knife'. He later committed a murder. 'These days I know that the situation when I committed the crime reminded me of things,' he explained. 'So lots of stuff was bubbling up in me.'[8] Indeed, *not* being able to point to a difficult childhood can cause problems in a culture where, as Christian Vinke put it in 2016, 'resocialization is discontinuing itself in favour of psychology.'[9] Walter was unable to tell the Kübbelers why he was in prison for armed robbery because, he confessed, he came from 'a normal middle-class working family' and could not recollect any serious childhood difficulties. Some of the women in Neufeld's project felt similarly that they 'didn't belong' in prison, because they came from good families.[10]

Nearly half of the people in prison who responded in the study of prison violence in 2011–12 said that they had been regularly beaten by their parents when they were children.[11] The prizewinning story in a prison writing competition in northern Germany in 1998 was 'Arthur' – the painful tale of a child abused by his war-damaged father.

> At home, the living room in his parents' house. His father stands swaying and slurring his words, a piece of garden hosepipe, about 40 cm long, in his right hand, threatening Arthur, who is crying and screaming but can't escape making the painful acquaintance of the misappropriated object.
>
> Cut.
>
> The kitchen in his parents' house. Darkness. His father lies delirious on the linoleum floor. He is singing very loudly, the old German national anthem . . .
>
> Cut.
>
> The kitchen again . . . 'Why is Daddy angry?' Arthur hears himself ask. 'Daddy's not angry, he's sick,' his mother answers tonelessly through a shallow stream of tears, 'the war made Daddy sick.'[12]

'My father was always drunk when he came home, and he'd start thrashing me like a madman,' recalled the writer and long-term prisoner Kenny Berger. In a later piece he added: 'He'd been fucking me since I was seven.' David, a young man in prison, told the story of his father's response the day he was sent home from school, aged fourteen, for smoking hashish. 'When I got there,' he remembered, 'my father was waiting for me eagerly. He didn't say anything, just swung his arm and hit me in the face as hard as he could. He beat me all the way from the living room to my bedroom.'[13]

Sometimes you need a good beating to teach you about discipline.

Can prison educate people who have been abused at home to get beyond those structures of violence? In 2007 a former member of the Red Army Faction, Klaus Jünschke, with Christiane Ensslin (sister of the late Gudrun Ensslin, another RAF member), went into the youth wing of Cologne prison to interview some of the young men held there. 'Did you know you had rights when you were arrested?' they asked one young man, Bilal. Yes, he responded, the police had read him his rights. 'Do you think it was ok how they did that, or was it brutal?' Bilal's answer described brutality, but without critique: the policemen's behaviour was, he said, 'normal'. 'Just the cuffs were too tight, they were positioned wrong, behind me on my back. I asked them to cuff me in front because it really made my shoulders hurt. On the way to the police station they accelerated on purpose, to make me fall backwards. He even said he knew it was hurting me.'[14]

Stories from the prison reveal violence as a normal part of what we call criminal justice. In a short story by Ralf Axel Simon, the protagonist similarly asks a policeman to loosen his cuffs, which are hurting him, but 'the copper pulled the cuffs tighter with the comment: "this isn't a finishing school!"'[15] Simon is an author with a political mindset, and he uses his story to critique and expose brutality. But for the youngster Bilal, being violently 'put in his place' was par for the course. 'It was completely normal,' he told his interviewers. 'It's not like you can do anything about that stuff.' His fellow prisoner, Carlos, agreed. When he arrived in prison, the officers 'didn't exactly shout at me but spoke to me in a tone that was meant to say that you're lower than them, that you're right at the bottom. You just have to obey.'[16] The young men's pragmatism spoke of a familiarity with the 'business narratives' of street culture, which present violence as 'a rational solution to a practical problem' – namely, the problem of asserting and maintaining dominance.[17] But the rules of hierarchical violence are learned not only on the street but at home. The young men in Cologne described the violence of their fathers, and their mothers' boyfriends, with a kind of resigned acceptance – even, sometimes, with approval. 'You learn something from it,' said one, and another expanded: 'What counts in life above all is discipline. And sometimes you need a good beating to teach you about discipline.' In that worldview, violence is a legitimate form of education, and even a sentencing judge can appear as the hard hand of paternal authority. 'The judge wants to see you totally fall apart, so that you learn – and you do learn.'[18]

The question of *what* you learn is never explicitly addressed, but there are clues. Selim explained why a boy will tolerate being relieved of his belongings by a bigger boy: namely, in anticipation of one day taking the dominant role himself. 'For us, it was kind of normal, we grew up with it,' he explained: 'When we were small, the big boys took our stuff and beat us up. And when we got a bit bigger we regarded that as normal.' Baschar described how, in return for voluntary servitude to older boys, he had been protected by them. From the perspective of these young men, prison seemed to offer a kind of continuity in that 'chain of command', rather than change – Ismail described becoming the protector of another young prisoner who was being victimized. All of them saw violent hierarchies as ladders to be climbed, and gentler approaches as obtuse: 'If I get asked, by some kind of psychologist, if he comes at me with some kind of why-did-you-do-it stuff and tries to take charge, I just say to him, kiss my ass,' said Kerim.[19] In prison as outside, boys and men learn that accepting and deferring to superior force is a rational step on the way to securing their own place in a violent hierarchy.

It's not the people you help to gain freedom you need to be afraid of. The people to fear are the people you've made afraid.

'Someone who has been punished rather than helped over a long period . . . he's not going to be able to lead a social life "outside" – that's a skill prison has made him forget. It's strengthened his bad sides and made him terribly afraid – he'll bite as soon as he can,' warned a prisoner in 2013. 'It's not the people you help to gain freedom you need to be afraid of. The people to fear are the people you've made afraid.'[20]

German prisons, concluded the weekly broadsheet *Die Zeit* in 2012, have a 'dramatic problem: they make people worse, not better.'[21] 'I learned in prison that the world outside is a jungle, and you won't survive unless you belong to a wolf pack' – Tom, who grew up in a village ('all very cosy'), summarized his prison education in the 2010s. 'And you have to fight for your place in the pack. Best thing is to fight your way to the top. It's like that inside, and it's exactly the same outside. I took that lesson to heart.'[22]

And still some people describe positive outcomes, often in the most basic sense. 'I've learned a lot in prison,' Ralph told the Kübbelers. 'Being in a secure psychiatric unit probably saved my life,' said Claudia Franck, who first participated in Neufeld's writing project and then ran the 16 Bars Project with him. Oliver, who was interviewed during that project, saw things similarly: 'Prison gave me the opportunity to have a good think about things,' he explained. 'The positive thing about going to prison was that I've turned forty. If I'd stayed in my old milieu I wouldn't have made it that long.'[23] 'A lot of women think through properly, for the first time, why it is that they're in prison,' echoed Katharina. 'Lots of them come to a sense, for the first time, that what they did wasn't right. And a lot of them are then very sorry for the things they did.' 'You see what's right and wrong,' explained Stefanie – 'Things we didn't see outside.'[24]

Some people describe finding help in therapy while they are in prison. Erwin, a repeat offender, described how he saw the light. 'Like I said, I was never willing to go into therapy. And precisely because of that I kept going back to drugs, because I wasn't ready to change. Now I know that my relapses were the reason I kept reoffending.' Martin's therapy helped him understand why he agreed to smuggle drugs: 'I didn't realize what I was doing there. But now, because of the therapy, I know why I said yes. Because of my past – my childhood – I never managed to say no.' An older prisoner declared himself 'so glad to have got a handle on my life in here'. The notion of getting a handle on life reflects what criminologists call *self-efficacy*: the ability to make choices, take decisions and generally manage life's challenges that helps people move away from crime.[25] But the likelihood of developing self-efficacy in prison is low, argues Stefan Augenstein, because the system offers 'zero opportunities for decision-making'. Prison, agrees 'John Doe' – using the pseudonym of a nobody – turns people into 'performing apes who can only respond to commands. They've been un-abled to think for themselves.'[26]

Some people recover from addiction inside. 'As my drug consumption got less and less in here I became more and more myself,' wrote Max Z. But while some overcome substance abuse in prison, others learn it there. In Santa Fu, explained Reiner, hashish was tolerated ('on hash you're a quiet prisoner and cause no trouble'), but he also discovered barbiturates, combined with strong coffee for maximum effect. Sonja, who was already familiar with drugs in tablet form when she entered prison, started using heroin.[27]

> *You'll ask yourself, quite rightly, how on earth drugs get into prisons . . . But even if I knew I couldn't tell you. Not even just between ourselves.*[28]
>
> J. B. Maelach, 2018

Every day tens or hundreds of people – prison officers, visitors, lawyers, probation officers, volunteers, delivery drivers – enter and leave prisons, making the problem of controlling what else enters and leaves a prison practically insoluble. In 2020 there were prisons where 80 per cent of the residents were struggling with addiction, noted Manuel Matzke as spokesperson for the Prisoners' Union.[29] Estimates say that over two-thirds of people in German prisons use drugs, one-third of them hard drugs such as heroin. Some prisons provide disposable syringes to reduce the spread of infections such as HIV or hepatitis. And there are legal drugs – in 2018 Linus Förster, a Social Democratic politician who began a three-year prison sentence in 2017 (he was released in August 2019), described the generous distribution of psychiatric meds, sedatives and sleeping pills to help keep the population calm. A similar policy had been in operation in Santa

Fu in the 1990s, wrote Niemeyer – after the riot, 'further outbreaks of violence were prevented by the prisoners' massive drug addiction.'[30]

I've never understood how people in here are supposed to
become better, nor do I think I'll ever know the answer –
what actually happens is they get worse.[31]

Around thirty of Germany's 180 prisons have introduced facilities known as 'love cells' for longer, unsupervised visits (in Hesse Weiterstadt prison in 2016, one man reported, a 'sex ban' had officers checking on couples to see that there was no erotic activity).[32] The story of losing a lover or spouse to the pressures of prison relationships remains common. 'I'm proud to be this far along,' wrote Daniel Teich, a Drewitz prizewinner in 2015. 'Into a new, better life!' But his confidence, he went on, was also being undermined by prison – by 'the feeling of being at someone else's mercy, the arbitrariness you're exposed to. Ever since they put me in prison this feeling of helplessness has been with me.' And even his hope for the future – for his new, better life – was tempered by anger, because that future would not include his family. His wife had left him for a man who could be part of her daily life. 'How can a system speak of resocialization when families are being torn apart and destroyed?' Teich exploded. 'When every prospect you ever had bursts like a soap bubble from one day to the next.'[33] 'I've just been dumped,' confessed J. B. Maelach, in prison in 2018. 'She waited three years patiently and then lost strength just as the end was in sight . . . Found someone to go for walks with, someone she could talk to. Wasn't me.'

What do I say to you in my letters?
What do I say to you on the phone?
What do I say to you during visits?
What do I say to you when I come home?
What do I say to your question why I wasn't there
when you needed me?
What do I say when you tell me
you had to lie at school, so no-one would know

where you really were?
What do I say when you sadly tell me
how the other children spoke proudly of their Dads,
and you had to keep silent.
I'm speechless when you tell me all
the things you'd like to have done with me.
What should I answer when you ask me if the drugs
really mean or meant more to me than you do?
What should I answer when you ask
what I'm doing for you now.
What do I say when you say you don't
believe me, because I've already disappointed you so often.[34]

Contact with family members is known to be absolutely key to successful resocialization – but for the children of people in prison the effects can go the other way. 'It's a strange thing: when children are abused the public is instantly outraged,' writes Bernd Maelicke, 'but hardly anyone troubles themselves with the damaging consequences for children of locking up their parents.' Maelicke was ministerial head of prisons in Schleswig-Holstein for fifteen years, and is now a prominent critic of the system.[35] Linus Förster described seeing children cry when they were encouraged to kiss their fathers during visits – because they no longer recognized them.

In Germany as elsewhere, most women in prison have children – but in January 2020 there were only 68 places in secure units for mothers with children (there is one father–child unit, in Waldheim prison in Saxony.)[36] Echoing the German researchers Uta Klein and Gertrud Hardtmann in the late 1970s, EU researchers in 2005 noted with concern that the women they interviewed had strong feelings of failure.[37] 'I don't know how I'll deal with it if my children ask me one day why I abandoned them,' worried Nancy, speaking ten years later with the 16 Bars Project. Karina described being in prison on her daughter's birthday – 'my middle child is fifteen today, and I'm not there! Do I even still exist?' The birth of her granddaughter brought home her own absence from her family even more painfully. 'Today I became a grandmother. I know it, but I can't feel it. I couldn't be

Mother and child in the women's prison Munich-Stadelheim.

there.' As the months passed her sense of her absence in the life of the baby, and of the baby's absence in hers, became intolerable – 'I haven't seen her yet, haven't smelled her. Haven't had her in my arms. Please, please let me out of here. I can't stand another minute of being cut off like this.' 'Feel very guilty,' she concluded.[38]

I have a question for the people
in whose name I'm here:
What happens in your name
after I get out?
Will you take me back into your people –
or will I be
judged, again, in
looks, gestures, talk?[39]

Around 40 per cent of people in German prisons serve sentences of less than a year, and one-fifth serve less than six months. In his entry for the Ingeborg Drewitz Prize in 2018, Linus Förster reflected on his former beliefs about prison and rehabilitation. In prison, he met a man serving a six-month sentence – outside he had been self-employed as a handyman. Six months in prison had changed everything, but not in a way that promised a better future – prison had lost him the customer base he had built up over years, and his home. Another man had a marijuana-related conviction. Outside he had been in an apprenticeship scheme, but his short stretch in prison had lost him his place as an apprentice. He was lucky, he told Förster, to have met a drug dealer inside. He would need to get a job quickly when he got out, to pay his legal and other debts, and the dealer had promised to set him up with connections.[40]

Prison produces the problem of *what-then*: what happens when the prison gates open and a prisoner is released? People leaving prison in the post-war decades, in both of the Germanies, described being rejected and excluded from employment 'outside'. Sometimes prison started to look like the more liveable option. From Ewald's perspective in the early 2000s, not much had changed: 'I know life in prison. And I know freedom outside. I know standing in line at the job centre,' he told the Kübbelers. 'And when someone gets out of prison who really wants to try to go straight, the first thing that happens is that he's unemployed.'[41] Employment helps people released from prison to get a secure footing back in society. But Jens, 32 years old in twenty-first-century Germany, had no hope at all: 'I can't see myself still having chances in life.' Without professional training he faced unskilled labour at best – but he did not believe that anyone would employ him with a criminal record: 'It's going to be hard for me to get back on a normal path in life.'[42]

A study published in 2016 showed that almost every second person released from prison in the Federal Republic re-offends.[43] 'Prison wrecks your head,' writes Dieter Wurm in *Lichtblick*. 'It's counterproductive to have to start a better life outside when you're in that mental state, with a garbage bag in your hand.'[44] Frank Niemeyer spoke with a fellow prisoner during the Hamburg riot of 1990. 'I've been inside for nearly nine years, and in four months I'm out,' the man told him. 'In all this time I've never been on day release. When I get out I'll have 800 DM resettlement money, no work, and nowhere to live.' The editors of *Lichtblick* describe a common pattern: 'prison, release, no money, nowhere to live, prison again'. 'In the worst case scenario a prisoner's release looks like something from a movie,' writes Bernd Maelicke. 'The prison gates behind him, the great prospect of freedom before him. In his hand a cardboard box containing whatever he had with him when he started his sentence. No one there to meet him.'[45] He (or she) might also have debts in the thousands or tens of thousands of Euros, incurred through trial and legal costs, fines, child maintenance and other things – all waiting to be settled when the prison gates open.

Attentive readers might recall an ironic short story written by one of Birgitta Wolf's connections in the 1960s, W. G., about an ex-con who startled a judge by requesting re-entry into prison. More than fifty years later, fiction became reality when, in 2019, a man was released after serving seventeen years. He was 64 and had been resisting his discharge from prison for three years. Soon after his unwilling return into the community he arrived back at the gates of Aachen prison in North Rhine–Westphalia, asking to be re-admitted. The prison refused.[46]

Where I am now, M was too.
Last October, after many years,
he left this place,
Resocialized!
Six weeks later he jumped
in front of a speeding train.[47]

After more than twenty years in custody, one man wrote a desperate letter to the Critical Working Group. 'I always worked when I was in prison, but no pension contributions were ever made for me,' he explained. 'Please tell me if a law has now been formulated and passed to rectify that.'[48] In fact the prison reform laws of 1976–7 envisaged new legislation that would include people in prison in a pension scheme – but it was never realized. Prison labourers in Germany pay unemployment benefit contributions, and provided that they have worked for twelve months over the previous two years, they can claim that benefit after release. But prison work does not (in 2021, at the time of writing) entail pension contributions, and people released after the retirement age often face poverty. In 2018 Germany's national conference of state ministers for justice decided that people in prison *should* be included in the legal regulation of pension provision, and asked the Federal ministry of justice to petition for the appropriate legislation. But the Federal Parliament threw the problem back to the individual states, with a reminder that they were financially responsible for their prisons. To date there has been no movement on the issue.[49]

Nonetheless, prison labour, insofar as it is available, is still a requirement in most states (though it can sometimes be replaced by education or apprenticeships). Low rates of pay make contemporary prisons competitive suppliers of labour. In 2018, there was more demand from industry than one Bavarian governor found he could supply – in defence of the low wages that continued to be paid to labourers in his prison, he pointed to the cost of running the institution. In the spirit of the Standard Minimum Rules that were agreed by the UN in 1955, prison work is supposed to be useful or meaningful. 'Counting rubber bands and bagging them. Polishing phone handsets. Glueing paper bags, sorting parcel tape. The kind of work no one outside would do. Day after day, month after month, year on year' – Frank Niemeyer described 'meaningful work' in Santa Fu in the 1990s. Refusing to work entailed disciplinary measures such as the loss of TV rights and social time.[50] Inge Viett saw the same thing in Koblenz, twenty years after she had first been incarcerated there in the 1970s: 'twenty years ago the women here were glueing paper bags. They're still doing that today.' In 2011 Germany's National Office for the Prevention of Torture reminded the women's prison in Frankfurt that training opportunities for women needed to go beyond domestic labour. Prisoners, Friedrich Peters observed in his *Prison Diary of 2014*, are 'last in line in society'[51] – but women in prison often seem to be at the very back of that line.

In Berlin in 2014, the Prisoners' Union was founded, not least to campaign for the minimum wage. In 2020, for people outside, that was 9 euros and 35 cents per hour. People serving prison sentences in 2020 earned between 1 and 3 euros per hour.[52] In 2015 Hamburg's higher regional court ruled that people in prison had no claim to the minimum wage, because they are not, formally speaking, employees.

Believe in yourself and never give up, fight for your dreams.[53]

'The struggle for freedom, for a certain independence and a more carefree financial life, alongside the recognition that I had failed in my family life, was the main motive that took me into criminality,' explained a man in prison in 2015. Another man, Walter, described becoming ill through overwork – 'I wanted to raise my standard of living,' he explained, 'I wanted luxury.' When his illness lost him his job he robbed a supermarket rather than tell his wife.[54] Being arrested took off the pressure of providing a high-status consumer lifestyle for his family. Walter was critical of himself, but never of the society that forced him to equate money with freedom.

'There is no such thing as society,' Margaret Thatcher told the UK in 1987. 'There are individual men and women, and there are families . . . and people must look after themselves first.'[55] Just as the spirit of '68 shaped stories from the prison in the 1970s and earlier '80s, the spirit of late capitalism and neoliberalism is present in prison and society in the noughties and beyond. 'Every violent offender is ultimately responsible for his own actions,' wrote Reinhard Nolle and Anke Hildebrandt in their introduction to a volume of writing by young men in prison.[56] 'I have no intention of complaining because I was in prison. It's entirely my responsibility,' Friedrich Peters wrote in his introduction to his *Prison Diary of 2014*. A young offender called Philipp saw things similarly: 'Looking at the reasons for my existence as a prisoner I find it more than justified that I'm not free.' 'I can't blame the prison officers or other people for the fact that I'm here. It's completely my own fault,' declared Ralph. 'Anyone who turns criminal in here', added Dietmar, 'has chosen that himself.'[57] Accepting responsibility matters. But in recent years there no longer seems to be any suggestion that people or society on the outside might accept responsibility too. In earlier decades, back covers promised stories of resistance to a flawed system and society, but in the noughties and beyond there are only flawed individuals. Readers are invited to sit back and enjoy the spectacle of (someone else's) self-help.

Dale Carnegie's self-help classic *Stop Worrying and Start Living* (1948) entered the top ten in Germany's non-fiction bestseller lists in 1984, and in the decade after unification it moved from tenth to first place in non-fiction bestsellers, until it was displaced in the early 2000s by self-help guides written by German authors.[58] In prisons in the 1980s self-help had been part of the project of resistance. 'I always say to my fellow prisoners, "listen, you're the only person who can help yourself out of this mess,"' Winand Buchacker wrote to Ingeborg Drewitz. For anyone to leave prison and never go back was, he argued, one in the eye for the system: 'The state and the courts want you to come back. They need your failure as an alibi, a legitimation to cover up their own violence.' In 2012 Dieter Wurm would characterize self-help in less militant terms: 'In here everyone has to look after himself and use prison as an opportunity,' he urged, 'to get away from drugs, to come off alcohol, to sort out your messed-up health or to get mentally more stable.'[59]

> *I want to live! Live! To get out of here at some point and live,*
> *not just rot away behind this wall.*[60]

Across the decades, one way of surviving prison is to write. 'Writing can take you to freedom,' declared Peter Feraru – 'the opportunity writing offers to change something, both in yourself and in your environment, is huge.' 'I have to get a command of this damned language, that's why I read and write constantly,' explains the Kurdish-speaking writer Metin Günes. For him, being seen to belong is critically important: 'I want to impress German society . . . These days writing is almost a life-or-death necessity.'[61]

Writing about the senselessness or arbitrariness of prison life can paradoxically produce a kind of coherence or meaning. It can return writers to a sense of themselves, of being someone. 'Communicating your experience is resistance. Resistance to a power that is taking away your subject status,' wrote Karin Amann, a former writer in prison and now a jury member for the Drewitz Prize. 'All the pressure that built up inside me was released via my pen.' There are different possible responses to pressure. 'I can trash the cell when I'm desperate,' explained Karlheinz Barwasser, 'or I can give the screw or another prisoner a smack in the mouth. That happens from time to time. But all those explosions come from the same place as my explosions on paper.'[62] Over and over again, writers in prison confirm that writing is a viable alternative to violence.

Indeed, Thomas Galli, a former prison governor and a patron of the Drewitz Prize, has described writing as the opposite of violence. 'Anyone who hurts or does severe harm to others is dividing people, creating fissures, digging trenches, causing injury,' observes Galli. 'Anyone who punishes another human being by incarcerating them is dividing people, creating fissures, digging trenches, causing injury. Literature, by contrast, brings us together.'[63]

Afterword: The Mirror and the Microcosm

A nation should not be judged by how it treats its highest citizens, but its lowest ones.
Nelson Mandela[1]

'Prison is a microcosm, a reflection of life outside', wrote Peter Zingler in 2016.[2] As society outside grows more punitive, violence has also escalated inside prisons, with significantly increased levels reported across Germany and in other countries. Both incarcerated people and prison officers are at risk. But is anybody looking? After fourteen months spent as a reseacher in a maximum-security prison in the USA, Fred Alford challenged Foucault's characterization of the prison as a panopticon: a structure where inmates feel permanently under observation. In contemporary prisons, writes Alford, the threat of being observed is much less real than the risk that no one is looking – the real power that is expressed by the system and society is 'the power not to look and not to care'.

Pathways through Prison calls it 'the silent convention of looking away',[3] and it is a convention observed outside as well as inside prisons. From her window in Mainz prison in the early 1970s, Marianne Herzog saw how passers-by exercised their power not to look and not to care: 'yesterday something fell over in the laundry. It sounded like a metal container rolling. Down on the street a woman was passing. She heard the noise, looked towards the prison, saw the bars, quickly looked away and walked on.'[4] Rather than looking away, people outside need to wonder what is reflected in the steady growth of the world prison population. Prison systems around the world are bursting at the seams, and in the absence of any proven capacity of prisons to produce law-abiding citizens we must assume that the swell in numbers primarily reflects a punitive will to incarcerate, not a genuine belief that prison works.

> *It's like we've been hidden away in a drawer. We're cut off from society. And society doesn't feel responsible. People don't want to know.*[5]
>
> Harry, 2016

In the 1960s a young prisoner called A. P. wrote a fictive letter to the state prosecutor. He described the case of a young offender, X, who grew up in care homes and borstals and 'continued his education – in prison'. He was eventually declared asocial and a psychopath. Not only the justice system, A. P. declares, but every single person who had contact with the boy in an official capacity had 'failed disgracefully. Not one of them managed to instil any sense of social responsibility in a person they had had charge of since he was fourteen years old. Don't anyone tell me that it was all the boy's fault.' A non-fictional letter from a twenty-year-old man, published in the same collection, made the same point. 'Yes, we're abandoned, we're excluded from human society,' the writer admitted. 'But do we really bear the entire burden of guilt?'[6] Birgitta Wolf responded to his question in her foreword: 'we talk a lot about our depraved young people. But is anyone asking who made them depraved, if that is what they are?' She interrogates the self-righteous decision to punish:

> What exactly are we punishing?
> Genetic factors?
> He didn't choose his parents.
> His upbringing?
> He was brought up by adults.
> Bad influences in his environment?
> We all co-produce the conditions that exist in state and society.[7]

'When you look at us it's like you're looking into a mirror of your society,' a man serving life told the journalists who interviewed him. 'Dear God, where do you think we come from? We're not from the moon, we come straight out of your damn society and everything we carry with us in here we learned out there.' 'All those people in preventive detention, or who keep coming back as repeat offenders have something in common,' agrees Klaus Jünschke, a former left-wing terrorist who is now a political commentator; 'they have been in care, in children's homes, youth homes, YOIS, adult prisons. Raised by the state and brutalized in its care.'[8] Prison, wrote the sociologist Gresham Sykes, is shaped by its social environment – it 'reacts to and is acted upon by the free community'.[9]

> *The destruction of a man's rights, the killing of the juridical person in him, is a prerequisite for dominating him entirely.*[10]
>
> Hannah Arendt

In his Auschwitz memoir, *If This Is a Man*, Primo Levi describes a moment soon after his arrival in the camp when, driven by thirst, he reached outside the window to break off an icicle. 'At once a large, heavy guard prowling outside brutally snatched it away from me. "*Warum?*" I asked him in my poor German. "*Hier ist kein warum*" (there is no why here), he replied.'[11] Arbitrariness – the practice of coercing or harming another human being in one's power *without saying why* – belongs to the politics of domination and characterizes authoritarian regimes. 'Never in my entire time in prison did anyone read me the paragraph I was convicted under,' wrote Erich Loest, who spent seven and a half years in East Germany's notorious Bautzen II.[12] Most of what happened in East German prisons only emerged after the Wall fell: if prisons are society's hidden institutions,[13] the GDR made them hermetic. Prison in the GDR meant being denied access to the criminal or penal codes of the state that had incarcerated you, and permanent unclarity about what the future might hold. You might be released; equally you might find yourself in long-term solitary without any explanation given. Loest was held in solitary for two and a half years without being offered a reason. André Baganz spent five years in solitary confinement. He asked why, and was told that his captors did not need a reason.[14] The nostalgia (or 'Ostalgia') some now feel for the East German past is not shared by anyone who spent time in an East German prison. Going to prison in West Germany was by no means a walk in the park, but the exacerbated hiddenness of penal practices in the communist East, and the authoritarian bent of the state, made for cruel and arbitrary conditions that are regularly described as torture by those who experienced them.

Arbitrariness disempowers people because they cannot make sense of events – where making sense of events is, beyond food and water, perhaps the most basic of human needs. Stasi detainees were routinely left waiting for hours without being told why they had been detained or what, if anything, they were waiting for. Carola Schacht, who was arrested on suspicion of planning to leave the GDR and spent six months in a Stasi interrogation centre before she was sentenced to two and a half years in prison, remembers dreaming about an interrogation. In the dream, her questioners

> had found in my room in Erfurt a little square table with rounded-off corners, one I really owned. They kept on asking me what had happened to the glass top that belonged to the table. But in reality there was no glass top for that table, and I told them that. But they kept on asking in their enervating way; they wanted me to tell them where the glass top was. I remember exactly how I kept answering in desperation in the dream – there isn't any glass top, there isn't any glass top!

Kerstin Hegert, who served three prison sentences in East Germany, even now cannot make sense of the 'suicide' of her boyfriend Matthias Domaschk, who died suddenly in a Stasi remand prison in 1981, two days after his arrest, in circumstances that have never been explained.[15]

One woman was crying. They told her to stop or she'd be sent to the seg. She was next to me in my cell. She didn't stop crying and two officers came with a bucket of ice-cold water.

They poured it over her and then sent her down the block.
Just because she cried too loudly.[16]
Rita, 2018

In some ways it is comfortable to see arbitrariness as a thing of the past: a historical feature of the Nazi or Communist states. Both of those systems have been historically discredited – however appalling the stories, we can feel that they do not reflect on 'us', but on others. But one part of what prison shows us is the continuing presence of the past – not only but not least in the sites that are still in use. 'The building is still infused with all that suffering,' wrote a resident in Hamburg's 'Santa Fu' prison, built on the site of a concentration camp. Berlin's Tegel II is, in the words of another writer, 'a panoptically constructed, four-winged star-shaped building from the time of Bismarck, holding just under 400 men'. And Klaus Jünschke noted that Siegburg, where the young Hermann Heibach died so horribly, was 'locking up young people in the same space used to detain youngsters in the Empire, in the Weimar period and in National Socialism'.[17] In the USA, the notorious San Quentin State prison has been in use since 1854, and the UK's 'monster mansion', HMP Wakefield, dates back to 1594, though the current buildings are Victorian.

Thomas Galli has concluded from his fifteen years in the prison service that Germany's prison system actually belongs to the past:

> Our criminal law is not reasonable. It is based far more on beliefs, prejudices, the emotions of fear and anger, than on knowledge or any kind of considerations that are properly thought-through . . . Particularly the practice of withdrawing people's freedom in total institutions is utterly out of date when considered in the light of day.[18]

We are no longer human beings. We are prison beings.[19]

'People coming out of prison have no self-confidence – they are broken men,' Schleswig-Holstein's former ministerial head of prisons, Bernd Maelicke, told *Spiegel* magazine in 2017. Some of them are broken women – 'the real damage prison has done is to make me completely unable to live independently,' wrote Sabine Thiesen. 'I'm trying to say how glad I am to be back inside. Ouch!!! That sentence is horrifying and is the pure truth. Who am I? Where is the Sabine I once was?'[20] 'Prison's objective is to break people', asserts Ralf Axel Simon, and Thiesen confirms the outcome if not the objective: 'much of my lightness of being, all my optimism, my unshakeable belief in a better future are irretrievably gone. Resocialization achieved – client (or patient?) dead!'[21] Even in one of the world's less punitive nations, prison does not seem to be working.

FOR DECADES, PEOPLE in prison have been 'writing back', contradicting, expanding and correcting the stories told by the system, the media and the state. But their versions of the story have largely been ignored – they have had, in words of Paul St John, a prisoner in Eastern New York Correctional Facility in 1994, 'the credibility of elves'.[22] Just recently, however, the status of writing from the prison seems to be shifting: H. Bruce Franklin, a professor of American literature who in the late 1970s introduced readers in the USA to writing from the prison, noticed with a little surprise in 2008 that a standard anthology of American literature now included a section called 'Prison Literature'.[23] In the same year the *Publications of the Modern Language Association of America* made incarceration the topic of its May issue, and *Texas Studies in Literature and Language* produced a special issue on 'Cultures of Detention' in the autumn. In 2015, the *American Book Review* issued a number on prison writing. And in 2021, the UK scholars Michelle Kelly and Claire Westall edited a collection of essays, *Prison Writing and the Literary World*.[24]

It is time to look again at the nations we think we know – from the inside.

The prison writers have done their bit. Now it's the public's turn.[25]
Helmut H. Koch, 2008

View from a cell in ‘Santa Fu’, 2006.

References

The epigraph is from A. P., 'Der Gefangene', in *Die vierte Kaste. Junge Menschen im Gefängnis*, ed. Birgitta Wolf (Hamburg, 1963), p. 64. Trans. Naomi Reiss.

Preface

1 Anon., 'Der Kreislauf', in *Gemeinsam einsam*, ed. Ingeborg-Drewitz-Literaturpreis (Münster, 2015), pp. 36–41 (p. 36).
2 This and the sections that follow in Roman are from Harald A. Dreßler, '*betr.: alltagsrealität im knast*', in *Risse im Fegefeuer*, ed. Ingeborg-Drewitz-Literaturpreis (Hagen, 1989), pp. 63–5.
3 Dirk Glebe, *Handbuch Knast und Strafvollzug: (Über-)leben im deutschen Gefängnis*, 2nd edn (Norderstedt, 2011), p. 17.
4 Rositta, 'Zugang', in *Menschen im Gefängnis: Literarische Selbstzeugnisse, authentische Texte und Materialien für den schulischen und außerschulischen Unterricht*, ed. Nicola Keßler, Uta Klein, Helmut H. Koch and Elisabeth Theine (Bonn, 1996), p. 27. Cited with kind permission of Carl Werner Wendland, Forum Verlag Godesberg.
5 Anon., 'Der Kreislauf' in *Gemeinsam einsam*, ed. Ingeborg-Drewitz-Literaturpreis (Münster, 2015), pp. 36–41 (pp. 36–9).
6 Katharina, 'Man geht mit dem, womit man angefangen hat, mit einer Lüge', in *Ich muß zurück ins Rattenloch: Unerhörte Geschichten aus dem Frauenknast*, ed. Reimund Neufeld and Helmut Koch (Oberhausen, 2010), pp. 113–27 (p. 114).

Foreword

1 *World Prison Brief* data for China in 2018, www.prisonstudies.org, accessed 5 August 2021.
2 Institute for Criminal Policy Research, 'Global Prison Population Soars', Birkbeck, University of London, www.bbk.ac.uk, 7 November 2018.
3 See the *World Prison Brief*, 'Highest to Lowest – Prison Population Rate', www.prisonstudies.org, accessed 5 August 2021.
4 Concurrently there has been an increase in suspended short sentences, 12–24 months, but with more people serving longer sentences. See

Helmut Kury, Theodore Ferdinand and Joachim Obergell-Fuchs, 'Punitivity in Germany: Attitudes to Punishment, Sentencing, and Prison Rates', in *International Perspectives on Punitivity*, ed. Kury and Ferdinand (Bochum, 2008), pp. 107–34 (pp. 107 and 123–33).

5 Oliver, in *16 Bars Project: Unterdrückte graue Schatten*, ed. Reimund Neufeld, Claudia Franck and Julia Schönstadt (Oberhausen, 2016), p. 16.

6 The data is as published in the *World Prison Brief* (2021). The most recent data for the USA is from June 2018. See www.prisonstudies.org, accessed 2 August 2021.

7 Hans Kaltenbach [Bericht], in *Strafvollzug in Deutschland: Situation und Reform*, ed. Dietrich Rollmann (Frankfurt am Main, 1967), pp. 25–32 (p. 25)

8 Ewald, in *Knast: Eine Dokumentation*, ed. Brigitte and Dieter Kübbeler (Oldenburg, 2003), pp. 84–92 (p. 91); Peter Feraru, *Das Messer der Hoffnung* [1983] (Frankfurt am Main, 1985).

9 Marion Döbert and Peter Hubertus, *Ihr Kreuz ist die Schrift. Analphabetismus und Alphabetisierung in Deutschland* (Münster, 2000), p. 69.

10 Unless I know the date when a story was actually told, the one I give is the date it was recorded or published.

11 Mary Fulbrook, *Dissonant Lives: Generations and Violence through the German Dictatorships* (Oxford, 2011).

12 Anon. [Karlheinz Barwasser], 'Sich als starke Mauern begreifen – Schreiben im Knast', in *Ungehörte Worte. Gefangene schreiben: Eine Dokumentation*, ed. Helmut H. Koch and Regine Lindtke (Münster, 1982), pp. 107–11 (pp. 109–10).

13 Dietmar, in *Knast*, ed. Kübbeler and Kübbeler, pp. 197–8; Tom, in *16 Bars Project*, ed. Neufeld, Franck and Schönstadt, p. 60.

14 Anon., in *Inside-Magazin: Gefangenenzeitung der JVA Rheinbach* (Christmas 2017), p. 25. All reasonable attempts were made to contact the copyright holder.

15 Dario Melossi, 'Overcoming the Crisis in Critical Criminology: Toward a Grounded Labeling Theory', *Criminology*, XXIII/2 (1985), pp. 193–208.

16 See www.prisonstudies.org for the *World Female Imprisonment List* (3rd edn).

17 Tobias Wunschik, *Knastware für den Klassenfeind: Häftlingsarbeit in der DDR, der Ost-West-Handel und die Staatssicherheit (1970–1989)* (Göttingen, 2014), p. 71.

18 In a high-profile case in Germany in 2016, a trans person who had already acquired legal status as a woman was nonetheless held in a men's prison. See Heike Romme, 'Transgender im Männerknast', *Südwest Presse*, www.swp.de, 17 September 2016. See also 'Informationen für Trans*Menschen in Haft und Freund_innen und Unterstützer_innen', transundhaft.blogspot.de.

19 Dirk Baier and Marie Christine Bergmann, 'Gewalt im Strafvollzug – Ergebnisse einer Befragung in fünf Bundesländern', *Forum Strafvollzug*, LXII/2 (2013), pp. 76–83 (p. 77).

20 In 2019, 26 per cent of Germany's general population had what is

called a 'migration background', meaning that either they or at least one of their parents was born without German citizenship.

21 Gregor Mayntz, 'Zahl der Ausländer in Gefängnissen auf Rekordhoch', *Rheinische Post*, rp-online.de, 4 February 2019; Thomas Galli, *Knast oder Heimat? Erzählungen von Recht und Unrecht* (Zell/Mosel, 2019), p. 7.

22 Sonja John, 'Gefängnismedizin', *Der Lichtblick*, CCCLXIV (2015), pp. 36–9 (p. 36). See also Jürgen, in *Knast*, ed. Kübbeler and Kübbeler, p. 25; and Aneta, 'Die Mauer', in *Ich muss zurück ins Rattenloch: Unerhörte Geschichten aus dem Frauenknast*, ed. Reimund Neufeld and Helmut Koch (Oberhausen, 2010), pp. 99–100 (p. 99).

23 Gill Green, Nigel South and Rose Smith, '"They Say that You Are a Danger but You Are Not": Representation and Construction of the Moral Self in Narratives of "Dangerous Individuals"', *Deviant Behaviour*, XXVII (2006), pp. 299–328 (p. 314).

24 Stefanie, in *Knast*, ed. Kübbeler and Kübbeler, pp. 97–103 (p. 98).

25 Sabine Bomeier, 'Frauen im Knast', *Der Lichtblick*, CCCLXIV (2015), pp. 32–3 (p. 33). See also Maren Michels, 'Straffällig gewordenene Frauen', in *Das Gefängnis auf dem Prüfstand: Zustand und Zukunft des Strafvollzugs*, ed. Bernd Maelicke and Stefan Suhling (Wiesbaden, 2018), pp. 381–401 (p. 387).

26 Bomeier, 'Frauen im Knast', p. 33; Ann Lloyd, *Doubly Deviant, Doubly Damned: Society's Treatment of Violent Women* (London, 1995).

27 Nancy, in *16 Bars Project*, ed. Neufeld, Franck and Schönstadt, p. 207.

28 Karina, 'Ich muss zurück ins Rattenloch', in *Ich muss zurück ins Rattenloch*, ed. Neufeld and Koch, pp. 44 and 49.

29 Committee on Women's Rights and Gender Equality (rapporteur: Marie Panayotopoulos-Cassiotou), *Report on the Situation of Women in Prison and the Impact of the Imprisonment of Parents on Social and Family Life* (Brussels, 2008), p. 4.

30 *Wege durch den Knast*, ed. Redaktionskollektiv (Berlin, 2016), pp. 107–8.

31 Katharina, 'Man geht mit dem, womit man angefangen hat', in *Ich muss zurück ins Rattenloch*, ed. Neufeld and Koch, p. 124.

32 Christiane Jesse, Susanne Jacob and Susann Prätor, 'Opferorientierung im Strafvollzug: Theoretische Grundlagen, empirische Befunde und Leitlinien für eine praktische Umsetzung', in *Das Gefängnis auf dem Prüfstand*, ed. Maelicke and Suhling, pp. 159–74.

33 Petra, 'Zorn', in *16 Bars Project*, ed. Neufeld, Franck and Schönstadt, pp. 108–9.

34 Sabine, 'Der Irrsinn des Systems', ibid., pp. 222–4 (p. 222).

35 Dieter Wurm, 'Knast macht krank – Gesundheitsschädliche Folgen des Knasts und miserable Krankenfürsorge im humanen Strafvollzug in Deutschland, oder wie aus einstigen Tätern Opfer werden. Ein subjektiver Bericht', *Der Lichtblick*, CCCLII (2012), reprinted www.schattenblick.de, accessed 10 August 2021.

36 'Über 70 Tuberkulose-Fälle in Berlins Gefängnissen', *Esanum*, www.esanum.de, 21 October 2019. See also Sonja John, 'Gefängnismedizin', *Der Lichtblick*, CCCLXIV (2015), pp. 36–9; and Murat Gerçek, 'Sucht, Infektionen und Hygiene in deutschen Gefängnissen', *Der Lichtblick*, CCCLII (2012), reprinted www.schattenblick.de, accessed 10 August 2021.

37 The figures are cited by Wurm, 'Knast macht krank', in *Der Lichtblick*, CCCLII (2012); similar figures were cited in 2019 by Hildburg Bruns, 'Abwesend wegen Krankheit! Berlins Behörden sind ein Fall fürs Wartezimmer', *Berliner Zeitung*, www.bz-berlin.de, 30 September 2019.

38 Jürgen Reissig and Norbert Kieper, 'Drogen', in *Der Lichtblick*, CCCLXXIII (2017), pp. 4–6 (p. 6); *Wege durch den Knast*, ed. Redaktionskollektiv, pp. 308–10.

39 Gilbert Koester, 'Ameisensäure', in *Schrei Deine Worte nicht in den Wind: Verständigungstexte von Inhaftierten*, ed. Karlheinz A. Barwasser (Tübingen, 1982), p. 133. All reasonable attempts were made to contact the copyright holder.

40 See the statistics cited in the German government's draft response to a parliamentary question: 'Antwort der Bundesregierung auf die Kleine Anfrage der Abgeordneten Ulla Jelpke, Dr. André Hahn, Göray Akbulut, weiterer Abgeordneter und der Fraktion DIE LINKE, dserver.bundestag.de, 9 July 2021; Jumbo, 'So geht's mit Pädophilen in der JVA', in *16 Bars Project*, ed. Neufeld, Franck and Schönstadt, pp. 26–9 (p. 29); and Julian Jestadt, 'Mehr Suizide in Gefängnissen', *TAZ*, www.taz.de, 20 July 2021.

41 Thanks to Andy Watson (Geese Theatre) and Andrew Wilkie (National Prison Radio) for helping me find the right terminology in English.

42 Tessa Murphy, 'Solitary Confinement Is Cruel and All Too Usual. Why Is It Only Getting Worse?' Amnesty International Canada, www.amnesty.ca, 14 October 2014.

43 Ivan Jelinic, 'WENN Wände erzählen könnten . . .', in *Wenn Wände erzählen könnten*, ed. Ingeborg-Drewitz-Literaturpreis (Münster, 1999), pp. 79–83 (p. 81).

44 Nationale Stelle zur Verhütung von Folter, *Jahresbericht 2010/2011* (Wiesbaden, 2011), pp. 43–4; see also Nationale Stelle zur Verhütung von Folter, *Jahresbericht 2020* (Wiesbaden, 2020), p. 84.

45 Helmut Pammler, 'Sicherheitsverwahrung', in *Geräusche der Nacht*, ed. Ingeborg-Drewitz-Literaturpreis, p. 61. Cited with kind permission of Agenda Verlag.

46 Friedhelm, 'Verurteilt wegen Rauschgifthandels und Diebstahls', in *Knast*, ed. Kübbeler and Kübbeler, pp. 72–8 (p. 72).

47 See Human Rights Watch, 'New Orleans: Prisoners Abandoned to Floodwaters', www.hrw.org, accessed 5 August 2021; Jürgen Reissig and Norbert Kiefer, 'Brand JVA Tegel', *Der Lichtblick*, CCCLXXIV (2018), pp. 26–8 (p. 26).

48 Anon., 'Der Kreislauf', in *Gemeinsam einsam*, ed. Ingeborg-Drewitz-Literaturpreis (Münster, 2015), pp. 36–41 (p. 37); Markus Lennemann, 'Knastrap in der Nacht: Haftanstalt', in *Geräusche der Nacht: Literatur aus dem deutschen Strafvollzug*, ed. Ingeborg-Drewitz-Literaturpreis (Münster, 2008), p. 87; Marianne Herzog, *Nicht den Hunger verlieren* (Berlin, 1980), p. 65.

49 Rainer, in *Knast*, ed. Kübbeler and Kübbeler, pp. 174–8 (p. 175); Anon., cited in Benjamin Schulz, 'Gefängnisalltag in Deutschland: Weggesperrt und vergessen', *Spiegel Online*, www.spiegel.de, 15 January 2013;

Jumbo, 'So geht's mit Pädophilen in der JVA', in *16 Bars Project*, ed. Neufeld, Franck and Schönstadt, pp. 26–9 (p. 29).
50 And have one, in the UK context: Alison Liebling, David Price and Guy Shefer, *The Prison Officer* [2011], 2nd edn (Abingdon, 2012).
51 See Baier and Bergmann, 'Gewalt im Strafvollzug',.
52 Jutta Giersch, 'Wir hungern noch, wir hungern noch', in *Hohenecker Protokolle: Aussagen zur Geschichte der politischen Verfolgung von Frauen in der DDR*, ed. Ulrich Schacht, 2nd edn (Leipzig, 2009), pp. 45–67.
53 Herzog, *Nicht den Hunger verlieren*, p. 152.
54 Anon., *Der Lichtblick* CCCLXXI (2017), p. 29.
55 Howard S. Becker, 'Whose Side Are We On?', *Social Problems*, XIV/3 (1967), pp. 239–47 (p. 241); and Catharine MacKinnon, *Feminism Unmodified: Discourses on Life and Law* (Cambridge, MA, 1987), p. 164.
56 Peter Dittrich, 'Alibi', in *Schrei Deine Worte,* ed. Barwasser, p. 132. All reasonable attempts were made to contact the copyright holder.
57 Peter Jörnschmidt, 'Alter: 30. Verurteilt: 1968', in *Lebenslänglich: Protokolle aus der Haft*, ed. Klaus Antes, Christiane Ehrhardt and Heinrich Hannover (Munich, 1972), pp. 42–84 (p. 76); Michelle, 'Tagebuch einer Chaosqueen', in *Ich muss zurück ins Rattenloch*, ed. Neufeld and Koch, pp. 73–6 (p. 73).
58 Brigitte and Dieter Kübbeler, 'Vorwort', in *Knast*, ed. Kübbeler and Kübbeler, pp. 7–8 (p. 8).
59 Karina, 'Ich muss zurück ins Rattenloch', in *Ich muss zurück ins Rattenloch*, ed. Neufeld and Koch, pp. 37–64 (p. 59).
60 Peter-Paul Zahl, 'Der große Reso-Schwindel', in *Schrei Deine Worte,* ed. Barwasser, pp. 64–7 (p. 64).

UNITY, RIGHTS AND FREEDOM: WEST GERMANY, 1949–68

1 A New Start?

1 Harry G., 'Alles in Ordnung', in *Rückkehr in die Freiheit: Ängste und Hoffnungen*, ed. Bundeszusammenschluß für Straffälligenhilfe (Bonn, 1981), pp. 80–86 (p. 81).
2 August Klemp, 'Alter: 45. Verurteilt: 1949 – begnadigt: 1971', in *Lebenslänglich: Protokolle aus der Haft*, ed. Klaus Antes, Christiane Ehrhardt and Heinrich Hannover (Munich, 1972), pp. 85–115 (p. 104); and D. E., in *Aussagen: Briefe von Strafgefangenen*, ed. Birgitta Wolf (Ebenhausen bei München, 1968), pp. 123–6 (p. 123).
3 Walter A. Lunden, 'United States Army Supervision of Civil Prisons in Bavaria', *Journal of Criminal Law and Criminology*, XXXVIII/4 (1947), pp. 358–68.
4 'Directive No. 19: Principles for Administration of German Prisons', in Allied Control Authority, Germany, *Enactments and Approved Papers of the Control Council and Coordinating Committee* (Legal Division, Office of Military Control for Germany [USA], 1945). See Library of Congress Military Legal resources, CORC/P(45) 136.

5 Myrl E. Alexander and John W. Roberts, 'Rebuilding a Prison System: Germany, 1945–46', *Federal Prisons Journal*, II/2 (1991), pp. 37–40. Alexander misremembers the number of the Directive as Directive 17. See also Lunden, 'United States Army Supervision of Civil Prisons in Bavaria', p. 365.
6 Alexander and Roberts, 'Rebuilding a Prison System', p. 41.
7 Klemp, 'Alter: 45. Verurteilt: 1949 – begnadigt: 1971', in *Lebenslänglich*, ed. Antes, Ehrhardt and Hannover, pp. 90 and 94.
8 Ibid., p. 111.
9 See Thomas Würtenberger, 'Criminology and Penology in Western Germany', *British Journal of Delinquency*, XXVI (1953–4), pp. 26–38 (pp. 33–4); and Lunden, 'United States Army Supervision of Civil Prisons in Bavaria', p. 364.
10 Adenauer, cited in Georg Bönisch, 'Amnesie Und Amnestie', *Spiegel Special: Die Fünfziger Jahre – Vom Trümmerland Zum Wirtschaftswunder* (21 February 2006), pp. 112–18 (p. 116). With thanks to Kathrin Wunderlich for the reference.
11 Jürgen Callberg, 'Alter: 35. Verurteilt: 1958' in *Lebenslänglich*, ed. Antes, Ehrhardt and Hannover, pp. 115–41 (pp. 116 and 138).
12 Anon., 'Haß auf die Gesellschaft. Ein Tonbandprotokoll', in *Prügelknaben der Gesellschaft: Häftlingsberichte*, ed. Ernst Klee (Düsseldorf, 1971), pp. 41–56 (p. 45).
13 P.A.B., '. . . und sein Vorher war die Angst', in *Die vierte Kaste. Junge Menschen im Gefängnis*, ed. Birgitta Wolf (Hamburg, 1963), pp. 154–81 (p. 161).
14 Thomas Krause, *Geschichte des Strafvollzugs: Von den Kerkern des Altertums bis zur Gegenwart* (Darmstadt, 1999), p. 89; Geoffrey J. Giles, '"The Most Unkindest Cut of All": Castration, Homosexuality and Nazi Justice', *Journal of Contemporary History*, XXVII/1 (1992), pp. 41–61.
15 E. B., in *Aussagen*: *Briefe von Strafgefangenen*, ed. Birgitta Wolf (Ebenhausen bei München, 1968), p. 137. Wolf uses initials to protect her correspondents' anonymity.
16 Ibid.
17 Christian Pfeiffer, 'Birgitta Wolf – Nachruf', www.nothilfe-birgitta-wolf.de, accessed 20 March 2022.
18 D. E., in *Aussagen*, ed. Wolf, 140–42.
19 E. E., ibid., pp. 140–46 (pp. 142–3).
20 Ibid., p. 146. E. E. is citing from *Der homosexuelle Nächste*, ed. Hermanus Bianchi (Hamburg, 1965).
21 E. A., in *Aussagen*, ed. Wolf, p. 136.
22 Günther H. Koepping, 'Bericht', in *Strafvollzug in Deutschland*: *Situation und Reform*, ed. Dietrich Rollmann (Frankfurt am Main, 1967), pp. 35–9 (p. 36).
23 E. E., in *Aussagen*, ed. Wolf, pp. 140–46 (p. 146); and E. C., ibid., p. 138. Italics in original.
24 Pfeiffer, 'Birgitta Wolf – Nachruf'.
25 Hannah Arendt, *Eichmann in Jerusalem: A Report on the Banality of Evil* (London, 1963).

26 J. A., in *Aussagen*, ed. Wolf, pp. 190–96.
27 Ibid., pp. 195–6. Emphasis in original.
28 Birgitta Wolf, 'Einführung', in *Die vierte Kaste*, ed. Wolf, pp. 7–53 (p. 38).
29 The cell was known as 'die Glocke'. Birgitta Wolf, 'Orientierung', in *Aussagen*, ed. Wolf, pp. 7–44 (p. 25).
30 Wolf, 'Einführung', in *Die vierte Kaste*, ed. Wolf, pp. 10 and 27.
31 Ibid., p. 15; Wolf, 'Orientierung', in *Aussagen*, ed. Wolf, pp. 14–16.
32 Cited in Birgitta Wolf, 'Der Strafgefangene: Gefahren seiner Isolierung', in *Strafvollzug in Deutschland*, ed. Rollmann, pp. 160–70 (p. 166).
33 Wolf, 'Orientierung', in *Aussagen*, ed. Wolf, pp. 16–24; and Wolf, 'Nachwort', in *Anklage erhoben: Gedichte und Grafiken von Strafgefangenen*, ed. Birgitta Wolf (Gelnhausen, 1972), pp. 139–44 (p. 141).
34 Wolf, 'Orientierung', in *Aussagen*, ed. Wolf, p. 9.

2 The Rubble Children

1 Manfred Heigand, 'Alter: 33. Verurteilt: 1962', in *Lebenslänglich: Protokolle aus der Haft*, ed. Klaus Antes, Christiane Ehrhard and Heinrich Hannover (Munich, 1972), pp. 142–79 (p. 142).
2 D. F., 'Für das Gefängnis geschriebener Lebenslauf', in *Aussagen: Briefe von Strafgefangenen*, ed. Birgitta Wolf (Ebenhausen bei München, 1968), pp. 129–30 (p. 129).
3 Thomas Würtenberger, 'Criminology and Penology in Western Germany', *British Journal of Delinquency*, XXVI (1953–4), pp. 26–38 (pp. 26–7).
4 B. C., in *Aussagen*, ed. Wolf, pp. 61–5 (p. 61).
5 Ibid., pp. 82–93 (p. 87).
6 B. C., in *Aussagen*, ed. Wolf, pp. 62–5.
7 Bruce Lambert, 'Myrl E. Alexander Is Dead at 83; Former Director of U.S. Prisons', *New York Times* (17 January 1993), p. 38; Myrl E. Alexander and John W. Roberts, 'Rebuilding a Prison System: Germany, 1945–46', *Federal Prisons Journal*, II/2 (1991), pp. 37–42 (pp. 41–2).
8 See, for example, Sonya Winterberger, *Wir sind die Wolfskinder: Verlassen in Ostpreußen* (Munich, 2012).
9 G. C., in *Aussagen*, ed. Wolf, pp. 163–8 (p. 164).
10 Ibid., pp. 164–6.
11 Ibid., pp. 166–8.
12 B. E., letter to Birgitta Wolf, in *Aussagen*, ed. Wolf, pp. 68–74 (p. 73).
13 Peter Jörnschmidt 'Alter: 30. Verurteilt: 1968', in *Lebenslänglich*, ed. Antes, Ehrhardt and Hannover, pp. 42–84 (p. 46).
14 E. E., in *Aussagen*, ed. Wolf, pp. 140–46 (pp. 140–41).
15 H. A., ibid., pp. 171–7 (pp. 171–4).
16 Ibid., pp. 173–4.
17 Felix Kamphausen, 'Lebenslänglich: Vom Versuch, die Haft zu überleben', in *Eingesperrt: Innenaussichten aus dem Gefängnis: Ein*

Lesebuch, ed. Helmut Ortner (Frankfurt am Main, 1984), pp. 203–11 (p. 205).
18 'H., 20 Jahre', in *Die vierte Kaste. Junge Menschen im Gefängnis*, ed. Birgitta Wolf (Hamburg, 1963), p. 276; and Jürgen J., 'Kaum ein Bonbon, jedoch Isolation', in *Rückkehr in die Freiheit*, ed. Bundeszusammenschluß für Straffälligenhilfe, pp. 164–77 (p. 165).
19 Jürgen J., 'Kaum ein Bonbon, jedoch Isolation', in *Rückkehr in die Freiheit*, ed. Bundeszusammenschluß für Straffälligenhilfe, pp. 164–77 (pp. 167–70).
20 Ulrike Meinhof, 'Jürgen Bartsch und die Gesellschaft', in *konkret*, 1 (1968), reprinted in Meinhof, *Die Würde des Menschen: Aufsätze und Polemiken* [1980] (Berlin, 1995), pp. 112–16 (p. 112).
21 Cited in Jürgen Roth, *Heimkinder: Ein Untersuchungsbericht über Säuglings- und Kinderheime in der Bundesrepublik* (Cologne, 1973), pp. 46–57 (p. 47).
22 B. E., in *Aussagen*, ed. Wolf, pp. 68–74 (pp. 68–9).
23 Cited in Ulrike Meinhof, 'Guxhagen – Mädchen in Fürsorgeerziehung: Ein Heim in Hessen' (Hessischer Rundfunk, typescript, November 1969), p. 6.
24 A. A., in *Aussagen*, ed. Wolf, pp. 45–52 (p. 48).
25 B. E., ibid., pp. 72–3; 'H., 21 Jahre', in *Die vierte Kaste*, ed. Wolf, p. 275; and A. A., in *Aussagen*, ed. Wolf, pp. 47–9.
26 Peter Wensierski, *Schläge im Namen des Herrn: Die verdrängte Geschichte der Heimkinder in der Bundesrepublik* (Munich and Hamburg, 2006), back cover; *Und alle haben geschwiegen* (TV movie, Germany, 2012). See also Ingrid Müller-Münch, *Die geprügelte Generation: Kochlöffel, Rohrstock und die Folgen* (Munich, 2013). The Ryan Report is available online via www.childabusecommission.ie, accessed 9 August 2021.

3 First Calls for Reform

1 *United Nations Congresses on Crime Prevention and Criminal Justice, 1955–2015*, ed. United Nations Information Service, www.un.org, Vienna, 2015; United Nations, 'Standard Minimum Rules for the Treatment of Prisoners, Adopted by the First United Nations Congress on the Prevention of Crime and the Treatment of Offenders'. See www.unodc.org, accessed 9 August 2021; United Nations, *The Integration of Prison Labour with the National Economy, Including the Remuneration of Prisoners* (New York, 1960), p. 45.
2 The account was called a *Rücklage*. See Birgitta Wolf, 'Einführung', in *Die vierte Kaste. Junge Menschen im Gefängnis*, ed. Birgitta Wolf (Hamburg, 1963), pp. 7–53 (p. 45).
3 Günter Blau, 'Arbeit im Gefängnis', in *Strafvollzug in Deutschland: Situation und Reform*, ed. Dietrich Rollmann (Frankfurt am Main, 1967), pp. 74–86 (pp. 81–3); see also Wolf, 'Einführung,' in *Die vierte Kaste*, ed. Wolf, p. 39. Figures are based on an average salary in 1967 of DM 32, cited in 'Tariflohn-Entwicklung – Monatslohn pro Monat', www.was-war-wann.de, accessed 9 August 2021; '[Der Staat] sorgt

dafür, daß jeder Gefangene sinnvolle und nützliche Arbeit verrichten kann.' Dienst- und Vollzugsordnung (DvollzO), 1962, Nr. 81 Abs. 1. See also Blau, 'Arbeit im Gefängnis', p. 77.

4 Andreas Predöhl and Hans-Jürgen Schmahl, 'An Economic Crisis?', *Intereconomics*, I/10 (1966); available online at https://50years.intereconomics.eu.

5 D. B., in *Aussagen: Briefe von Strafgefangenen*, ed. Birgitta Wolf (Ebenhausen bei München, 1968), pp. 112–20 (pp. 112–13).

6 See B. F., ibid., pp. 74–82 (p. 75); also Wolf, 'Einführung,' in *Die vierte Kaste*, ed. Wolf, p. 15, and Wolf, 'Orientierung', in *Aussagen*, ed. Wolf, p. 12.

7 *Sühne* and *Vergeltung*. See, for example, the critique by Heinrich Hannover, 'Stellungnahme eines Juristen' in *Lebenslänglich: Protokolle aus der Haft*, ed. Klaus Antes, Christiane Ehrhardt and Heinrich Hannover (Munich, 1972), pp. 181–232 (p. 232).

8 Kaltenbach, 'Bericht', in *Strafvollzug in Deutschland*, ed. Rollmann, pp. 25–32 (p. 29).

9 H. G., in *Aussagen*, ed. Wolf, pp. 187–8.

10 F. B., ibid., pp. 150–53.

11 Wolf, editorial note, ibid., p. 153.

12 Anon., in *Prügelknaben der Gesellschaft: Häftlingsberichte*, ed. Ernst Klee (Düsseldorf, 1971), p. 56.

13 D. B., in *Aussagen*, ed. Wolf, pp. 112–20 (p. 113). See also Wolf, 'Orientierung', ibid., p. 11.

14 Birgitta Wolf, 'Eine Einführung', in *Anklage erhoben: Gedichte und Grafiken von Strafgefangenen*, ed. Birgitta Wolf (Gelnhausen, 1972), pp. 6–9 (pp. 7–8).

15 Anon., 'Aus dem Tagebuch eines 21jährigen', in *Die vierte Kaste*, ed. Wolf, pp. 284–6 (p. 284); and Klemp, 'Alter: 45. Verurteilt: 1949 – begnadigt: 1971', in *Lebenslänglich*, ed. Antes, Ehrhardt and Hannover, p. 85.

16 Wolf, 'Einführung,' in *Die vierte Kaste*, ed. Wolf, p. 43.

17 Klemp, 'Alter: 45. Verurteilt: 1949 – begnadigt: 1971', in *Lebenslänglich*, ed. Antes, Ehrhardt and Hannover, pp. 85–6.

18 Cited in Birgitta Wolf, 'Grundgesetz und Strafvollzug. Ein Vergleichsversuch anhand von Beispielen', *vorgänge*, VI (1969), pp. 211–15.

19 Ibid.

20 Manfred Heigand, 'Alter: 33. Verurteilt: 1962', in *Lebenslänglich*, ed. Antes, Erhardt and Hannover, pp. 142–79 (p. 174).

21 Anon., 'Haß auf die Gesellschaft', in *Prügelknaben der Gesellschaft*, ed. Klee, pp. 48 and 42.

22 Wolf, 'Der Strafgefangene: Gefahren seiner Isolierung', in *Strafvollzug in Deutschland*, ed. Rollmann, pp. 160–70 (p. 161); Wolf, 'Orientierung', in *Aussagen*, ed. Wolf, p. 23.

23 A. B., in *Aussagen*, ed. Wolf, pp. 52–3 (p. 53); and Wolf, 'Orientierung', ibid., p. 23.

24 E. S., 'Ein Leben lang', in *Anklage erhoben*, ed. Wolf, p. 116.

25 H. F., in *Aussagen*, ed. Wolf, p. 184; and Behr, 'Alter: 32. Verurteilt: 1964', in *Lebenslänglich*, ed. Antes, Erhardt and Hannover, pp. 39–40.

26 B. C., in *Aussagen*, ed. Wolf, pp. 61–5 (p. 62).

27 Wolf, 'Einführung', in *Die vierte Kaste*, ed. Wolf, p. 13.
28 D. E., in *Aussagen*, ed. Wolf, pp. 123–6.
29 D. H., ibid., pp. 132–5 (pp. 133–5).
30 W. G., 'Man fragt doch, wenn man Logik hat . . .: Aus einem Romanmanuskript', in *Die vierte Kaste*, ed. Wolf, pp. 93–109 (p. 99).
31 W. G., 'Humanitas', ibid., pp. 262–4 (p. 263).
32 See Thomas Vormbaum, *Einführung in die moderne Strafrechtsgeschichte*, 3rd edn (Heidelberg, 2016), p. 175; and Thomas Würtenberger, 'Criminology and Penology in Western Germany', *British Journal of Delinquency*, XXVI (1953–4), pp. 26–38 (pp. 26–7).
33 W. G., 'Urlaub aus Burstadt', in *Die vierte Kaste*, ed. Wolf, pp. 223–53 (p. 252); and W. B., 'Die fünfte Kaste', ibid., pp. 139–43 (pp. 141–2).
34 P.A.B., 'Die Überraschung', in *Die vierte Kaste*, ed. Wolf, pp. 150–53 (p. 151).
35 Jungmann, 'Bericht', in *Strafvollzug in Deutschland*, ed. Rollmann, p. 34; and Borchert, 'Bericht', ibid., p. 22.

A MODEL AND LOOKING GOOD? WEST GERMANY, 1968–89

4 The German Model

1 Jeffrey J. Anderson, 'Modell Deutschland: From the Bonn to the Berlin Republic', in *The Routledge Handbook of German Politics and Culture*, ed. Sarah Colvin (London and New York, 2015), pp. 71–84.
2 *Regierungserklärung von Bundeskanzler Willy Brandt vor dem Deutschen Bundestag in Bonn*, 28 October 1969. See www.willy-brandt.de, accessed 9 August 2021.
3 See Thomas Würtenberger, 'Criminology and Penology in Western Germany', *British Journal of Delinquency*, XXVI (1953–4), pp. 26–38 (p. 30); Albin Eser, 'Major Stages of Criminal Law Reform in Germany', *Israeli Law Review*, XXVIII (1996), pp. 28–35 (p. 30); Thomas Vormbaum and Michael Bohlander, eds, *A Modern History of German Criminal Law*, trans. Margaret Hiley (Heidelberg, 2014), pp. 223 and 226.
4 Günter Blau, 'Die Entwicklung des Strafvollzuges seit 1945', in *Strafvollzug in der Praxis*, ed. Hans-Dieter Schwind and Günter Blau (Berlin, 1976), pp. 23–35 (p. 28). See also *A Modern History of German Criminal Law*, ed. Vormbaum and Bohlander, p. 226–8.
5 In the so-called 'Strafgefangenen-Entscheidung'; see BVerfG 33,1 v. 14.3.1972.
6 Helga Einsele, cited in Anja Vomberg, *Hinter Schloss und Riegel: Gefangenenzeitungen aus Nordrhein-Westfalen und Brandenburg zwischen Anspruch und Wirklichkeit* (Mönchengladbach, 2000), p. 41.
7 See *Strafvollzug in der Praxis: Eine Einführung in die Probleme und Realitäten des Strafvollzuges und der Entlassenenhilfe*, ed. Hans-Dieter Schwind and Günter Blau (Berlin, 1976), p. 26; and Klaus Antes and Christiane Ehrhardt, 'Vorwort', in *Lebenslänglich: Protokolle aus der Haft*, ed. Klaus Antes, Christiane Ehrhardt and Heinrich Hannover (Munich, 1972), pp. 9–10.

8 Klaus Antes, back-cover blurb for *So wächst die Mauer zwischen Mensch und Mensch: Stimmen aus dem Knast und zum Strafvollzug*, ed. Ingeborg Drewitz and Johann P. Tammen (Bremerhaven, 1980).
9 The newspaper was *Die weiße Frau*, in Schwäbisch-Gmünd prison. The exchange of letters was published as Ingeborg Drewitz and Winand Buchacker, *Mit Sätzen Mauern eindrücken: Briefwechsel mit einem Strafgefangenen* (Düsseldorf, 1979).
10 Peter-Jürgen Boock and Peter Schneider, *Ratte – tot . . . Ein Briefwechsel* (Darmstadt, 1985). All reasonable attempts were made to contact the copyright holder.
11 The Piper volume was *Lebenslänglich*, ed. Antes, Ehrhardt and Hannover; see also *Schatten im Kalk. Lyrik und Prosa aus dem Knast*, ed. Ingeborg Drewitz (Stuttgart, 1979) and *So wächst die Mauer*, ed. Drewitz and Tammen; *Gefängnis: Eine Einführung in seine Innenwelt*, ed. Helmut Ortner (Weinheim, 1988).
12 Helmut Ortner, 'Das Beispiel Massachussets', in *Eingesperrt: Innenaussichten aus dem Gefängnis: Ein Lesebuch*, ed. Helmut Ortner (Frankfurt am Main, 1984), pp. 257–66 (p. 266).
13 Peter Feraru, 'Schreib-Prozesse', in *Schrei Deine Worte nicht in den Wind: Verständigungstexte von Inhaftierten*, ed. Karlheinz A. Barwasser (Tübingen, 1982), pp. 9–14 (p. 9); and Sigrid Weigel, '*Und selbst im Kerker frei . . .!' Schreiben im Gefängnis* (Marburg, 1980), p. 7.
14 See Helmut H. Koch, 'Schreiben und Lesen in sozialen und psychischen Krisensituationen: Eine Annäherung', in *Schreiben im Kontext von Schule, Universität, Beruf, und Lebensalltag*, ed. Johannes Berning, Nicola Keßner and Helmut H. Koch (Berlin, 2006), pp. 127–59 (p. 129); and *Ungehörte Worte: Gefangene schreiben: Eine Dokumentation aus deutschen Gefangenenzeitungen*, ed. Helmut H. Koch and Regine Lindtke (Münster, 1982), back cover.
15 Peter Feraru, 'Ich bin in Worten', in *Gefangenenliteratur: Sprechen – Schreiben – Lesen in deutschen Gefängnissen*, ed. Uta Klein and Helmut Koch (Hagen, 1988), p. 118.
16 The benefits of biographical storytelling have since been examined in detail in Shadd Maruna's influential study *Making Good: How Ex-Convicts Reform and Rebuild Their Lives* (Washington, DC, 2001).
17 Ingeborg Drewitz, 'Nachwort', in *Rückkehr in die Freiheit: Ängste und Hoffnungen. Gefangene schreiben*, ed. Bundeszusammenschluß für Straffälligenhilfe (Bonn, 1981), pp. 178–80 (p. 178); and Peter Feraru, 'Ich bin in Worten', in *Gefangenenliteratur*, ed. Klein and Koch, p. 118.
18 Anon., 'Bunker', in *Ungehörte Worte*, ed. Koch and Lindtke, pp. 60–69 (p. 60).
19 R. H. 'Vietnam – Träume' (Vietnam – Dreams), in *Anklage erhoben: Gedichte und Grafiken von Strafgefangenen*, ed. Birgitta Wolf (Gelnhausen, 1972), p. 21. All reasonable attempts were made to contact the copyright holder.
20 Anon., 'Der Bunker', in *Laßt mich leben: Frauen im Knast*, ed. Luise Rinser (Hagen, 1987), pp. 81–3 (p. 83). The use of lower case follows the concrete poets who hoped, in poet Chris Bezzel's words, 'to

revolutionize language itself in the medium of language'. Bezzel, 'dichtung und revolution', in *Text und Kritik*, xxv (1970), p. 34.

21 Ulf G. Stuberger, 'Vorwort zur vierten Ausgabe', in Stuberger, *Die ausgeschlossenen Eingeschlossenen: Straffälligkeit und Strafvollzug* [1974], 4th edn (Stuttgart, 2014), p. 5.

22 Initiativgruppe Durchblick, 'Vorwort der Herausgeber', in *Presse und Informationsfreiheit im Knast: Am Beispiel der Gefangenenzeitung 'Durchblick'. Eine Dokumentation*, ed. Initiativgruppe Durchblick (Redaktionskollektiv Durchblick, 1977), pp. 3–4 (p. 3).

23 The poll was published in *Der Spiegel*, VIII (1971).

24 Section 2(1) StVollzG. See also Klaus Laubenthal, *Strafvollzug*, 6th edn (Heidelberg, 2011), p. 69; and *A Modern History of German Criminal Law*, ed. Vormbaum and Bohlander, p. 237.

25 *Angleichungsgrundsatz*, *Gegensteuerungsgrundsatz* and *Integrationsgrundsatz*. §3 StVollzG.

26 U. K., 'gestern – heute – morgen', in *Schatten im Kalk*, ed. Drewitz, pp. 111–13 (p. 112). All reasonable attempts were made to contact the copyright holder.

27 *Presse- und Informationsfreiheit im Knast*, ed. Initiativgruppe Durchblick, p. 16.

28 Ibid., p. 19.

29 Anon. 'Überbelegung', in *Ungehörte Worte*, ed. Koch and Lindtke, p. 32. Emphasis in original.

30 Lothar Ra., 'Rückkehr in die Freiheit – Ängste und Hoffnungen' in *Rückkehr in die Freiheit*, ed. Bundeszusammenschluß für Straffälligenhilfe, pp. 99–105 (p. 104).

31 August Klemp, 'Alter: 45. Verurteilt: 1949 – begnadigt: 1971', in *Lebenslänglich*, ed. Antes, Ehrhardt and Hannover, pp. 85–115 (p. 110); and Günter Hartzen, 'Im Bunker', *Kaschott*, IV (1973), reprinted in *Knast-Reportagen*, ed. Ernst Klee (Stein, 1973), pp. 66–9 (p. 68).

32 Wolf, 'Eine Einführung', in *Anklage erhoben*, ed. Wolf, pp. 8–9; and Monika Sperr, 'Big Sister sieht alles: Eindrücke im Aichacher Frauengefängnis', in *So wächst die Mauer*, ed. Drewitz and Tammen, pp. 77–82 (pp. 79–81).

33 Helmut Ortner, 'Vorwort von Draußen', in *Gefängnis*, ed. Ortner, pp. 9–11 (pp. 9–10).

34 Fred Kreisler 'Die Zeit danach', in *Eingesperrt*, ed. Ortner, pp. 247–53 (p. 251); and Jürgen J., in *Rückkehr in die Freiheit*, ed. Bundeszusammenschluß für Straffälligenhilfe, p. 175.

35 Anon. 'Vollzugslyrik', in *Ungehörte Worte*, ed. Koch and Lindtke, p. 95.

36 §41 StVollzG: (1). See also Anon., 'Verpflichtung zur Arbeit', in *Ungehörte Worte*, ed. Koch and Lindtke, pp. 76–7 (p. 77).

37 Winand Buchacker, 'das knastpensum', in *So wächst die Mauer*, ed. Drewitz and Tammen, pp. 33–5 (p. 35).

38 Paul Gleye, *Behind the Wall: An American in East Germany, 1988–89* (Carbondale, IL, 1991), p. 193.

39 Czenki, 'Ein Tag von eintausendfünfhundert', in *Eingesperrt*, ed. Ortner, p. 66; and Peter Fritze, 'Rein in die Kiste . . . Die ersten Tage hinter Gittern', ibid., pp. 33–42 (p. 41).

40 Kollektiv Rote Hilfe München, 'Am Tag ein paar Pfennige' [1976], in *Eingesperrt*, ed. Ortner, pp. 45–56 (p. 46).
41 Helmut Ortner, 'Zu diesem Buch', in *Eingesperrt*, ed. Ortner, pp. 9–12 (pp. 11–12).
42 Helga Einsele, cited in *Schatten im Kalk*, ed. Drewitz, back cover; and Helga Einsele, *Mein Leben mit Frauen in Haft* (Stuttgart, 1994), p. 351.
43 Werner Schlegel, 'Reisen in der Verbannung: Als Gefangener "auf Transport"', in *Eingesperrt*, ed. Ortner, pp. 73–85 (p. 79); Peter Fritze, 'Rein in die Kiste . . . Die ersten Tage hinter Gittern', in *Eingesperrt*, ed. Ortner, pp. 33–42 (p. 37); and Anon., 'Mein Wohnklo', in *Ungehörte Worte*, ed. Koch and Lindtke, p. 29.
44 In German, 'Imi und Ata' (Imi and Ata were well-known cleaning products manufactured by Henkel, which also manufactured Persil). Marianne Herzog, *Nicht den Hunger verlieren* (Berlin, 1980), p. 109.
45 Alex, 'Die Arbeit', in *Alltag hinter Gittern*, ed. Gefangenenzeitung U-Bahn (Darmstadt, 1980), pp. 39–43 (p. 39); and Manfred, 'Zweieinhalbtausend Kugelschreiber am Tag', in Ortner ed., *Gefängnis*, pp. 70–72 (p. 70).
46 Peter-Paul Zahl, 'Der große Reso-Schwindel', in *Schrei Deine Worte*, ed. Barwasser, pp. 64–7 (p. 64).
47 Anon., 'Wir wollen Freiheit', in *Ungehörte Worte*, ed. Koch and Lindtke, p. 81.
48 Uschi Keutsch, 'ResoCIAlisierungs-Märchen', in *Schrei Deine Worte*, ed. Barwasser, p. 62.

5 Terrorist Interventions

1 Gilbert Koester, 'Zeit wird's!', in *Schrei Deine Worte nicht in den Wind: Verständigungstexte von Inhaftierten*, ed. Karlheinz A. Barwasser (Tübingen, 1982), p. 135.
2 Holger Meins, a member of the Red Army Faction, died of malnutrition in Wittlich prison on 9 November 1974, Ulrike Meinhof was found hanged in her cell in Stuttgart-Stammheim prison on 9 May 1976 and three more RAF members died the following year: Andreas Baader and Jan-Carl Raspe were found shot in the head in Stuttgart-Stammheim on 18 October 1977, and Gudrun Ensslin was found hanged in her cell the same day.
3 Ulrike Meinhof, 'Die Aktion des Schwarzen September in München' [1972], in *Rote Armee Fraktion: Texte und Materialien zur Geschichte der RAF*, ed. Martin Hoffmann (Berlin, 1997), p. 158; and Marianne Herzog, *Nicht den Hunger verlieren* (Berlin, 1980), p. 125.
4 Ulrike Meinhof, 'aus der zeit: 16.6.72 – 8.2.73'. Typescript. Hamburger Institut für Sozialforschung, Me,U/009,002. Reprinted as 'Das Gefühl', in *Freiheit gestreift – Texte gegen den Knast: Überwachen, Strafen, Widerstand*, ed. Unrast-Kollektiv and Anares Nord (Münster, 1994), pp. 178–9.
5 Meinhof, letter regarding solitary confinement (26 February 1973); see Meinhof, 'briefe ulrikes aus dem trakt, 73/74', typescript. Hamburger Institut für Sozialforschung, Me,U/008,002, p. 18.

6 Amnesty International, *Amnesty International's Work on Prison Conditions of Persons Suspected or Convicted of Politically Motivated Crimes in the Federal Republic of Germany: Isolation and Solitary Confinement* (May 1980), see www.amnesty.org, accessed 9 August 2021.
7 Werner Schlegel, 'Grabgesang', in *So wächst die Mauer zwischen Mensch und Mensch: Stimmen aus dem Knast und zum Strafvollzug*, ed. Ingeborg Drewitz and Johann P. Tammen (Bremerhaven, 1980), pp. 39–41 (p. 41). Cited with kind permission of Monika Thiele, Schünemann Verlag.
8 The new legislation, article 129a StGB, was introduced on 18 August 1976. See Erhard Blankenburg, 'Changes in Political Regimes and Continuity of the Rule of Law in Germany', in Herbert Jacob et al., *Courts, Law, and Politics in Comparative Perspective* (New Haven, CT, 1996), pp. 249–314 (p. 294)
9 Heinz-Holger Stumme, 'Gesundheitspflege', in *Schatten im Kalk. Lyrik und Prosa aus dem Knast*, ed. Ingeborg Drewitz (Stuttgart, 1979), p. 63. All reasonable attempts were made to contact the copyright holder.
10 Winand Buchacker, letter to Ingeborg Drewitz of 6 June 1976, in Ingeborg Drewitz and Winand Buchacker, *Mit Sätzen Mauern eindrücken: Briefwechsel mit einem Strafgefangenen* (Düsseldorf, 1979), p. 58.
11 Ibid., p. 64.
12 Ibid., p. 43.
13 Anon., 'Vaterland', in *Ungehörte Worte: Gefangene schreiben: Eine Dokumentation aus deutschen Gefangenenzeitungen*, ed. Helmut H. Koch and Regine Lindtke (Münster, 1982), p. 61.
14 *Presse und Informationsfreiheit im Knast: Am Beispiel der Gefangenenzeitung 'Durchblick'. Eine Dokumentation*, ed. Initiativgruppe Durchblick (Redaktionskollektiv Durchblick, 1977), p. 57 (capitals in original).
15 Jürgen Callberg, 'Alter: 35 Verurteilt: 1958', in *Lebenslänglich: Protokolle aus der Haft*, ed. Klaus Antes, Christiane Ehrhardt and Heinrich Hannover (Munich, 1972), pp. 114–41 (p. 121).
16 Czenki, 'Ein Tag von eintausendfünfhundert: Bericht aus einem Frauengefängnis', in *Eingesperrt: Innenaussichten aus dem Gefängnis: Ein Lesebuch*, ed. Helmut Ortner (Frankfurt am Main, 1984), pp. 59–70 (pp. 59 and 65); and Anon., 'man muß das system fressen', in *Laßt mich leben: Frauen im Knast*, ed. Luise Rinser (Hagen, 1987), p. 78.
17 Anon., 'Wir bestimmen, was Kultur ist. Am Beispiel Tegel', in *Ungehörte Worte*, ed. Koch and Lindtke, pp. 82–8 (p. 86).
18 Michel Foucault, *Überwachen und Strafen. Die Geburt des Gefängnisses* (Frankfurt am Main, 1976).
19 Uschi Keutsch, 'Operation: Gehirneingriff', in *Schrei Deine Worte*, ed. Barwasser, p. 57. All reasonable attempts were made to contact the copyright holder.
20 Holger Meins, 'Bericht zur Zwangsernährung, Wittlich 11. Oktober 1974'. Reprinted (in German) on the Social History Portal, www.socialhistoryportal.org, accessed 9 August 2021.

21 Letter from Holger Meins to Manfred Grashof, published in *Der Spiegel*, XLVII (1974), p. 30; and Anon. [Karlheinz Barwasser], 'Sich als starke Mauern begreifen – Schreiben im Knast', in *Ungehörte Worte,* ed. Koch and Lindtke, pp. 107–11 (p. 108).
22 Buchacker, letter to Ingeborg Drewitz, in Drewitz and Buchacker, *Mit Sätzen Mauern eindrücken*, p. 148.
23 Christian Schneider, 'Omnipotente Opfer: Die Geburt der Gewalt aus dem Geist des Widerstands', in *Die RAF und der linke Terrorismus*, ed. Wolfgang Kraushaar (Hamburg, 2006), vol. II, pp. 1328–42 (p. 1341).
24 Herzog, *Nicht den Hunger verlieren*, p. 37.
25 Dieter Bock, 'Eingefahren', in *Alltag hinter Gittern*, ed. Gefangenenzeitung U-Bahn (Darmstadt, 1980), pp. 21–4 (p. 22); and Buchacker, letter to Ingeborg Drewitz, in Drewitz and Buchacker, *Mit Sätzen Mauern eindrücken*, p. 17.
26 Günter Machura, 'Endstation für Träumer', in *So wächst die Mauer*, ed. Drewitz and Tammen, pp. 115–19 (p. 118).
27 Peter-Jürgen Boock, letter to Peter Schneider, in Peter-Jürgen Boock and Peter Schneider, *Ratte – tot . . . Ein Briefwechsel* (Darmstadt, 1985), p. 102.
28 'Nötigung mit Gewalt'. See also Gisela Notz, 'Klara Maria Fassbinder (1890–1974) und die Westdeutsche Frauenfriedensbewegung (WFFB)', in *Frauen und Frieden? Zuschreibungen – Kämpfe – Verhinderungen*, ed. Franziska Dunkel and Corinna Schneider (Opladen, 2015), pp. 87–103 (pp. 94–5).
29 Rinser's reputation was shifted dramatically by a biography published in 2011, which claimed that she had falsified her own history under the Nazis. See José Sánchez de Murillo, *Luise Rinser: Ein Leben in Widersprüchen* (Frankfurt am Main, 2011).
30 'Jeanne d'Arc der Friedensbewegung'. See Malte Herwig, 'Luise Rinser: Ein Mensch eigener Art', *Deutschlandfunk Kultur*, www.deutschlandfunkkultur.de, 4 September 2011.
31 It grew from a prison newspaper, the *Cuckoo's Egg – Das Kuckucksei* – from Schwerte prison. Padligur would also publish the first of the Ingeborg Drewitz Prize anthologies in 1989, and a number of volumes on prisoner writing and prison issues, before the publishing house folded in the changing climate of the 1990s.
32 Jutta von Ochsenstein, 'Liebe Familie', in *Laßt mich leben*, ed. Rinser, pp. 26–33 (p. 30); and Andrea Pfeiffer, 'Erfahrungsbericht', ibid., p. 34.
33 Kathrin Rodi, 'Die Entmündigung', in *Laßt mich leben*, ed. Rinser, p. 80; and Maria Braig, 'Tagebuchaufzeichnung', ibid., pp. 35–6 (p. 35).
34 Jutta von Ochsenstein, 'Liebe Familie', in *Laßt mich leben*, ed. Rinser, pp. 26–33 (pp. 32 and 27).
35 Braig, 'Tagebuchaufzeichnung', in *Laßt mich leben*, ed. Rinser, p. 35; Rodi, 'Die Entmündigung', ibid., p. 80; and Ochsenstein, 'Tagebuchaufzeichnung', ibid., p. 79.

6 'How do you bear it?'

1 Ludwig Lugmeier, 'verlust', in *Themenheft: Literatur aus dem Knast*, ed. Haberfeld/Die Palette, *Die Palette*, III (1987), p. 54. When he kindly gave permission for the use of his poem, Ludwig Lugmeier (in an email to the author) remembered another story – the grey snails that inspired him to write it, which were crawling in front of the prison laundry, the room where the anti-Nazi activist Sophie Scholl was beheaded.
2 Monika Sperr, 'Big Sister sieht alles: Eindrücke im Aichacher Frauengefängnis', in *So wächst die Mauer zwischen Mensch und Mensch: Stimmen aus dem Knast und zum Strafvollzug*, ed. Ingeborg Drewitz and Johann P. Tammen (Bremerhaven, 1980), pp. 77–82 (p. 77).
3 Anon., 'Leserbrief', in *Ungehörte Worte: Gefangene schreiben: Eine Dokumentation aus deutschen Gefangenenzeitungen*, ed. Helmut H. Koch and Regine Lindtke (Münster, 1982), pp. 56–7.
4 Anon., 'Trennungen', ibid., p. 53.
5 Anon., 'Liebe hinter Gittern', ibid.; and Alex, in *Alltag hinter Gittern*, ed. Gefangenenzeitung U-Bahn (Darmstadt, 1980), p. 43.
6 Anon., 'Leserbrief', in *Ungehörte Worte*, ed. Koch and Lindtke, pp. 56–7 (p. 57).
7 See 'Strafvollzug/Intimitäten: Wie im Hotel', in *Der Spiegel*, VII (1970), available online at www.spiegel.de, accessed 9 August 2021.
8 Boock, letter to Peter Schneider, in Peter-Jürgen Boock and Peter Schneider, *Ratte – tot . . . Ein Briefwechsel* (Darmstadt, 1985), p. 120; and Boock, 'Es ist viel schlimmer, die Fähigkeit zu lieben zu verlieren, als eingesperrt zu sein!', in *Menschen im Gefängnis: Literarische Selbstzeugnisse, authentische Texte und Materialien für den schulischen und außerschulischen Unterricht*, ed. Nicola Keßler, Uta Klein, Helmut H. Koch and Elisabeth Theine (Bonn, 1996), pp. 49–50.
9 Anon., 'Sex im Knast', in *Ungehörte Worte*, ed. Koch and Lindtke, pp. 47–8 (p. 47); and Harry Graf, 'Aus meinem Gefängnistagebuch', in *So wächst die Mauer zwischen Mensch und Mensch: Stimmen aus dem Knast und zum Strafvollzug*, ed. Ingeborg Drewitz and Johann P. Tammen (Bremerhaven, 1980), pp. 31–3 (p. 31).
10 Detlef Kruklinski, 'Fleisch', in *Themenheft: Literatur aus dem Knast*, ed. Haberfeld/Die Palette, *Die Palette*, III (1987), pp. 39–45 (pp. 40–41).
11 Gaby Krücken, 'kann nicht ewig alles hochziehen', in *Laßt mich leben: Frauen im Knast*, ed. Luise Rinser (Hagen, 1987), p. 120. All reasonable attempts were made to contact the copyright holder.
12 See Gertrud Hardtmann, 'Straftäter müßte man sein', in *Frauen im Gefängnis*, ed. Marlis Dürkop and Gertrud Hardtmann (Frankfurt am Main, 1978), p. 167; and Helga Einsele and Hanna Dupuis, 'Die Mutter-Kind-Situation im Frauengefängnis', ibid., pp. 58–66 (pp. 58–9).
13 Irene Dreier, 'Meine Gedanken', in *Laßt mich leben*, ed. Rinser, p. 114. All reasonable attempts were made to contact the copyright holder.
14 monika h., 'Tatsachenbericht', in *Laßt mich leben*, ed. Rinser, pp. 45–50 (pp. 48–9).

15 Winand Buchacker, 'der wandel', in *So wächst die Mauer*, ed. Drewitz and Tammen (Fachverlag NW in Carl Ed. Schünemann KG), pp. 112–13. Cited with kind permission of Monika Thiele, Schünemann Verlag.
16 Jürgen Callberg, 'Alter: 35 Verurteilt: 1958', in *Lebenslänglich: Protokolle aus der Haft*, ed. Klaus Antes, Christiane Ehrhardt, and Heinrich Hannover (Munich, 1972), pp. 114–41 (pp. 117–18).
17 Anon., 'Der Homosexuelle ist ein Mensch', in *Ungehörte Worte*, ed. Koch and Lindtke, pp. 60–61 (p. 60); and Marc Wiltzius, 'Offen schwul im Knast', in *Schrei Deine Worte nicht in den Wind: Verständigungstexte von Inhaftierten*, ed. Karlheinz A. Barwasser (Tübingen, 1982), pp. 155–9 (pp. 156–7).
18 Peter-Jürgen Boock, 'Es ist viel schlimmer, die Fähigkeit zu lieben zu verlieren, als eingesperrt zu sein!', in *Menschen im Gefängnis*, ed. Keßler, Klein and Koch, pp. 49–50.
19 Klaus D. Mahn, 'Esmeralda', in *So wächst die Mauer*, ed. Drewitz and Tammen, pp. 101–11 (p. 111).
20 Winand Buchacker, 'verdammte schweinerei, sagte der schließer', in *Schatten im Kalk. Lyrik und Prosa aus dem Knast*, ed. Ingeborg Drewitz (Stuttgart, 1979), pp. 16–18 (p. 18). All reasonable efforts were made to contact the copyright holder.
21 Buchacker, letter to Ingeborg Drewitz, in Ingeborg Drewitz and Winand Buchacker, *Mit Sätzen Mauern eindrücken: Briefwechsel mit einem Strafgefangenen* (Düsseldorf, 1979), p. 12. Unlike Drewitz, Birgitta Wolf knew about swallowing and had mentioned it in 1967 among the dangers facing prisoners in isolation. See Birgitta Wolf, 'Der Strafgefangene: Gefahren seiner Isolierung', in *Strafvollzug in Deutschland: Situation und Reform*, ed. Dietrich Rollmann (Frankfurt am Main, 1967), pp. 160–70 (p. 161).
22 Peter Feraru, 'Die Gruft', in *Schrei Deine Worte*, ed. Barwasser, pp. 35–40 (p. 36).
23 Winand Buchacker, 'die schlucker', in *Schatten im Kalk*, ed. Drewitz, p. 21. All reasonable attempts were made to contact the copyright holder.
24 Werner Schlegel, 'Requiem für Werner D. gest. 13.2.1976 ca. 2 Uhr', in *So wächst die Mauer*, ed. Drewitz and Tammen, p. 131. Cited with kind permission of Monika Thiele, Schünemann Verlag.
25 Anon., 'Für Lothar S', in *Ungehörte Worte*, ed. Koch and Lindtke, p. 62.
26 R. H., 'Zellennachbar', in *Anklage erhoben: Gedichte und Grafiken von Strafgefangenen*, ed. Birgitta Wolf (Gelnhausen, 1972), p. 44. All reasonable attempts were made to contact the copyright holder.
27 Heinrich Behr, 'Alter: 32. Verurteilt: 1964', in *Lebenslänglich: Protokolle aus der Haft*, ed. Klaus Antes, Christiane Ehrhardt and Heinrich Hannover (Munich, 1972), pp. 13–41 (p. 41).
28 Johan Galtung, 'Violence, Peace, and Peace Research', *Journal of Peace Research*, VI (1969), pp. 167–91 (p. 175). See also Craig Haney, Curtis Banks and Philip Zimbardo, 'Interpersonal Dynamics in a Simulated Prison', *International Journal of Criminology and Penology*, I (1973), pp. 69–97.

29 Harry Graf, 'Ausgestiegen', in *So wächst die Mauer*, ed. Drewitz and Tammen, pp. 138–9.
30 Horst Rakow, 'Strafantrag', in *'Selbst'-Mord in U-Haft: Briefe und Dokumente*, ed. Arbeitsgemeinschaft Sozialpolitischer Arbeitskreise (Berlin, 1976), pp. 7–14. Emphasis in original.
31 Uta Klein and Helmut Koch, 'Nur Lesen reicht nicht', in *Themenheft: Literatur aus dem Knast*, ed. Haberfeld/Die Palette, *Die Palette*, III (1987), pp. 62–4 (p. 62).
32 Strafgefanger T, Strafgefangener V and Strafgefangener Y, 'Sexuelle Gewalt', in *Ungehörte Worte*, ed. Koch and Lindtke, pp. 50–52 (p. 50); and Jochen Quentmaier, 'Vergewaltigung – Betriebsunfall im Strafvollzug?', letter to Helmut Koch of 28 July 1997, in *Mit der Flaschenpost gegen einen Ozean: Briefe aus dem Knast,* ed. Helmut Koch (Münster, 1998), p. 122.
33 Peter-Paul Zahl, 'Der große Reso-Schwindel', in *Schrei Deine Worte*, ed. Barwasser, pp. 64–7 (p. 64); Koch, 'Vorwort', in *Ungehörte Worte*, ed. Koch and Lindtke, pp. 7–8 (p. 7); and Martin Walser, 'Sich schreibend behaupten', in *Wenn Wände erzählen könnten*, ed. Ingeborg-Drewitz-Literaturpreis (Münster, 1999), pp. 9–11 (p. 10).

RISEN FROM THE RUINS: EAST GERMANY, 1949–89

1 Cited in Falco Werkentin, *Politische Strafjustiz in der Ära Ulbricht* (Berlin, 1995), p. 381.
2 Horst Fichter, 'Lebendig begraben', in *Gefangen in Hohenschönhausen: Stasi-Häftlinge berichten*, ed. Hubertus Knabe (Berlin, 2007), pp. 154–63 (p. 162).

7 Bearing Witness

1 Composed by Hanns Eisler with lyrics by Johannes R. Becher. English translation cited after Wikipedia.
2 Erika Riemann (with Claudia Hoffmann), *Die Schleife an Stalins Bart: ein Mädchenstreich, acht Jahre Haft und die Zeit danach* [2002] (Hamburg, 2017).
3 Wolfgang H. A. Löffler, in *Das gelbe Elend: Bautzen-Häftlinge berichten 1945–1956*, ed. Bautzen-Komitee (Halle, 1992), pp. 212–16 (p. 213). See also Marion Sonnenmoser, 'Traumatisierung politischer Gefangener in der DDR: Schweres Erbe', *Deutsches Ärzteblatt*, VIII (2009), p. 406; and Riemann, *Die Schleife*, pp. 40–41 and p. 73.
4 See Klára Pinerová, 'Vergleich der Strafvollzugsysteme in der Tschechoslowakei und der DDR in den 1950er Jahren', in *Die ČSSR und die DDR im historischen Vergleich. Gemeinsamkeiten und Unterschiede zweier staatssozialistischer Systeme in Mitteleuropa*, ed. Miloš Řezník and Katja Rosenbaum (Leipzig and Berlin, 2014); and Jörg Müller, 'Das Haftsystem der SBZ/DDR von 1945 bis zur Mitte der 1970er Jahre unter besonderer Berücksichtigung der Haftbedingungen politischer

Häftlinge', see www.bundesstiftung-aufarbeitung.de, accessed 9 August 2021.

5 Greg Eghigian, *The Corrigible and the Incorrigible: Science, Medicine and the Convict in Twentieth-Century Germany* (Ann Arbor, MI, 2015), pp. 59 and 62. See also Leonore Ansorg, *Politische Häftlinge im Strafvollzug der DDR: Die Strafvollzugsanstalt Brandenburg* (Berlin, 2005), pp. 32–3.

6 *Im Namen des Volkes? Über die Justiz im Staat der SED*, ed. Bundesministerium der Justiz (Leipzig, 1994), p. 61.

7 Erich Loest, *Durch die Erde ein Riß: Ein Lebenslauf* (Hamburg, 1981), p. 404.

8 Ibid., pp. 363 and 384, pp. 360–61.

9 See Tobias Wunschik, 'Politischer Strafvollzug und Haftanstalten in der DDR', in *Orte des Erinnerns: Gedenkzeichen, Gedenkstätten und Museen zur Diktatur in SBZ und DDR*, ed. Annette Kaminsky (Berlin, 2007), pp. 517–21 (p. 520). See also *Im Namen des Volkes?*, ed. Bundesministerium der Justiz, p. 211.

10 Cited in Falco Werkentin, *Politische Strafjustiz in der Ära Ulbricht* (Berlin, 1995), p. 381.

11 Petra Koch, *Menschenwege: Politisch inhaftiert auf Burg Hoheneck: Eine wahre Geschichte* (Berlin, 2002), pp. 16 and 140.

12 §99 StVG. See Birgit Schlicke, *Knast-Tagebuch: Erinnerung einer politischen Gefangenen an Stasi-Haft und das Frauenzuchthaus Hoheneck* (Wiesbaden, 2001), p. 98.

13 *Beschluß des Staatsrates der DDR über die weitere Entwicklung der Rechtspflege vom 30. Januar 1961*. Cited in Heinz Szkibik, *Sozialistischer Strafvollzug* (Berlin, 1969). With thanks to Nick Courtman for the reference.

14 Szkibik, *Sozialistischer Strafvollzug*, p. 10.

15 *Strafvollzugs- und Wiedereingliederungsgesetz (SVWG) vom 12. Januar 1968*. See www.verfassungen.de/ddr/strafgesetzbuch74.htm, accessed 9 August 2021.

16 Riemann, *Die Schleife*, p. 128; and Mario Mann, in *'Ich kam mir vor wie'n Tier' – Knast in der DDR*, ed. Torsten Heyme and Felix Schumann (Berlin, 1991), pp. 134–44 (p. 137).

17 'Besserungswillige' and 'Besserungsunwillige'. Thomas Ziegler, 'Der Strafvollzug in der DDR'. See www.justiz.sachsen.de, accessed 9 August 2021; Kim Richmond, 'Negotiating "Femininity" in the GDR Prison Narrative: Discourses of Character Development and Incorrigibility in Elisabeth Graul's *Die Farce* (1991)', *German Life and Letters*, LXIII (2010), pp. 345–53; and Greg Eghigian, *The Corrigible and the Incorrigible*.

18 Renate Werwigk-Schneider, 'Man behandelte mich wie eine Verbrecherin, ich war auf einer Stufe mit Kriminellen. Das war für mich die größte Strafe', in *Der dunkle Ort: 25 Schicksale aus dem DDR-Frauengefängnis Hoheneck*, ed. Dirk von Nayhauß and Maggie Riepl (Berlin-Brandenburg, 2012), pp. 54–5.

19 Koch, *Menschenwege*, p. 57.

20 Werwigk-Schneider, 'Man behandelte mich wie eine Verbrecherin',

in *Der dunkle Ort*, ed. Nayhauß and Riepl, pp. 54–5. Until 1977 a price per prisoner was calculated based on factors that included their educational level. Later there was a set rate, which rose to around 96,000 DM. See Katja Iken, 'Häftlingsdeals mit der DDR – Menschen gegen Maisladungen: 40.000 D-Mark für die Freiheit', *Spiegel Online*, www.spiegel.de, 24 October 2011; and Ludwig A. Rehlinger, *Freikauf. Die Geschäfte der DDR mit politisch Verfolgten* (Frankfurt, 1991).

21 Koch, *Menschenwege*, p. 58.

22 Elke Lehmann, 'Entlassungstermin in die DDR', in *Hohenecker Protokolle: Aussagen zur Geschichte der politischen Verfolgung von Frauen in der DDR*, ed. Ulrich Schacht, 2nd edn (Leipzig, 2009), pp. 137–51 (p. 147).

23 André Baganz, *Endstation Bautzen II: Zehn Jahre lebenslänglich* (Halle, 2011), p. 72; Schlicke, *Knast-Tagebuch*, p. 67.

24 Birgitta Wolf, 'Einführung', in *Die vierte Kaste. Junge Menschen im Gefängnis*, ed. Birgitta Wolf (Hamburg, 1963), pp. 7–53 (p. 10).

25 Ulrich Schacht, 'Hoheneck. Nachdenken über ein Stichwort: Vorwort zur Erstausgabe', in *Hohenecker Protokolle*, ed. Schacht, p. 43.

26 Wendelgard Trampota, 'Russische zehn Minuten', in *Hohenecker Protokolle*, ed. Schacht, pp. 80–98 (pp. 84–7).

27 Jutta Giersch, 'Wir hungern noch, wir hungern noch', in *Hohenecker Protokolle*, ed. Schacht, pp. 45–67 (pp. 45 and 53); and Anita Goßler, 'Meine Tochter hat mir nie geglaubt, dass ich unschuldig in Hoheneck war', in *Der dunkle Ort*, ed. Nayhauß and Riepl, pp. 38–41 (pp. 40–41).

28 Monika Schneider, 'Das Schlimmste war für mich die Ungewißheit, was mit meinen Kindern passiert ist', in *Der dunkle Ort*, ed. Nayhauß and Riepl, pp. 102–3 (p. 102); and Freya Klier, 'Tagebuch einer Haft', in *Gefangen in Hohenschönhausen: Stasi-Häftlinge berichten*, ed. Hubertus Knabe (Berlin, 2007), pp. 334–47 (p. 343).

29 See 'Die Kinder fest verwurzeln', *Der Spiegel* LII (1975). Reprinted www.spiegel.de, accessed 9 July 2021.

30 Gunhild Gerth, 'Angst vor soviel Macht', in *Hohenecker Protokolle*, ed. Schacht, pp. 118–36 (p. 135); and Koch, *Menschenwege*, pp. 144.

31 Matthias Bath, *Gefangen und freigetauscht: 1197 Tage als Fluchthelfer in DDR-Haft* (Munich, 1981), p. 12. Bath was a member of the centre-right youth organization Junge Union, and also part of the post-war New Right. The designation 'middle Germany' (*Mitteldeutschland*) for the GDR is a clear rejection of its status as an independent state, even though the SPD Chancellor Willy Brandt had formally recognized that status in 1972. The book was reissued by a Berlin publisher, Jaron, in 2007.

32 Bath, *Gefangen und freigetauscht*, p. 72.

33 Ibid., p. 17.

34 Baganz, *Endstation Bautzen II*, p. 108.

35 The abolition of the death penalty in the GDR was timed to coincide with Honecker's first state visit to the FRG. See *Im Namen des Volkes?*, ed. Bundesministerium der Justiz, p. 217. See also Roland Garve, *Unter Mördern: Gefängnisalltag in der DDR* [1999] (Berlin, 2014), pp. 212–13.

36 André Baganz, *Lebenslänglich Bautzen II: Als Farbiger in der DDR* (Berlin, 1993). All references are to the later edition, *Endstation Bautzen II*.
37 Baganz, *Endstation Bautzen II*, pp. 62, 119, 57, 261.
38 Ibid., p. 99.
39 Bath, *Gefangen und freigetauscht*, p. 97.
40 Garve, *Unter Mördern*, pp. 22–6; 'die reinste Mördergrube'; see also Koch, *Menschenwege*, p. 86; and Schlicke, *Knast-Tagebuch*, p. 96.
41 Garve, *Unter Mördern*, pp. 132–3, 233 and 45.
42 Günter Grau, 'The Policy of the SED and the Laws Against Homosexuality in Eastern Germany between 1946 and 1968', *Journal of Homosexuality*, XXXVII (2008), pp. 1–21 (p. 2).
43 Carola Schacht, 'Ich wurde während des Prozesses fast nur angeschrien', in *Hohenecker Protokolle*, ed. Schacht, pp. 152–91 (p. 168); Regina Ebert, 'Beim Anblick der Burg bekam ich Angst', in *Hohenecker Protokolle*, ed. Schacht, pp. 192–204 (p. 200); and Schlicke, *Knast-Tagebuch*, pp. 99 and 140.
44 Grau, 'The Policy of the SED and the Laws Against Homosexuality', p. 2.
45 Garve, *Unter Mördern*, p. 127.
46 Mann, in *'Ich kam mir vor wie'n Tier'*, ed. Heyme and Schumann, p. 143; Garve, *Unter Mördern*, pp. 184–5; and Mann, in *'Ich kam mir vor wie'n Tier'*, ed. Heyme and Schumann, p. 143.
47 *Unabhängige Untersuchungskommission gegen Amtsmißbrauch und Korruption*. See Torsten Heyme, 'Einleitung', in *'Ich kam mir vor wie'n Tier'*, ed. Heyme and Schumann, p. 11
48 Wunschik, 'Politischer Strafvollzug und Haftanstalten in der DDR', p. 520.
49 Steffen Seidel, in *'Ich kam mir vor wie'n Tier'*, ed. Heyme and Schumann, pp. 67–115 (pp. 86–7).
50 Lucie Fischer, 'Wir wurden alle immer nur erniedrigt, belogen und beleidigt', in *Der dunkle Ort*, ed. Nayhauß and Riepl, pp. 36–7 (p. 37); Ute Steinhäuser, 'Die Haft war traumatisch, und ich habe viele Jahre gebraucht, bis ich über diese Zeit reden konnte', in *Der dunkle Ort*, ed. Nayhauß and Riepl, pp. 84–5; and Baganz, *Endstation Bautzen II*, p. 166.
51 Nora Strejilevich, 'Testimony: Beyond the Language of Truth', *Human Rights Quarterly*, XXVIII (2006), pp. 701–13 (p. 702).
52 Mann, in *'Ich kam mir vor wie'n Tier'*, ed. Heyme and Schumann, pp. 137–9.
53 Schlicke, *Knast-Tagebuch*, p. 2.
54 Ibid., p. 67; Koch, *Menschenwege*, pp. 30 and 23 (emphasis in original); and Bath, *Gefangen und freigetauscht*, p. 7.
55 Schlicke, *Knast-Tagebuch*, p. 2.

8 Stasi Stories

1 Hubertus Knabe, 'Einführung', in *Gefangen in Hohenschönhausen: Stasi-Häftlinge berichten*, ed. Hubertus Knabe (Berlin, 2007), p. 15.

2 Carola Schacht, 'Ich wurde während des Prozesses fast nur angeschrien', in *Hohenecker Protokolle: Aussagen zur Geschichte der politischen Verfolgung von Frauen in der DDR*, ed. Ulrich Schacht, 2nd edn (Leipzig, 2009), pp. 152–91 (p. 155); Jutta Giersch, 'Wir hungern noch, wir hungern noch', ibid., pp. 45–67 (p. 66); and Matthias Bath, *Gefangen und freigetauscht: 1197 Tage als Fluchthelfer in DDR-Haft* (Munich, 1981), p. 44.
3 Knabe, 'Einführung', in *Gefangen in Hohenschönhausen*, ed. Knabe, p. 13.
4 Kurt Müller, 'Der geplante Schauprozeß', in *Gefangen in Hohenschönhausen*, ed. Knabe, pp. 101–29 (p. 103); and Walter Janka, *Spuren eines Lebens* [1991] (Reinbek bei Hamburg, 1992), p. 322.
5 Fritz Sperling, 'Opfere dich für die Partei!' in *Gefangen in Hohenschönhausen*, ed. Knabe, pp. 147–53 (pp. 149–50).
6 Horst Fichter, 'Lebendig begraben', in *Gefangen in Hohenschönhausen*, ed. Knabe, pp. 154–63 (p. 163); and Roland Garve, *Unter Mördern: Gefängnisalltag in der DDR* [1999] (Berlin, 2014), p. 32.
7 Elke Lehmann, 'Entlassungstermin in die DDR', in *Hohenecker Protokolle*, ed. Ulrich Schacht, pp. 137–51 (pp. 141–2).
8 Janka, *Spuren eines Lebens*, pp. 329–30.
9 Mario Mann, in *'Ich kam mir vor wie'n Tier' – Knast in der DDR*, ed. Torsten Heyme and Felix Schumann (Berlin, 1991), pp. 134–44 (pp. 137–8); and Brigitte Ballnow, '1974 war das schlimmste Jahr', in *Der dunkle Ort: 25 Schicksale aus dem DDR-Frauengefängnis Hoheneck*, ed. Dirk von Nayhauß and Maggie Riepl (Berlin-Brandenburg, 2012), pp. 58–61 (p. 60).
10 See, for example, Gerth, 'Angst vor soviel Macht', in *Hohenecker Protokolle*, ed. Ulrich Schacht, pp. 118–36 (p. 119).
11 Petra Koch, *Menschenwege: Politisch inhaftiert auf Burg Hoheneck: Eine wahre Geschichte* (Berlin, 2002), p. 92; Anne Niendorf, 'Für den Westen ohne Einnäher', in *Hohenecker Protokolle*, ed. Ulrich Schacht, pp. 99–117 (p. 106); Catharina Mäge, 'Was mich am meisten erschreckte, waren die Gesichter der Gefangenen', in *Der dunkle Ort*, ed. Nayhauß and Riepl, pp. 76–7 (p. 76).
12 Koch, *Menschenwege*, p. 86
13 Helgard Krumm, 'Es ist nicht erlaubt, Ihre Eltern zu umarmen', in *Hohenecker Protokolle*, ed. Schacht, pp. 205–28 (p. 215); and Birgit Schlicke, *Knast-Tagebuch: Erinnerung einer politischen Gefangenen an Stasi-Haft und das Frauenzuchthaus Hoheneck* (Wiesbaden, 2001), p. 188.
14 Trampota, 'Russische zehn Minuten', in *Hohenecker Protokolle*, ed. Ulrich Schacht, p. 83.
15 Bettina Gilek, 'Amnestie als Auslegungssache', in *Hohenecker Protokolle*, ed. Ulrich Schacht, pp. 229–44 (p. 238); Renate Werwigk-Schneider, 'Man behandelte mich wie eine Verbrecherin, ich war auf einer Stufe mit Kriminellen', in *Der dunkle Ort*, ed. Nayhauss and Riepl, pp. 54–5 (p. 54).
16 Gerth, 'Angst vor soviel Macht', *Hohenecker Protokolle*, ed. Ulrich

Schacht, pp. 121, 126 and 123; Niendorf, 'Für den Westen', in *Hohenecker Protokolle*, ed. Schacht, pp. 108 and 112–15.
17 Lehman, 'Entlassungstermin in die DDR', ibid., p. 150; and Schlicke, *Knast-Tagebuch*, p. 140.
18 Niendorf, 'Für den Westen ohne Einnäher', in *Hohenecker Protokolle*, ed. Schacht, p. 107; Werwigk-Schneider, 'Man behandelte mich wie eine Verbrecherin', in *Der dunkle Ort*, ed. Nayhauß and Riepl, p. 54; Gerth, 'Angst vor soviel Macht', in *Hohenecker Protokolle*, ed. Schacht, p. 123.
19 Gerth, 'Angst vor soviel Macht', in *Hohenecker Protokolle*, ed. Schacht, pp. 123–7.
20 Carola Schacht, 'Ich wurde während des Prozesses fast nur angeschrien', in *Hohenecker Protokolle*, ed. Schacht, p. 188.
21 Ariel Dorfman, *Some Write to the Future: Essays on Contemporary Latin American Fiction* (Durham, NC, 1991), p. 137.
22 Schlicke, *Knast-Tagebuch*, p. 108.
23 Koch, *Menschenwege*, p. 130; and Gerth, 'Angst vor soviel Macht', in *Hohenecker Protokolle*, ed. Schacht, p. 125.
24 Niendorf, 'Für den Westen', in *Hohenecker Protokolle*, ed. Schacht, pp. 112–15; Giersch, 'Wir hungern noch', ibid., p. 56; and Erika Riemann (with Claudia Hoffmann), *Die Schleife an Stalins Bart: ein Mädchenstreich, acht Jahre Haft und die Zeit danach* [2002] (Hamburg, 2017), p. 128.
25 Garve, *Unter Mördern*, p. 80.
26 Seidel, 'Steffen Seidel', in *'Ich kam mir vor wie'n Tier' – Knast in der DDR*, ed. Torsten Heyme and Felix Schumann (Berlin, 1991), pp. 67–115 (p. 85). See also Torsten Heyme, 'Knast in der DDR – eine Bestandsaufnahme', ibid., pp. 12–24 (p. 13).
27 Theatre-makers in the GDR regularly created subversive performances that managed to evade censorship. See Laura Bradley, *Cooperation and Conflict: GDR Theatre Censorship, 1961–1989* (Oxford, 2010).
28 Alexandra Dust-Wiese, 'O Gott, waren wir begeistert, daß Stalin tot war', in *Hohenecker Protokolle*, ed. Ulrich Schacht, pp. 68–79 (p. 75).
29 Mäge, 'Was mich am meisten erschreckte', in *Der dunkle Ort*, ed. Nayhauß and Riepl, p. 76.
30 Trampota, 'Russische zehn Minuten', in *Hohenecker Protokolle*, ed. Ulrich Schacht, p. 87.
31 Anneliese Gabel, 'Wir waren eine Gemeinschaft, in der eine für die andere da war', in *Der dunkle Ort*, ed. Nayhauß and Riepl, pp. 32–3 (p. 32); Carola Schacht, 'Ich wurde während des Prozesses fast nur angeschrien', in *Hohenecker Protokolle*, ed. Ulrich Schacht, p. 190; Trampota, 'Russische zehn Minuten', ibid., p. 91.
32 Giersch, 'Wir hungern noch', in *Hohenecker Protokolle*, ed. Schacht, pp. 57–8 and 63; and Koch, *Menschenwege*, p. 142.
33 Erica Wallach, 'Ein Grab voller Erinnerungen', in *Gefangen in Hohenschönhausen*, ed. Knabe, pp. 130–46 (pp. 137–9). The extract is from her autobiography, *Licht um Mitternacht* (Munich, 1969).
34 Dust-Wiese, 'O Gott, waren wir begeistert', in *Hohenecker Protokolle*, ed. Schacht, p. 71; and Koch, *Menschenwege*, p. 96.

35 André Baganz, *Endstation Bautzen II: zehn Jahre lebenslänglich* (Halle, 2011), p. 177; and Erich Loest, *Durch die Erde ein Riß: Ein Lebenslauf* (Hamburg, 1981), p. 394.
36 Loest, *Durch die Erde*, p. 393.
37 Roland Garve, *Unter Mördern: Gefängnisalltag in der DDR* [1999] (Berlin, 2014), pp. 129 and 213.
38 Ulrich Mählert, *Kleine Geschichte der DDR* [1998] (Munich, 2001), p. 29.
39 Dust-Wiese, 'O Gott, waren wir begeistert', in *Hohenecker Protokolle*, ed. Ulrich Schacht, pp. 76–7. See also Mählert, *Kleine Geschichte der DDR*, p. 76.
40 Giersch, 'Wir hungern noch', in *Hohenecker Protokolle*, ed. Ulrich Schacht, p. 65. See also Jorg Müller, *Strafvollzugspolitik und Haftregime in der SBZ und in der DDR: Der sächsische Raum in der Ära Ulbricht* (Göttingen, 2012), p. 191.
41 Riemann, *Die Schleife*, p. 149.
42 Garve, *Unter Mördern*, pp. 9 and 133–5.
43 Ibid., p. 238.
44 Riemann, *Die Schleife*, p. 66.
45 Baganz, *Endstation Bautzen II*, pp. 128–32.

9 The Big Prison

1 Birgit Schlicke, *Knast-Tagebuch: Erinnerung einer politischen Gefangenen an Stasi-Haft und das Frauenzuchthaus Hoheneck* (Wiesbaden, 2001), p. 215
2 Karl Heinz Lange, in *'Ich kam mir vor wie'n Tier' – Knast in der DDR*, ed. Torsten Heyme and Felix Schumann (Berlin, 1991), pp. 186–209 (p. 190).
3 Schlicke, *Knast-Tagebuch*, p. 51.
4 Hans-Eberhard Zahn, 'Das Spitzelnetz', in *Gefangen in Hohenschönhausen: Stasi-Häftlinge berichten*, ed. Hubertus Knabe (Berlin, 2007), pp. 192–203 (pp. 196 and 194); and Petra Koch, *Menschenwege: Politisch inhaftiert auf Burg Hoheneck: Eine wahre Geschichte* (Berlin, 2002), p. 110.
5 'Zwei Frauen in Hoheneck', in *'Ich kam mir vor wie'n Tier'*, ed. Heyme and Schumann, pp. 124–6; and Anne Niendorf, 'Für den Westen ohne Einnäher', in *Hohenecker Protokolle: Aussagen zur Geschichte der politischen Verfolgung von Frauen in der DDR*, ed. Ulrich Schacht, 2nd edn (Leipzig, 2009), pp. 99–117 (p. 113).
6 Prisoner A, cited in Heyme, 'Gespräch mit Gefangenen in Bautzen I', in *'Ich kam mir vor wie'n Tier'*, ed. Heyme and Schumann, p. 36; Mario Mann, ibid., p. 137; and Robert Goldstein, ibid., pp. 148–59 (p. 148).
7 Robert Goldstein, in *'Ich kam mir vor wie'n Tier'*, ed. Heyme and Schumann, pp. 148–59 (pp. 148 and 150); and Axel Wiesner, ibid., pp. 210–21 (p. 210)
8 Steffen Seidel, in *'Ich kam mir vor wie'n Tier'*, ed. Heyme and Schumann, pp. 68–71 and p. 75.
9 Steffi Weiß, in *'Ich kam mir vor wie'n Tier'*, ed. Heyme and Schumann, pp. 160–61 (p. 161).

10 Seidel, in *'Ich kam mir vor wie'n Tier'*, ed. Heyme and Schumann, pp. 81–2; and Mann, ibid., p. 139.
11 Seidel, in *'Ich kam mir vor wie'n Tier'*, ed. Heyme and Schumann, p. 85.
12 Prisoner B, cited in Heyme, 'Gespräch mit Gefangenen in Bautzen I', in *'Ich kam mir vor wie'n Tier'*, ed. Heyme and Schumann, pp. 34–45 (p. 37).
13 Mann, in *'Ich kam mir vor wie'n Tier'*, ed. Heyme and Schumann, p. 141. See also Greg Eghigian, *The Corrigible and the Incorrigible: Science, Medicine and the Convict in Twentieth-Century Germany* (Ann Arbor, MI, 2015), p. 68.
14 Anke and Doren, cited in 'Zwei Frauen in Hoheneck', in *'Ich kam mir vor wie'n Tier'*, ed. Heyme and Schumann, pp. 127–9; Sylvia Stark, ibid., pp. 182–5.
15 Doren, cited in 'Zwei Frauen in Hoheneck', in *'Ich kam mir vor wie'n Tier'*, ed. Heyme and Schumann, p. 129.
16 See Edward Schramm, *Ehe und Familie im Strafrecht: Eine strafrechtsdogmatische Untersuchung* (Tübingen, 2011), p. 76.
17 See Roland Garve, *Unter Mördern: Gefängnisalltag in der DDR* [1999] (Berlin, 2014), p. 81; Niendorf, 'Für den Westen', in *Hohenecker Protokolle*, ed. Ulrich Schacht, p. 110; Gerth, 'Angst vor soviel Macht', ibid., pp. 118–36 (p. 121); Erich Loest, *Durch die Erde ein Riß: Ein Lebenslauf* (Hamburg, 1981), p. 384; Doren, cited in 'Zwei Frauen in Hoheneck', in *'Ich kam mir vor wie'n Tier'*, ed. Heyme and Schumann, p. 125.
18 Schlicke, *Knast-Tagebuch*, pp. 172 and 174; Doren, cited in 'Zwei Frauen in Hoheneck', in *'Ich kam mir vor wie'n Tier'*, ed. Heyme and Schumann, p. 125.
19 *Wachtmeister, Leutnant, Hauptmann, Major, Oberst.* See Thomas Ziegler, 'Der Strafvollzug in der DDR', www.justiz.sachsen.de, p. 2.
20 Gerth, 'Angst vor soviel Macht', in *Hohenecker Protokolle*, ed. Ulrich Schacht, pp. 126–7.
21 Erika Riemann (with Claudia Hoffmann), *Die Schleife an Stalins Bart: Ein Mädchenstreich, acht Jahre Haft und die Zeit danach* [2002] (Hamburg, 2017), pp. 127 and 157.
22 Trampota, 'Russische zehn Minuten', in *Hohenecker Protokolle*, ed. Ulrich Schacht, p. 90; Bettina Gilek, 'Amnestie als Auslegungssache', ibid., pp. 229–44 (p. 231).
23 Anke, cited in 'Zwei Frauen in Hoheneck', in *'Ich kam mir vor wie'n Tier'*, ed. Heyme and Schumann, p. 130.
24 Schlicke, *Knast-Tagebuch*, p. 156 (ellipsis in original); Bath, *Gefangen und freigetauscht*, p. 129.
25 Sperling, 'Opfere dich für die Partei!', in *Gefangen in Hohenschönhausen*, ed. Knabe, p. 151.
26 Garve, *Unter Mördern*, pp. 32 and 72.
27 Ibid., pp. 98–9.
28 See Chapter Eleven.
29 Garve, *Unter Mördern*, p. 122.
30 Sigrid Paul, 'Mauer durchs Herz', in *Gefangen in Hohenschönhausen*, ed. Knabe, pp. 236–47 (p. 244).

31 Bath, *Gefangen und freigetauscht*, pp. 101 and 108–9.

32 Ellen Thiemann, 'Eine besondere Schikane waren die Körperrazzien und die nächtlichen Feueralarmübungen', in *Der dunkle Ort: 25 Schicksale aus dem DDR-Frauengefängnis Hoheneck*, ed. Dirk von Nayhauß and Maggie Riepl (Berlin-Brandenburg, 2012), pp. 64–5 (p. 64).

33 Waltraud Krüger, 'Im Haftkrankenhaus' in *Gefangen in Hohenschönhausen*, ed. Knabe, pp. 303–17 (pp. 304–5). See also Tobias Wunschik, 'Politischer Strafvollzug und Haftanstalten in der DDR', in *Orte des Erinnerns: Gedenkzeichen, Gedenkstätten und Museen zur Diktatur in SBZ und DDR*, ed. Annette Kaminsky (Berlin, 2007), pp. 517–21 (p. 519); and Jörg Arnold, 'Einige normative Aspekte der Entwicklung des StGB der DDR', in *Das Strafgesetzbuch: 130 Jahre Strafgesetzgebung – eine Bilanz*, ed. Thomas Vormbaum and Jürgen Welp (Berlin, 2004), pp. 423–55 (p. 437).

34 'Standard Minimum Rules for the Treatment of Prisoners Adopted by the First United Nations Congress on the Prevention of Crime and the Treatment of Offenders, held at Geneva in 1955, and approved by the Economic and Social Council by Its Resolutions 663 C (XXIV) of 31 July 1957 and 2076 (LXII) of 13 May 1977', 28 (1).

35 Loest, *Durch die Erde*, p. 405.

36 Steffen Seidel, in *'Ich kam mir vor wie'n Tier'*, ed. Heyme and Schumann, p. 85. See also Ronny Heidenreich, *Aufruhr hinter Gittern: Das 'Gelbe Elend' im Herbst 1989* (Leipzig, 2009), p. 46.

37 *Ordner, Brigadiere, Schichtleiter*; see Garve, *Unter Mördern*, pp. 85–6 and 60.

38 See Ulrich Schacht, 'Hoheneck: Nachdenken über ein Stichwort: Vorwort zur Erstausgabe', in *Hohenecker Protokolle*, ed. Schacht, p. 42; and Schlicke, *Knast-Tagebuch*, p. 171.

39 Zahn, 'Das Spitzelnetz', in *Gefangen in Hohenschönhausen*, ed. Knabe, p. 203; Alexandra Dust-Wiese, 'O Gott, waren wir begeistert, daß Stalin tot war', in *Hohenecker Protokolle*, ed. Schacht, pp. 68–79 (p. 79). See also Ulrich Schacht, 'Hoheneck: Nachdenken über ein Stichwort: Vorwort zur Erstausgabe', in *Hohenecker Protokolle*, ed. Schacht, p. 40.

40 Niendorf, 'Für den Westen ohne Einnäher', pp. 113–14; Schlicke, *Knast-Tagebuch*, p. 109; ibid., pp. 143–4, 204 and 229.

41 Schlicke, *Knast-Tagebuch*, p. 108.

42 Fischer, 'Wir wurden alle immer nur erniedrigt', in *Der dunkle Ort*, ed. Nayhauß and Riepl, p. 36; Koch, *Menschenwege*, p. 26; Gilek, 'Amnestie als Auslegungssache', in *Hohenecker Protokolle*, ed. Schacht, p. 232; Schlicke, *Knast-Tagebuch*, p. 225.

43 André Baganz, *Endstation Bautzen II: Zehn Jahre lebenslänglich* (Halle, 2011), p. 140; Garve, *Unter Mördern*, p. 137; Mann, in *'Ich kam mir vor wie'n Tier'*, ed. Heyme and Schumann, p. 139; Seidel, ibid., p. 115; Schlicke, *Knast-Tagebuch*, p. 232.

44 Silke Klewin and Klaus-Dieter Müller, 'Vorwort', in Heidenreich, *Aufruhr hinter Gittern*, p. 7.

45 Baganz, *Endstation Bautzen II*, pp. 303–4. See also Arnold, 'Einige

normative Aspekte', pp. 446–7; and Heidenreich, *Aufruhr hinter Gittern*, pp. 85 and 130.
46 Klewin and Müller, 'Vorwort', p. 7. Klewin works for the Bautzen memorial site and Müller for the Foundation for Saxony's Memorial Sites (Stiftung Sächsische Gedenkstätten). See also Pierre Nora, 'Between Memory and History: Les Lieux de Mémoire', *Representations*, XXVI (1989), pp. 7–24.
47 *Das gelbe Elend: Bautzen-Häftlinge berichten 1945–1956*, ed. Bautzen-Komitee (Halle, 1992). See also www.bautzen-komitee.de, accessed 9 August 2021.

WIND OF CHANGE: GERMANY AFTER 1989

1 Sonja John, 'Überwachen und Verschlafen', *Der Lichtblick*, CCCLXIII (2015), pp. 40–41 (p. 41).

10 Wind of Change or *Plus ça Change*?

1 Christian Vinke, 'Die Gewalt Fabrik', letter in *Der Lichtblick*, CCCLXVII (2016), p. 38.
2 *Der Spiegel*, XXV (1990), available at www.spiegel.de, accessed 5 August 2021.
3 Inge Viett, *Einsprüche: Briefe aus dem Gefängnis* (Hamburg, 1996), p. 14.
4 Ibid., pp. 19–20.
5 Ibid., pp. 63 and 67.
6 Ibid., pp. 10 and 14–15.
7 Ibid., p. 11.
8 Ibid., p. 25.
9 Around two-thirds did apply, and around half of those were successful. See Erhard Blankenburg, 'Changes in Political Regimes and Continuity of the Rule of Law in Germany', in Herbert Jacob et al., *Courts, Law, and Politics in Comparative Perspective* (New Haven, CT, 1996), pp. 249–314 (p. 275).
10 Anton Karge, 'Maßregelvollzug' (letter of 6 September 1996), in *Mit der Flaschenpost gegen einen Ozean: Briefe aus dem Knast*, ed. Helmut Koch (Münster, 1998), pp. 100–102 (pp. 100–101); and Markus Finke, 'Arrest', in *Mit der Flaschenpost*, ed. Koch, pp. 82–4 (p. 83).
11 Manuel Matzke, cited in Moritz Geier, 'Sexuelle Gewalt in Gefängnissen: "Keiner kontrolliert, was in den Zellen geschieht"', *Süddeutsche Zeitung*, www.sueddeutsche.de, 25 June 2020.
12 Robert P. Weiss, 'Humanitarianism, Labour Exploitation, or Social Control? A Critical Survey of Theory and Research on the Origin and Development of Prisons', *Social History*, XII (1987), pp. 331–50 (p. 335).
13 Gruppe Respekt, 'Der Schlimmste', in *Geräusche der Nacht: Literatur aus dem deutschen Strafvollzug*, ed. Ingeborg-Drewitz-Literaturpreis (Münster, 2008), pp. 79–80 (p. 79); Mario Steiner, '23 Stunden in der Zelle sind nicht gut!', *Der Lichtblick*, CCCLXIII (2015), pp. 26–7 (p. 26); and see *Der Lichtblick*, CCCLXXII (2017), p. 33.

14 Corinna, 'Schuldig?', in *Ich muss zurück ins Rattenloch: Unerhörte Geschichten aus dem Frauenknast*, ed. Reimund Neufeld and Helmut Koch (Oberhausen, 2010), pp. 181–91 (p. 190); Rainer, 'Verurteilt wegen Totschlags', in *Knast: Eine Dokumentation*, ed. Brigitte and Dieter Kübbeler (Oldenburg, 2003), pp. 174–8 (p. 175); Katharina, 'Man geht mit dem, womit man angefangen hat', in *Ich muss zurück ins Rattenloch*, ed. Neufeld and Koch, p. 116; and Sigrun, 'Intimität', ibid., pp. 206–9 (p. 207).

15 See Nationale Stelle zur Verhütung von Folter, *Jahresbericht 2020* (Wiesbaden, 2020), pp. 16 and 84.

16 E. S., in *Anklage erhoben: Gedichte und Grafiken von Strafgefangenen*, ed. Birgitta Wolf (Gelnhausen, 1972), p. 130.

17 Dirk Glebe, *Handbuch Knast und Strafvollzug: (Über-)leben im deutschen Gefängnis*, 2nd edn (Norderstedt, 2011), p. 15; and Hubertus Becker, *Ritual Knast: Die Niederlage des Gefängnisses – eine Bestandsaufnahme* (Leipzig, 2008), pp. 65–6.

18 Becker, *Ritual Knast*, pp. 65–6.

19 Gresham M. Sykes, *The Society of Captives: A Study of a Maximum Security Prison* [1958] (Princeton, NJ, 2007), p. 69; and see the poem 'Verniemandung' in Peter-Paul Zahl, *Alle Türen offen: Gedichte* (Berlin, 1977), pp. 9–15.

20 Peter Fritze, 'Rein in die Kiste . . . Die ersten Tage hinter Gittern', in *Eingesperrt: Innenaussichten aus dem Gefängnis: Ein Lesebuch*, ed. Helmut Ortner (Frankfurt am Main, 1984), pp. 33–42 (p. 37); and Anon., 'Der Kreislauf', in *Gemeinsam einsam*, ed. Ingeborg-Drewitz-Literaturpreis (Münster, 2015), pp. 36–41 (p. 40).

21 Rosemarie Müller, 'Was ist hier los?', in *Wenn Wände erzählen könnten*, ed. Ingeborg-Drewitz-Literaturpreis (Münster, 1999), pp. 115–20 (pp. 115–16).

22 Anon., 'Leserbrief aus Moabit', *Der Lichtblick*, CCCLXXXVI (2021), pp. 36–7 (p. 37).

23 U. K., 'gestern – heute – morgen', in *Schatten im Kalk. Lyrik und Prosa aus dem Knast*, ed. Ingeborg Drewitz (Stuttgart, 1979), pp. 111–13 (p. 112); Becker, *Ritual Knast*, p. 65.

24 Katharina, 'Man geht mit dem, womit man angefangen hat', in *Ich muss zurück ins Rattenloch*, ed. Neufeld and Koch, p. 114.

25 §18 StVG. In 2003 it was half of all prisoners, but in 2016 that had sunk to around 26 per cent. See Kirstin Drenkhahn, 'Entwicklung und Prognose der Gefangenenpopulation und ihrer Merkmale', in *Das Gefängnis auf dem Prüfstand: Zustand und Zukunft des Strafvollzugs*, ed. Bernd Maelicke and Stefan Suhling (Wiesbaden, 2018), pp. 51–72 (p. 63). See also National Stelle zur Verhütung von Folter, *Jahresbericht 2020*, p. 83.

26 Katharina, 'Man geht mit dem, womit man angefangen hat', in *Ich muss zurück ins Rattenloch*, ed. Neufeld and Koch, pp. 114 and 119.

27 Karina, 'Ich muss zurück ins Rattenloch', in *Ich muss zurück ins Rattenloch*, ed. Neufeld and Koch, pp. 37–64 (p. 59). Here, as in other areas, conditions vary from prison to prison.

28 Dieter Wurm, 'Knast macht krank - Gesundheitsschädliche Folgen des

Knasts und miserable Krankenfürsorge im humanen Strafvollzug in Deutschland, oder wie aus einstigen Tätern Opfer werden. Ein subjektiver Bericht', *Der Lichtblick*, CCCLII (2012), reprinted www.schattenblick.de, accessed 10 August 2021.

29 Marco Lobito, 'Warum man einen Menschen so quälen darf', in *Mit der Flaschenpost gegen einen Ozean*, ed. Koch, pp. 64–7 (p. 64–5).

30 Naim Kilig, 'Bin folterähnlich behandelt worden', in *Mit der Flaschenpost*, ed. Koch, pp. 69–72 (p. 72).

31 Anton, 'Das bin ich', in *Junge Gefangene – Wir sagen aus (Band 4): Biographische Geschichten, Gedichte und Rap-Songs von jungen Gewalttätern und Gefangenen*, ed. Reinhard Nolle and Maria Bauer (Kassel, 2008), pp. 9–11.

32 Hassan, 'Verurteilt wegen Diebstahls', in *Knast*, ed. Kübbeler and Kübbeler, pp. 169–73 (p. 173); and Metin Günes, 'Schreibend sterben', in *Wenn Wände erzählen könnten*, ed. Ingeborg-Drewitz-Literaturpreis, pp. 49–53 (p. 50).

33 Emphasis in original, document found on the *Arbeitskreis kritischer Strafvollzug* webpages in September 2018; the website has since been discontinued.

34 Christian Vinke, 'Die Gewalt Fabrik', letter in *Der Lichtblick*, CCCLXVII (2016), p. 38; letter from 27 prisoners in Berlin Tegel (10 February 2012), document found on the *Arbeitskreis kritischer Strafvollzug* webpages in September 2018; the website has since been discontinued.

35 See *Wege durch den Knast*, ed. Redaktionskollektiv, p. 141.

36 Carolyn Rowe and Ed Turner, 'Justice and Prisons Policy', in *Die Politik der Bundesländer: Zwischen Föderalismusreform und Schuldenbremse*, ed. Achim Hildebrandt and Frieder Wolf, 2nd expanded edn (Wiesbaden, 2016), pp. 87–114 (pp. 89–95; p. 111 et passim).

37 See Frank Arloth and Tobias Geiger, 'Der deutsche Strafvollzug nach der Föderalismusreform', in *Das Gefängnis auf dem Prüfstand: Zustand und Zukunft des Strafvollzugs*, ed. Bernd Maelicke and Stefan Suhling (Wiesbaden, 2018), pp. 73–88 (pp. 74–5).

38 The city-state of Hamburg emphasized the equivalence of the two principles. See Rowe and Turner, 'Justice and Prisons Policy', in *Die Politik der Bundesländer*, ed. Hildebrandt and Wolf, p. 95.

39 Friedrich Peters, *Alles auf blau: Knasttagebuch* (Leipzig, 2014), p. 104.

40 Closed institutions varied widely: one of those in the study had a victim rate of 5.2 per cent while in another it was 34.8 per cent. See Dirk Baier and Marie Christine Bergmann, 'Gewalt im Strafvollzug – Ergebnisse einer Befragung in fünf Bundesländern', *Forum Strafvollzug: Zeitschrift für Strafvollzug und Straffälligenhilfe*, LXII/2 (2013), pp. 81–2. Also Sylvette Hinz and Sven Hartenstein, 'Jugendgewalt im Strafvollzug. Eine retrospektive Untersuchung im Sächsischen Jugendstrafvollzug', *Zeitschrift für Jugendkriminalrecht und Jugendhilfe*, XXI (2010), pp. 176–82.

41 Rowe and Turner, 'Justice and Prisons Policy', in *Die Politik der Bundesländer*, ed. Hildebrandt and Wolf, pp. 100–104; Jürgen Reissig,

'Ist die Gerechtigkeit eine Frage der Geografie geworden?', *Der Lichtblick*, CCCLXXIII (2017), pp. 16–17.

42 Ulf G. Stuberger, *Die ausgeschlossenen Eingeschlossenen: Straffälligkeit und Strafvollzug* [1974], 4th edn (Stuttgart, 2014), p. 5; Katharina, 'Man geht mit dem, womit man angefangen hat, mit einer Lüge', in *Ich muss zurück ins Rattenloch*, ed. Neufeld and Koch, pp. 113–27 (p. 113).

43 Reinhard Neufeld, 'Einleitung', in *Ich muss zurück ins Rattenloch*, ed. Neufeld and Koch, pp. 11–12 (p. 11); Reimund Neufeld, 'Vorwort', in *16 Bars Project: Unterdrückte graue Schatten*, ed. Reimund Neufeld, Claudia Franck and Julia Schönstadt (Oberhausen, 2016), pp. 6–7 (p. 6).

44 In a letter from Heiko Bondieck to the *Arbeitkreis kritischer Strafvollzug* (24 February 2012), document found on the *Arbeitskreis kritischer Strafvollzug* webpages in September 2018; the website has since been discontinued.

45 Other online newspapers include *Janus* from Freiburg prison, *Inside* from Rheinbach, *Tr§tzdem* from Oldenburg and *HaftLeben* from the women's prison in Chemnitz. Prisoners themselves have only very limited and controlled access to the Internet, for specific tasks such as accessing courses at Germany's distance-learning university, Hagen.

46 Dirk Glebe, *Handbuch Knast und Strafvollzug: (Über-)leben im deutschen Gefängnis*, 2nd edn (Norderstedt, 2011); Peters, *Alles auf Blau*.

47 Unrast-Kollektiv, 'Vorwort', in *Freiheit gestreift. Texte gegen den Knast: Überwachen – Strafen – Widerstand*, ed. Unrast-Kollektiv, Anares Nord (Münster, 1995), pp. 7–8.

48 Frank R. Niemeyer, 'Knastrevolte in Santa Fu: Bericht über den Aufstand in der Justizvollzugsanstalt Hamburg-Fühlsbüttel von 28. bis 30. Mai 1990, sowie über die Vorgeschichte und die Folgen', in *Freiheit gestreift*, ed. Unrast-Kollektiv, pp. 35–132 (pp. 55, 67, 69, 82–3, 86).

49 Ibid., pp. 44–5.

50 Anon., 'Eine Krankenhausgeschichte', *Der Lichtblick*, CCCLXXII (2017), p. 17.

51 Wurm, 'Knast macht krank', in *Der Lichtblick*, CCCLII (2012), available online at www.schattenblick.de, accessed 10 August 2021.

52 Hubertus Gärtner, 'Neue Vorwürfe nach Häftlingstod in Herford', *Lippische Landes-Zeitung*, www.lz.de, 18 October 2014.

53 Verena Mayer, 'Tod in der Gefängniszelle: Das Rätsel von Bruchsal', *Stuttgarter Zeitung*, www.stuttgarter-zeitung.de, 16 September 2014; see also 'Karlsruhe Hungertod von Häftling: Verfahren gegen Ärztin eingestellt', www.ka-news.de, 18 July 2017.

54 Wurm, 'Knast macht krank', in *Der Lichtblick*, CCCLII (2012), available online at www.schattenblick.de, accessed 10 August 2021.

55 Christine Graebsch, cited in Torben Becker, Aiko Kempen, Sarah Ulrich, 'In deutschen Gefängnissen fehlt es an Geld, Personal und Medikamenten – mit teils dramatischen Folgen für die Häftlinge', *TAZ*, www.taz.de, 4 August 2020.

56 Niemeyer, 'Knastrevolte in Santa Fu', in *Freiheit gestreift*, ed. Unrast-Kollektiv, p. 45; and an anonymous letter, *Der Lichtblick*, CCCLXXI

(2017), p. 29. See also *Wege durch den Knast*, ed. Redaktionskollektiv, p. 395.
57 Letter, *Der Lichtblick*, CCCLXXI (2017), p. 29.
58 'Berichte von Gefangenen aus Plötzensee über die Corona Pandemie', www.criminalsforfreedom.noblogs.org (published 19 March 2020).
59 'Knast Tegel, Zustände durch Corona Pandemie', www.criminalsforfreedom.noblogs.org (published 26 March 2020); Manuel Matzke, cited in Döbber, 'Corona im Knast', *Focus*, www.focus.de, 13 October 2020; and Marvin D., 'Corona-Zeiten im offenen Vollzug der Berufsförderungsstätte Bochum-Langendreer und im geschlossenen Vollzug der JVA Bochum-Krümmede und der JVA Aachen', see https://ggbo.de (published 18 June 2020).
60 Matzke, cited in Döbber, 'Corona im Knast'.
61 Matzke, cited in Ina Hildebrandt, 'Berliner Gefängnisse: Wie Inhaftierte unter der Corona-Krise leiden', *Tip Berlin*, www.tip-berlin.de, 20 April 2020.
62 Kirstin Drenkhahn, 'Entwicklung und Prognose der Gefangenenpopulation und ihrer Merkmale', in *Das Gefängnis auf dem Prüfstand: Zustand und Zukunft des Strafvollzugs*, ed. Bernd Maelicke and Stefan Suhling (Wiesbaden, 2018), pp. 51–72 (p. 62). See also Uschi Götz, 'Haftanstalten – Hoffnungslos überfüllt', *Deutschlandfunk-Magazin*, www.deutschlandfunk.de, 3 January 2019.
63 'Knast Tegel, Zustände durch Corona Pandemie'; and Luisa Houben, 'Justizvollzug – Wie Corona das Leben im Gefängnis verändert', *ZDF*, www.zdf.de, 19 April 2020.
64 'Knast Tegel, Zustände durch Corona Pandemie'.
65 'Erste Corona-News aus Bützow', www.criminalsforfreedom.noblogs.org (published 20 March 2020).
66 Christine Schwenke, 'Gedanken, Gefühle und Ängste zur Corona-Krise', www.criminalsforfreedom.noblogs.org (published 7 April 2020).
67 Marvin D., 'Corona-Zeiten im offenen Vollzug der Berufsförderungsstätte Bochum-Langendreer und im geschlossenen Vollzug der JVA Bochum-Krümmede und der JVA Aachen.
68 Matzke, cited in Hildebrandt, 'Berliner Gefängnisse', *Tip Berlin* (20 April 2020).
69 Christian Döbber, 'Corona im Knast', *Focus*, www.focus.de, 13 October 2020; 'Alarm aus dem Knast! Corona-Ausbruch in der Außenstelle Boke der JVA Bielefeld', see https://ggbo.de (published 23 February 2021).
70 'Bayerische Tugenden in Corona-Zeiten', *Der Lichtblick*, CCCLXXXVI (2021), pp. 38–9.
71 'Das Corona – Debakel im Dezember 2020!' *Der Lichtblick*, CCCLXXXVI (2021), pp. 4–7 (p. 5).
72 Moritz Börner and Lena Kampf, 'Pandemie könnte Resozialisierung gefährden', *Tagesschau*, 6 May 2021.
73 'Bayerische Tugenden in Corona-Zeiten', *Der Lichtblick*, CCCLXXXVI (2021), pp. 38–9; Hildebrandt, 'Berliner Gefängnisse', *Tip Berlin*, 20 April 2020.
74 With thanks to Johannes Feest for confirming that this corresponds

to information he received following inquiries with all of the state ministries of justice.

75 Julian Jestadt, 'Mehr Suizide in Gefängnissen', *TAZ*, www.taz.de, 20 July 2021.

76 Börner and Kampf, 'Pandemie könnte Resozialisierung gefährden', *Tagesschau*, www.tagesschau.de, 6 May 2021.

77 Becker, Kempen and Ulrich, 'In deutschen Gefängnissen fehlt es an Geld, Personal und Medikamenten', *TAZ*, 4 August 2020. See also the press release of the state of Baden-Württemberg, 'Expertenkommission übergibt Medizinkonzept für Justizvollzug'.

11 Death in Siegburg and Other Stories

1 Rainer, in *Knast: Eine Dokumentation*, ed. Brigitte and Dieter Kübbeler (Oldenburg, 2003), p. 174–8 (p. 176).

2 *Wege durch den Knast*, ed. Redaktionskollektiv (Berlin, 2016), p. 97; Reiner, 'Nicht hinter der Mauer verrecken', in *Freiheit gestreift – Texte gegen den Knast: Überwachen, Strafen, Widerstand*, ed. Unrast-Kollektiv (Münster, 1995), pp. 142–3.

3 Anon., 'Un-frei und furcht-bar: Ein Essay', *Der Lichtblick*, CCCLIV (2013), available online at www.schattenblick.de, accessed 10 August 2021.

4 Karina, 'Ich muss zurück ins Rattenloch', in *Ich muß zurück ins Rattenloch: Unerhörte Geschichten aus dem Frauenknast*, ed. Reimund Neufeld and Helmut Koch (Oberhausen, 2010), p. 41; Katharina, 'Man geht mit dem, womit man angefangen hat, mit einer Lüge', ibid., pp. 113–27 (p. 117).

5 R. S., 'Wem ein Lächeln fehlt, dem fehlt ein Flügel', in *Geräusche der Nacht: Literatur aus dem deutschen Strafvollzug*, ed. Ingeborg-Drewitz-Literaturpreis (Münster, 2008), pp. 89–94 (p. 94); and Harald A. Dreßler, '*betr.: alltagsrealität im knast*', in *Risse im Fegefeuer*, ed. Ingeborg-Drewitz-Literaturpreis (Hagen, 1989), pp. 63–5 (p. 65).

6 Jan Reisner, 'meiner zelle gegenüber', in *Wenn Wände erzählen könnten*, ed. Ingeborg-Drewitz-Literaturpreis (Münster, 1999), p. 121.

7 Dieter Wurm, 'Der Hänger', in *Wenn Wände erzählen könnten*, ed. Ingeborg-Drewitz-Literaturpreis, p. 166. Cited with kind permission of Agenda Verlag.

8 Frank R. Niemeyer, 'Knastrevolte in Santa Fu: Bericht über den Aufstand in der Justizvollzugsanstalt Hamburg-Fühlsbüttel von 28. bis 30. Mai 1990, sowie über die Vorgeschichte und die Folgen', in *Freiheit gestreift*, ed. Unrast-Kollektiv, p. 48.

9 D. Radeloff et al., 'National Total Survey of German Adolescent Suicide in Prison', *European Child and Adolescent Psychiatry*, XXIV (2015), pp. 219–25 (pp. 223–4); Annette Opitz-Welke et al., 'Prison Suicides in Germany from 2000 to 2011', *International Journal of Law and Psychiatry*, XXXVI (2013), pp. 386–9 (p. 386). See also the statistics cited in the German government's draft response to a parliamentary question: 'Antwort der Bundesregierung auf die Kleine Anfrage der Abgeordneten Ulla Jelpke, Dr. André Hahn, Göray Akbulut, weiterer Abgeordneter und der Fraktion DIE LINKE', dserver.bundestag.de, 9 July 2021.

10 Stefan Adler, 'Drei Mal Drei', in *Begegnungen in der Welt des Widersinns*, ed. Ingeborg-Drewitz-Literaturpreis (Zell, 2018), pp. 159–72 (p. 163). See also *Der Lichtblick*, CCCLXXII (2017), p. 33; and letter, *Der Lichtblick*, CCCLXXI (2017), p. 29.
11 See the German government's draft response to a parliamentary question: 'Antwort der Bundesregierung auf die Kleine Anfrage der Abgeordneten Ulla Jelpke, Dr. André Hahn, Göray Akbulut, weiterer Abgeordneter und der Fraktion DIE LINKE', and Gregor Mayntz, 'Zahl der Ausländer in Gefängnissen auf Rekordhoch', *Rheinische Post*, www.rp-online.de, 4 February 2019.
12 Philipp Khabo Koepsell, 'Defending Dessau', in *Die Akte James Knopf: Afrodeutsche Wort- und Streitkunst* (Münster, 2010), p. 53. Orthography in original. Cited with kind permission of Philipp Khabo Koepsell and Unrast Verlag.
13 Ben Knight, 'New Evidence Contradicts German Police in Oury Jalloh Death', *Deutsche Welle*, www.dw.com, 16 November 2017; Elliot Douglas, 'Germany: New Accusations of Police Violence in Death of Asylum-Seeker', *Deutsche Welle*, www.dw.com, 11 November 2019.
14 Lena Wiese, cited on the webpage www.initiativeamad.blackblogs.org, accessed 8 August 2021.
15 See the Basic Rights Report for 2021: *Grundrechte-Report 2021*, ed. Benjamin Derin et al. (Frankfurt am Main, 2021), n. p.
16 See the Death in Custody website, doku.deathincustody.info
17 German prisoner in 2015, cited in Becker, 'In der Schattenwelt der Gefängnisse', document on the *Arbeitskreis kritischer Strafvollzug* webpages in September 2018; the website has since been discontinued.
18 Becker, 'In der Schattenwelt der Gefängnisse'.
19 Thomas Baumann-Hartwig, '"Kanaken wechselten die Straßenseite": Dresdner JVA-Beamter schickte Nazi-Botschaften per WhatsApp an Kollegen', *Leipziger Volkszeitung*, www.lvz.de, 2 April 2019; see also Göran Schattauer, 'JVA Dresden: Justizbeamte feiern in Chat Gewalt gegen ausländische Häftlinge', *Focus*, www.focus.de, 31 March 2021; and Rebecca Stange, cited ibid.
20 Timo Stukenberg, 'Rechte Netzwerke im Justizvollzug', *Deutschlandfunk*, www.deutschlandfunk.de, 10 September 2020.
21 Anon., 'Wir bestimmen, was Kultur ist. Am Beispiel Tegel', in *Ungehörte Worte. Gefangene schreiben: Eine Dokumentation*, ed. Helmut H. Koch and Regine Lindtke (Münster, 1982), pp. 82–8 (p. 84). See also Niemeyer, 'Knastrevolte in Santa Fu', in *Freiheit gestreift*, ed. Unrast-Kollektiv, p. 93.
22 Herm Klingstedt, 'Das Schloß am Ende der Straße', in *Wenn Wände erzählen könnten*, ed. Ingeborg-Drewitz-Literaturpreis, pp. 88–90 (pp. 88–9).
23 Ralf Axel Simon, 'moral ist der arglistige versuch der herrschenden . . .', in *Geräusche der Nacht*, ed. Ingeborg-Drewitz-Literaturpreis, pp. 95–110 (p. 101).
24 Harald A. Dreßler, '*betr.: alltagsrealität im knast*', in *Risse im Fegefeuer*, ed. Ingeborg-Drewitz-Literaturpreis (Hagen, 1989), pp. 63–5 (p. 65). Italics in original.

25 See Dirk Baier and Marie Christine Bergmann, 'Gewalt im Strafvollzug', *Forum Strafvollzug*, LXII/2 (2013), p. 81.
26 Jumbo, 'So geht's mit Pädophilen in der JVA', in *16 Bars Project: Unterdrückte graue Schatten*, ed. Reimund Neufeld, Claudia Franck and Julia Schönstadt (Oberhausen, 2016), pp. 26–9 (p. 26).
27 See 'Folter im Knast: Die schlimmsten Fälle', *Spiegel Online*, www.spiegel.de, 18 November 2006; 'Jugendgefängnis in Hameln: Häftlinge sollen Mitgefangenen misshandelt haben', *Spiegel Online*, www.spiegel.de, 13 November 2012; and Paula Trautmann, 'Gewalt hinter Gittern. In Bernau ist es in zwei Jahren hintereinander zu tödlichen Gewalttaten gekommen', *Süddeutsche Zeitung*, www.sueddeutsche.de, 23 November 2020.
28 Rainer, in *Knast*, ed. Kübbeler and Kübbeler, pp. 174–8 (p. 176); Dietmar, ibid., pp. 192–8 (p. 196). See also Baier and Bergmann, 'Gewalt im Strafvollzug', p. 81.
29 Tom, '1 Jahr', in *16 Bars Project*, ed. Neufeld, Franck and Schönstadt, pp. 52–60 (p. 55); Katharina, 'Man geht mit dem, womit man angefangen hat', in *Ich muss zurück ins Rattenloch,* ed. Neufeld and Koch, p. 122.
30 Dirk Glebe, *Handbuch Knast und Strafvollzug: (Über-)leben im deutschen Gefängnis*, 2nd edn (Norderstedt, 2011), p. 111; Martin, in *Knast*, ed. Kübbeler and Kübbeler, pp. 15–25 (p. 19); and Katharina, 'Man geht mit dem, womit man angefangen hat', in *Ich muss zurück ins Rattenloch*, ed. Neufeld and Koch, p. 125.
31 See *Wege durch den Knast*, ed. Redaktionskollektiv, p. 81–2; Bilal and Christian, in *Pop Shop*, ed. Jünschke, Hauenstein and Ensslin, pp. 141–2.
32 Ralf Wegner, '"Für Emotionen ist es nie zu spät!" Ein schwuler Gefangener zum Umgang mit Gefühlen hinter Gittern', in *Gemeinsam Einsam*, ed. Ingeborg-Drewitz-Literaturpreis, (Münster, 2015), pp. 151–2 (p. 151).
33 Michelle, 'Tagebuch einer Chaosqueen', in *Ich muss zurück ins Rattenloch*, ed. Neufeld and Koch, pp. 73–6 (p. 73).
34 Ibid., pp. 75–6.
35 Fred, in *Pop Shop: Gespräche mit Jugendlichen in Haft*, ed. Klaus Jünschke, Jörg Hauenstein and Christiane Ensslin (Hamburg, 2007), p. 122; Oliver K., Berlin, cited in *Tr§tzdem: Gefangenenzeitung der JVA Oldenburg*, 52 (December 2015), p. 59.
36 Manuel Matzke, cited in Moritz Geier, 'Sexuelle Gewalt in Gefängnissen: "Keiner kontrolliert, was in den Zellen geschieht"', *Süddeutsche Zeitung*, www.sueddeutsche.de, 25 June 2020.
37 Karin Steinberger, 'Gewalt im Jugendgefängnis', *Süddeutsche Zeitung*, www.sueddeutsche.de, 19 May 2010; Martin Kotynek, Stephan Lebert and Daniel Müller, 'Die Schlechterungsanstalt', *Zeit Online*, www.zeit.de, 16 August 2012, p. 5; see also 'Mord hinter Gittern', *Spiegel Online*, www.spiegel.de, 15 November 2006.
38 See *Bild*, www.bild.de, 4 October 2007; and Malte Arnsperger, 'BGH urteilt zu Gefängnis-Foltermord', *Stern*, www.stern.de, 13 August 2008.
39 Klaus Jünschke, 'Tod in Siegburg. Schlagzeilen – aber über die Ursachen wird öffentlich nicht diskutiert', *Neue Rheinische Zeitung Online Flyer*, 71, www.nrhz.de, 21 November 2006.

40 Gruppe Respekt, 'Eine Oma', in *Geräusche der Nacht*, ed. Ingeborg-Drewitz-Literaturpreis, p. 83.
41 Angela and Sandra, 'Kranke Gedanken, kranke Träume', in *Ich muss zurück ins Rattenloch*, ed. Neufeld and Koch, pp. 209–20.

12 The Desocialization Machine – Remixed

1 Dieter Wurm, 'Knast macht krank – Gesundheitsschädliche Folgen des Knasts und miserable Krankenfürsorge im humanen Strafvollzug in Deutschland, oder wie aus einstigen Tätern Opfer werden. Ein subjektiver Bericht', *Der Lichtblick*, CCCLII (2012), available online at www.schattenblick.de, accessed 5 August 2021.
2 Stefanie, in *Knast: Eine Dokumentation*, ed. Brigitte and Dieter Kübbeler (Oldenburg, 2003), pp. 97–103 (p. 98).
3 Sabine Bomeier, 'Frauen im Knast', *Der Lichtblick*, CCCLXIV (2015), pp. 32–3 (p. 33). See also Maren Michels, 'Straffällig gewordenene Frauen', in *Das Gefängnis auf dem Prüfstand: Zustand und Zukunft des Strafvollzugs*, ed. Bernd Maelicke and Stefan Suhling (Wiesbaden, 2018), pp. 381–401 (p. 387).
4 Sonja, 'Besser im Knast als bei meinem Mann', in *Die schlimmsten Gitter sitzen innen: Geschichten aus dem Frauenknast*, ed. Katrin Panier (Berlin, 2004), pp. 80–92 (pp. 92 and 90).
5 Marta, 'Kannst Du Dich noch erinnern?', in *Ich muss zurück ins Rattenloch: Unerhörte Geschichten aus dem Frauenknast*, ed. Reimund Neufeld and Helmut Koch (Oberhausen, 2010), pp. 13–15.
6 Manuela, 'Es begann, als ich 7 Jahre alt war', in *Ich muss zurück ins Rattenloch*, ed. Neufeld and Koch, pp. 144–6 (pp. 144–5).
7 Jürgen, in *Knast*, ed. Kübbeler and Kübbeler, pp. 25–34 (p. 32).
8 Martin, ibid., p. 15; Ralph, ibid., pp. 117–25 (pp. 117 and 120).
9 Christian Vinke, 'Die Gewalt Fabrik', letter, *Der Lichtblick*, CCCLXVII (2016), p. 38.
10 Walter, in *Knast*, ed. Kübbeler and Kübbeler, p. 158. See also the stories of Aneta ('dass ich hier nicht hingehöre'); and Beatrix ('aus gutem Hause'), in *Ich muss zurück ins Rattenloch*, ed. Neufeld and Koch, pp. 99 and 169.
11 The exact figure for respondents who had suffered parental violence was 46.7 per cent. See Dirk Baier and Marie Christine Bergmann, 'Gewalt im Strafvollzug – Ergebnisse einer Befragung in fünf Bundesländern', *Forum Strafvollzug: Zeitschrift für Strafvollzug und Straffälligenhilfe*, LXII/2 (2013), pp. 76–83 (p. 81).
12 Anon., 'Arthur', in *Knastgeflüster: Gereimtes und Ungereimtes aus dem Gefängnis*, ed. Uwe Quedens, Martin Hagenmaier and Dieter Boßmann (Sierksdorf, 1999), pp. 55–9 (p. 57).
13 Kenny Berger, 'Kalter Rauch', in *Wenn Wände erzählen könnten*, ed. Ingeborg-Drewitz-Literaturpreis (Münster, 1999), pp. 21–8 (p. 22); Berger, 'Mein Leben und ich – behind the sun', in *Begegnungen in der Welt des Widersinns*, ed. Ingeborg-Drewitz-Literaturpreis (Zell, 2018), pp. 77–8 (p. 77); and David, 'Meine erste Tat', in *Wir sagen aus (Band 2): Biographische Geschichten und Interviews jugendlicher Gefangener,*

ed. Reinhard Nolle and Anke Hildebrandt (Kassel, 2004), pp. 9–11 (p. 10).

14 Bilal, in *Pop Shop: Gespräche mit Jugendlichen in Haft*, ed. Klaus Jünschke, Jörg Hauenstein and Christiane Ensslin (Hamburg, 2007), p. 14.

15 Ralf Axel Simon, 'moral ist der arglistige versuch der herrschenden', in *Geräusche der Nacht: Literatur aus dem deutschen Strafvollzug*, ed. Ingeborg-Drewitz-Literaturpreis (Münster, 2008), p. 95.

16 Bilal, in *Pop Shop*, ed. Jünschke, Hauenstein and Ensslin, p. 14; Carlos, ibid., p. 175. See also Anke Neuber, 'Der Zusammenhang zwischen Gewalthandeln im Gefängnis und Männlichkeitsentwürfen aus einer subjekttheoretischen Perspektive', in *Entwicklung unter Kontrolle? Biographische Entwürfe und alltägliche Handlungsmuster junger Inhaftierter*, ed. Mechthild Bereswill (Baden-Baden, 2003), pp. 133–54.

17 See Sveinung Sandberg, Sébastien Tutenges and Heith Copes, 'Stories of Violence: a Narrative Criminological Study of Ambiguity', *British Journal of Criminology*, LV/6 (2015), pp. 1168–86 (p. 1174).

18 Baschar, Tamer and Horst, in *Pop Shop*, ed. Jünschke, Hauenstein and Ensslin, pp. 54, 92 and 189.

19 Selim, Baschar and Ismail, in *Pop Shop*, ed. Jünschke, Hauenstein and Ensslin, pp. 48 and 123; Kerim, ibid., p. 36.

20 Anon., 'Un-frei und furcht-bar: Ein Essay', *Der Lichtblick*, CCCLIV (2013), available online at www.schattenblick.de, accessed 10 August 2021.

21 Martin Kotynek, Stephan Lebert and Daniel Müller, 'Die Schlechterungsanstalt', *Zeit Online*, www.zeit.de, 16 August 2012, p. 4.

22 'Tom, '1 Jahr', in *16 Bars Project: Unterdrückte graue Schatten*, ed. Reimund Neufeld, Claudia Franck and Julia Schönstadt (Oberhausen, 2016), p. 55.

23 Ralph, in *Knast*, ed. Kübbeler and Kübbeler, pp. 117–25 (p. 123); Claudia, '4 Jahre', in *16 Bars Project*, ed. Neufeld, Franck and Schönstadt, p. 32; and Oliver, 'Lebenslänglich', ibid., pp. 12–18 (pp. 14–16).

24 Katharina, 'Man geht mit dem, womit man angefangen hat, mit einer Lüge', in *Ich muss zurück ins Rattenloch*, ed. Neufeld and Koch, pp. 113–27 (p. 124); Stefanie, in *Knast*, ed. Kübbeler and Kübbeler, p. 103.

25 Erwin, in *Knast*, ed. Kübbeler and Kübbeler, pp. 39–47 (p. 47); Martin, ibid., pp. 15–24 (p. 17); Ralph, ibid., 123. See also Fergus McNeill, Stephen Farrall, Claire Lightowler and Shadd Maruna, 'How and Why People Stop Offending: Discovering Desistance', Institute for Research and Innovation in Social Services 2012, https://eprints.gla.ac.uk.

26 Stefan Augenstein, 'Getrennt und doch vereint', in *Gemeinsam einsam*, ed. Ingeborg-Drewitz-Literaturpreis (Münster, 2015), p. 45; and John Doe, 'Pépé. Eine Begegnung der besonderen Art', in *Begegnungen in der Welt des Widersinns*, ed. Ingeborg-Drewitz-Literaturpreis, pp. 51–6 (p. 51).

27 Max Z., 'Die Einzigen, die mir geblieben sind, sind die Vögel am Fester', in *Jailbirds: Blicke zum Himmel über den Knast*, ed. Thomas Marin (Freiburg, 2014), pp. 68–9 (p. 69); Reiner, 'Nicht hinter der Mauer verrecken', in *Freiheit gestreift. Texte gegen den Knast: Überwachen – Strafen – Widerstand*, ed. Unrast-Kollektiv, Anares

Nord (Münster, 1995), p. 136; and Sonja, 'Besser im Knast als bei meinem Mann', in *Die schlimmsten Gitter sitzen innen*, ed. Panier, p. 89.

28 J. B. Maelach, 'Gefängnis, das ist kein Ort, es ist ein Zustand!', in *Begegnungen in der Welt des Widersinns*, ed. Ingeborg-Drewitz-Literaturpreis, pp. 29–49 (pp. 31–2).

29 Manuel Matzke, cited in Moritz Geier, 'Sexuelle Gewalt in Gefängnissen: "Keiner kontrolliert, was in den Zellen geschieht"', *Süddeutsche Zeitung*, www.sueddeutsche.de, 25 June 2020.

30 Linus Förster, 'Denn wer schreibt, hat noch die Hoffnung auf ein Weiterleben', in *Begegnungen in der Welt des Widersinns*, ed. Ingeborg-Drewitz-Literaturpreis, pp. 139–58 (pp. 148–9); Niemeyer, 'Knastrevolte in Santa Fu', in *Freiheit gestreift*, ed. Unrast-Kollektiv, p. 83. See also Bernd Maelicke, *Das Knast Dilemma: Wegsperren oder resozialisieren? Eine Streitschrift*, 2nd edn (Frankfurt am Main, 2015), pp. 164–5 and 185–6.

31 J. B. Maelach, 'Gefängnis, das ist kein Ort', in *Begegnungen in der Welt des Widersinns*, ed. Ingeborg-Drewitz-Literaturpreis, pp. 29 and 47.

32 Maelicke, *Das Knast Dilemma*, p. 194; Mario Steiner, 'Die Liebeszellen: über Langzeitbesuche', *Der Lichtblick*, CCCLXIV (2015), pp. 4–5; and see Norbert Kieper, 'Kleine Glosse über einen Langzeitbesuch in der JVA Weiterstadt', *Der Lichtblick*, CCCLXVII (2016), p. 36.

33 Daniel Teich, 'Die Reise ins Ungewisse', in *Gemeinsam Einsam*, ed. Ingeborg-Drewitz-Literaturpreis, pp. 67–8 (p. 68).

34 Helmut Pammler, 'Mein Kind – Fragen', in *Begegnungen in der Welt des Widersinns*, ed. Ingeborg-Drewitz-Literaturpreis, p. 97. Cited with kind permission of Melanie Oster-Daum, Rhein-Mosel Verlag.

35 See Maelicke, *Das Knast-Dilemma*, p. 102; Förster, 'Denn wer schreibt', in *Begegnungen in der Welt des Widersinns*, ed. Ingeborg-Drewitz-Literaturpreis, p. 144.

36 Till Haase, 'Haftstrafe: Mit Kind im Knast', *Deutschlandfunk Nova*, www.deutschlandfunknova.de, 14 January 2020.

37 Gertrud Hardtmann, 'Straftäter müßte man sein', in *Frauen im Gefängnis*, ed. Marlis Dürkop and Gertrud Hardtmann (Frankfurt am Main, 1978), p. 167; and Marta Cruells and Noelia Igareda, *Women, Integration and Prison: An Analysis of the Processes of Sociolabour Integration of Women Prisoners in Europe* (EU Directorate-General for Research, September 2005), p. 40.

38 Nancy, in *16 Bars Project*, ed. Neufeld, Franck and Schönstadt, p. 207; Karina, 'Ich muss zurück ins Rattenloch', in *Ich muss zurück ins Rattenloch*, ed. Neufeld and Koch, pp. 44 and 49–50.

39 Irene Dreier, 'Im Namen des Volkes', in *Themenheft: Literatur aus dem Knast*, ed. Haberfeld/Die Palette, *Die Palette*, III (1987), p. 23. All reasonable attempts were made to contact the copyright owner.

40 Förster, 'Denn wer schreibt', in *Begegnungen in der Welt des Widersinns*, ed. Ingeborg-Drewitz-Literaturpreis, p. 150.

41 D. H., in *Aussagen: Briefe von Strafgefangenen*, ed. Birgitta Wolf (Ebenhausen bei München, 1968), pp. 132–5 (p. 135); and Ewald, in *Knast*, ed. Kübbeler and Kübbeler, p. 89.

42 Jens, in *Knast*, ed. Kübbeler and Kübbeler, p. 94; and see for example Elisabeth Theine and Brigitte Elgeti-Starke, 'Bildung und Qualifizierung', in *Das Gefängnis auf dem Prüfstand*, ed. Maelicke and Suhling, pp. 109–28 (p. 123).

43 See Jörg-Martin Jehle et al., *Legalbewährung nach strafrechtlichen Sanktionen. Eine bundesweite Rückfalluntersuchung 2010 bis 2013 und 2004 bis 2013*, www.bmjv.de (Berlin, 2016).

44 Wurm, 'Knast macht krank', in *Der Lichtblick*, CCCLII (2012), reprinted www.schattenblick.de, accessed 10 August 2021.

45 Cited in Niemeyer, 'Knastrevolte in Santa Fu', in *Freiheit gestreift*, ed. Unrast-Kollektiv, p. 52; see also *Der Lichtblick*, CCCLXXIV (2018), p. 33; and Maelicke, cited in Tanja Karrasch, 'Resozialisierung nach der Haft: Draußen bist du allein', *Spiegel Online*, www.spiegel.de, 19 February 2017.

46 W. G., 'Humanitas', in *Die vierte Kaste. Junge Menschen im Gefängnis*, ed. Birgitta Wolf (Hamburg, 1963), pp. 262–4 (p. 263); and see '"Hartz 4"-Empfänger will zurück in den Knast – der Grund ist abstrus', *Der Westen*, www.derwesten.de, 6 December 2019.

47 Rero W., 'Gegen-Sätze', in *Gemeinsam Einsam*, ed. Ingeborg-Drewitz-Literaturpreis, p. 71. Cited with kind permission of Agenda Verlag.

48 Anon., letter to the *Arbeitskreis kritischer Strafvollzug* (12 May 2012), document on the *Arbeitskreis kritischer Strafvollzug* webpages in September 2018; the website has since been discontinued.

49 See *Wege durch den Knast*, ed. Redaktionskollektiv, p. 152. See also the press release of the Berlin Senate, 'JuMiKo beschließt Einbeziehung von Strafgefangenen und Sicherungsverwahrten in die gesetzliche Rentenversicherung', www.berlin.de/sen/justva/presse, accessed 7 August 2021; Britta Raabe, 'Auch 2020 noch aktuell: Die Forderung nach Einbeziehung von Strafgefangenen in die Rentenversicherung', www.grundrechtekomitee.de, accessed 5 August 2021; and Timo Stukenberg and Olaya Argüeso, '"Made in Germany" – Wer von der Arbeit in Gefängnissen profitiert', *Correctiv: Recherchen für die Gesellschaft*, www.correctiv.org, 21 July 2021.

50 Niemeyer, 'Knastrevolte in Santa Fu', in *Freiheit gestreift*, ed. Unrast-Kollektiv, p. 40. See also 'Entwicklung der durchschnittlichen Löhne/Gehälter 1995 – 2017', available as a PDF online via www.sozialpolitik-aktuell.de, accessed 5 July 2021. Six DM equates to around 3 euros; the average daily rate for a worker outside prison in 1995 was 67 euros. The conversion rate is based on the rate used for the introduction of the euro in 2002.

51 Inge Viett, *Einsprüche: Briefe aus dem Gefängnis* (Hamburg, 1996), p. 94. See also Nationale Stelle zur Verhütung von Folter, *Jahresbericht 2010/2011* (Wiesbaden, 2011), p. 42; and Friedrich Peters, *Alles auf blau: Knasttagebuch* (Leipzig, 2014), pp. 103–4.

52 In Bavaria in 2017, the entire prison estate apparently cost 417 million euros, where the total revenue from prisoner work was just one-tenth of that (41.5 million euros). See 'Im Gefängnis: Häftlinge arbeiten hinter Gittern', *Spiegel Online*, www.spiegel.de, 26 February 2018; and

Timo Stukenberg, 'Arbeitslohn für Strafgefangene', *Deutschlandfunk*, www.deutschlandfunk.de, 18 August 2020.

53 Ayiaz, in *Junge Gefangene – Wir sagen aus (Band 4): Biographische Geschichten, Gedichte und Rap-Songs von jungen Gewalttätern und Gefangenen*, ed. Reinhard Nolle and Maria Bauer (Kassel, 2008), p. 232.

54 Rudolf Josef Bremmer, 'Der Preis der Freiheit ist Einsamkeit', in *Gemeinsam Einsam*, ed. Ingeborg-Drewitz-Literaturpreis, pp. 109–13 (p. 112); Walter, in *Knast*, ed. Kübbeler and Kübbeler, pp. 159–60.

55 Douglas Keay, interview with Margaret Thatcher, *Woman's Own* (31 October 1987), pp. 8–10. See the record in the Thatcher Foundation archive: www.margaretthatcher.org, accessed 1 August 2021.

56 See Reinhard Nolle and Anke Hildebrandt, 'Einleitung', in *Wir sagen aus (Band 3): Biographische Geschichten und Interviews jugendlicher Gewalttäter und Gefangener*, ed. Reinhard Nolle and Anke Hildebrandt (Kassel, 2006), pp. 4–6 (p. 5).

57 Peters, *Alles auf Blau*, p. 5; Philipp von S., 'Provokation', in *Jailbirds*, ed. Marin, pp. 73–4 (p. 73); Ralph, in *Knast*, ed. Kübbeler and Kübbeler, p. 123; and Dietmar, ibid., p. 196.

58 The German title was *Sorge dich nicht, lebe!* See 'Jahresbestseller Sachbücher', 1989 to 1998, in *Der Spiegel*, www.spiegel.de.

59 Buchacker, letter to Drewitz, in Ingeborg Drewitz and Winand Buchacker, *Mit Sätzen Mauern eindrücken: Briefwechsel mit einem Strafgefangenen* (Düsseldorf, 1979), p. 24 (see Chapter Two); and Wurm, 'Knast macht krank', in *Der Lichtblick*, CCCLII (2012), available online at www.schattenblick.de, accessed 10 August 2021.

60 Reiner, 'Nicht hinter der Mauer verrecken', in *Freiheit gestreift*, ed. Unrast-Kollektiv, p. 141.

61 Peter Feraru, 'Ich bin in Worten' in *Gefangenenliteratur: Sprechen – Schreiben – Lesen in deutschen Gefängnissen*, ed. Uta Klein and Helmut Koch (Hagen, 1988), p. 118; Metin Günes, 'Schreibend sterben', in *Wenn Wände erzählen könnten*, ed. Ingeborg-Drewitz-Literaturpreis, pp. 51–3.

62 Karin Amann, 'Eindrücke eines Jury-Mitglieds: Anschreiben gegen die Ohnmacht', in *Gestohlene Himmel: Widerstehen im Knast*, ed. Ingeborg-Drewitz-Literaturpreis (Leipzig, 1995), pp. 12–15 (p. 13); and see Anon. [Karlheinz Barwasser], 'Sich als starke Mauern begreifen – Schreiben im Knast', in *Ungehörte Worte. Gefangene schreiben: Eine Dokumentation*, ed. Helmut H. Koch and Regine Lindtke (Münster, 1982), pp. 107–11 (pp. 107–8).

63 Thomas Galli, 'Von Mensch zu Mensch', in *Begegnungen in der Welt des Widersinns*, ed. Ingeborg-Drewitz-Literaturpreis (Zell, 2018), p. 11.

Afterword: The Mirror and the Microcosm

1 Nelson Mandela, *The Long Walk to Freedom: The Autobiography of Nelson Mandela* (Boston, MA, 1994), p. 201.

2 Peter Zingler, 'LESEN IM KNAST oder "Nur wer selbst will kommt weiter"', in *16 Bars Project: Unterdrückte graue Schatten*,

ed. Reimund Neufeld, Claudia Franck and Julia Schönstadt (Oberhausen, 2016), p. 8.

3 C. Fred Alford, 'What Would It Matter if Everything Foucault Said about Prison Were Wrong? *Discipline and Punish* after Twenty Years', *Theory and Society*, XXIX (2000), pp. 125–46 (p. 127); see also *Wege durch den Knast*, ed. Redaktionskollektiv (Berlin, 2016), p. 141.

4 Marianne Herzog, *Nicht den Hunger verlieren* (Berlin, 1980), p. 107.

5 Harry, in *16 Bars Project*, ed. Neufeld, Franck and Schönstadt, p. 148.

6 A. P., 'Brief an den Staatsanwalt', in *Die vierte Kaste. Junge Menschen im Gefängnis*, ed. Birgitta Wolf (Hamburg, 1963), pp. 144–9 (pp. 145–7); H., ibid., p. 274.

7 Birgitta Wolf, 'Einführung', in *Die vierte Kaste*, ed. Wolf, pp. 7–53 (pp. 7 and 24).

8 Peter, in *Lebenslänglich: Protokolle aus der Haft*, ed. Klaus Antes, Christiane Ehrhardt and Heinrich Hannover (Munich, 1972), p. 84; Klaus Jünschke, 'Amnestie für alle', TAZ, www.taz.de, 11 October 1990.

9 Gresham M. Sykes, *The Society of Captives: A Study of a Maximum Security Prison* [1958] (Princeton, NJ, 2007), p. 8.

10 Hannah Arendt, *The Origins of Totalitarianism* (New York, 1966), p. 451.

11 Primo Levi, *If This Is a Man*, trans. Stuart Woolf (London, 1979), p. 35. Emphasis in original.

12 Erich Loest, *Durch die Erde ein Riß: Ein Lebenslauf* (Hamburg, 1981), pp. 395–6.

13 See Michel Foucault, *Discipline and Punish: The Birth of the Prison*, trans. Alan Sheridan [1977] (London, 1991); and Michelle Brown, *The Culture of Punishment: Prison, Society, and Spectacle* (New York, 2009), p. 119.

14 André Baganz, *Endstation Bautzen II: Zehn Jahre lebenslänglich* (Halle, 2011), pp. 122–4; Erich Loest, *Durch die Erde ein Riß: Ein Lebenslauf* (Hamburg, 1981), pp. 395–6.

15 Carola Schacht, 'Ich wurde während des Prozesses fast nur angeschrien', in *Hohenecker Protokolle: Aussagen zur Geschichte der politischen Verfolgung von Frauen in der DDR*, ed. Ulrich Schacht, 2nd edn (Leipzig, 2009), pp. 152–91 (p. 159); Kerstin Hegert, 'Das Begreifen, daß die Dummen die Macht haben', ibid., pp. 245–56.

16 Rita, in *16 Bars Project*, ed. Neufeld, Franck and Schönstadt, p. 135.

17 Reiner, 'Nicht hinter der Mauer verrecken, war meine Perspektive. Sie haben es nicht geschafft, mich in diesem Gefühl zu brechen', in *Freiheit gestreift. Texte gegen den Knast: Überwachen – Strafen – Widerstand*, ed. Unrast-Kollektiv, Anares Nord (Münster, 1995), pp. 133–59 (p. 135); and see the description of Tegel II in *Der Lichtblick*, CCLXXII (2017), p. 33; and Klaus Jünschke, 'Tod in Siegburg', *Neue Rheinische Zeitung Online Flyer*, 71, www.nrhz.de, 21 November 2006.

18 Thomas Galli, 'Von Mensch zu Mensch', in *Begegnungen in der Welt des Widersinns*, ed. Ingeborg-Drewitz-Literaturpreis (Zell, 2018), p. 11.

19 Hartmut Kahle, 'One Day, Baby', in *Begegnungen in der Welt des Widersinns*, ed. Ingeborg-Drewitz-Literaturpreis, pp. 99–106 (p. 101).

20 Maelicke, cited in Tanja Karrasch, 'Resozialisierung nach der Haft:

Draußen bist du allein', *Spiegel Online*, www.spiegel.de, 19 February 2017; Sabine Thiesen, 'Wer bin ich?' in *Gemeinsam einsam*, ed. Ingeborg-Drewitz-Literaturpreis (Münster, 2015), pp. 119–20 (p. 120).

21 Ralf Axel Simon, *Worte sind meine brand-Sätze (sic) gegen eure Knastmachinerie und 5 Literaturpreise meine Steine gegen eure modernen Panzer* (Hamburg, 2012), p. 11; Thiesen, 'Wer bin ich?', in *Gemeinsam einsam*, ed. Ingeborg-Drewitz-Literaturpreis, p. 119.

22 Paul St John, 'Behind the Mirror's Face', in *Doing Time: 25 Years of Prison Writing*, ed. Bell Gale Chevigny (New York, 1999), pp. 119–25 (p. 121).

23 See H. Bruce Franklin, *The Victim as Criminal and Artist: Literature from the American Prison* (New York and London, 1978). A paperback (revised and expanded) edition was published as *Prison Literature in America: The Victim as Criminal and Artist* (Westport, CT, 1982); the anthology was the fifth edition of the *Heath Anthology of American Literature*. See Franklin, 'The Inside Stories of the Global American Prison', *Texas Studies in Literature and Language*, 50 (2008), pp. 235–42 (p. 239).

24 Phillip Barrish (guest editor), *Texas Studies in Literature and Language*, L (2008); *PMLA*, CXXIII (2008); *American Book Review*, XXXVI/3 (March/April 2015); Michelle Kelly and Claire Westall, eds, *Prison Writing and the Literary World: Imprisonment, Institutionality and Questions of Literary Practice* (London and New York, 2021).

25 Helmut H. Koch, 'Geräusche der Nacht: Anmerkungen zum Ingeborg-Drewitz-Literaturpreis 2008', in *Geräusche der Nacht*, ed. Ingeborg-Drewitz-Literaturpreis, pp. 113–23 (p. 122).

Further Reading

In English

Alexander, Myrl E., and John W. Roberts, 'Rebuilding a Prison System: Germany, 1945–46', *Federal Prisons Journal*, II/2 (1991), pp. 37–43

Colvin, Sarah, 'Dancing through the Next Minefield; or, How and Why Should We Read the Stories of German Women Prisoners?', *German Life and Letters*, CXVII (2014), pp. 589–603

—, 'Why Should Criminology Care about Literary Fiction? Literature, Life Narratives, and Telling Untellable Stories', *Punishment and Society*, XVII (2015), pp. 211–29

—, 'Unerhört? Prisoner Narratives as Unlistened-To Stories (and Some Reflections on the Picaresque)', in *Modern Language Review*, CXII (2017), pp. 440–58

Cradle Community, *Brick by Brick: How We Build a World without Prisons* (London, 2021)

Eghigian, Greg, *The Corrigible and the Incorrigible: Science, Medicine and the Convict in Twentieth-Century Germany* (Ann Arbor, MI, 2015)

Foucault, Michel, *Discipline and Punish: The Birth of the Prison*, trans. Alan Sheridan [1977] (London, 1991)

Franklin, H. Bruce, *Prison Literature in America: The Victim as Criminal and Artist* (Westport, CT, 1982)

Gelfand, Elissa D., *Imagination in Confinement: Women's Writings from French Prisons* (Ithaca, NY, 1983)

Giles, Geoffrey J., '"The Most Unkindest Cut of All": Castration, Homosexuality and Nazi Justice', *Journal of Contemporary History*, XXVII/1 (1992), pp. 41–61

Haslam, Jason, *Fitting Sentences: Identity in Nineteenth- and Twentieth-Century Prison Narratives* (Toronto, 2005)

Jones, Sara, *The Media of Testimony: Remembering the East German Stasi in the Berlin Republic* (Basingstoke, 2014)

Kelly, Michelle, and Claire Westall, eds, *Prison Writing and the Literary World: Imprisonment, Institutionality and Questions of Literary Practice* (London and New York, 2021)

Miller, D. Quentin, ed., *Prose and Cons: Essays on Prison Literature in the United States* (Jefferson, NC, 2005), pp. 246–71

Phillips, Coretta, *The Multicultural Prison: Ethnicity, Masculinity, and Social Relations among Prisoners* (Oxford, 2012)
Presser, Lois, *Been a Heavy Life: Stories of Violent Men* (Chicago, IL, 2008)
—, and Sveinung Sandberg, eds, *Narrative Criminology: Understanding Stories of Crime* (New York, 2015)
Richmond, Kim, *Women Political Prisoners in Germany: Narratives of Self and Captivity, 1915–91* (London, 2016)
Rodriguez, Dylan, *Forced Passages: Imprisoned Radical Intellectuals and the U.S. Prison Regime* (Minneapolis, MN, 2005)
Rowe, Carolyn, and Ed Turner, 'Justice and Prisons Policy', in *Die Politik der Bundesländer: Zwischen Föderalismusreform und Schuldenbremse*, ed. Achim Hildebrandt and Frieder Wolf, 2nd expanded edn (Wiesbaden, 2016), pp. 87–114
Schwan, Anne, *Convict Voices: Women, Class, and Writing about Prison in Nineteenth-Century England* (Durham, NH, 2014)
Sykes, Gresham M., *The Society of Captives: A Study of a Maximum Security Prison* [1958] (Princeton, NJ, 2007)
Vormbaum, Thomas, and Michael Bohlander, eds, *A Modern History of German Criminal Law*, trans. Margaret Hiley (Heidelberg, 2014)
Würtenberger, Thomas, 'Criminology and Penology in Western Germany', *British Journal of Delinquency*, XXVI (1953–4), pp. 26–38

In German

Baganz, André, *Endstation Bautzen II: Zehn Jahre lebenslänglich* (Halle, 2011)
Becker, Hubertus, *Ritual Knast: Die Niederlage des Gefängnisses – eine Bestandsaufnahme* (Leipzig, 2008)
Berndt, Sandra, *Haftautobiographik im 20. Jahrhundert* (Frankfurt am Main, 2016)
Dölling, Birger, *Strafvollzug zwischen Wende und Wiedervereinigung: Kriminalpolitik und Gefangenenprotest im letzten Jahr der DDR* (Berlin, 2009)
Einsele, Helga, *Mein Leben mit Frauen in Haft* (Stuttgart, 1994)
Galli, Thomas, *Knast oder Heimat? Erzählungen von Recht und Unrecht* (Zell/Mosel, 2019)
—, *Weggesperrt – Warum Gefängnisse niemandem nützen* (Hamburg, 2020)
Garve, Roland, *Unter Mördern: Gefängnisalltag in der DDR* [1999] (Berlin, 2014)
Glebe, Dirk, *Handbuch Knast und Strafvollzug: (Über-)leben im deutschen Gefängnis*, 2nd edn (Norderstedt, 2011)
Ingeborg-Drewitz-Literaturpreis für Gefangene, ed., *Risse im Fegefeuer* (Hagen, 1989)
—, *Fesselballon* (Münster, 1992)
—, *Gestohlener Himmel: Widerstehen im Knast* (Leipzig, 1995)
—, *Wenn Wände erzählen könnten* (Münster, 1999)
—, *Nachrichten aus Anderwelt* (Münster, 2002)
—, *Geräusche der Nacht: Literatur aus dem deutschen Strafvollzug 2008* (Münster, 2008)

—, *In jeder Nacht lacht der Teufel leise* (Oberhausen, 2011)
—, *Gemeinsam einsam* (Münster, 2015)
—, *Begegnungen in der Welt des Widersinns* (Zell, 2018)
Keßler, Nicola, *Schreiben, um zu überleben: Studien zur Gefangenenliteratur* (Mönchengladbach, 2001)
—, et al., eds, *Menschen im Gefängnis: Literarische Selbstzeugnisse, authentische Texte und Materialien für den schulischen und außerschulischen Unterricht* (Bonn, 1996)
Knabe, Hubertus, ed., *Gefangen in Hohenschönhausen: Stasi-Häftlinge berichten* (Berlin, 2007)
Koch, Petra, *Menschenwege: Politisch inhaftiert auf Burg Hoheneck: Eine wahre Geschichte* (Berlin, 2002)
Krause, Thomas, *Geschichte des Strafvollzugs: Von den Kerkern des Altertums bis zur Gegenwart* (Darmstadt, 1999)
Kübbeler, Brigitte, and Dieter Kübbeler, eds, *Knast: Eine Dokumentation* (Oldenburg, 2003)
Laubenthal, Klaus, *Strafvollzug*, 6th edn (Heidelberg, 2011)
Maelicke, Bernd, and Stefan Suhling, eds, *Das Gefängnis auf dem Prüfstand: Zustand und Zukunft des Strafvollzugs* (Wiesbaden, 2018)
Marin, Thomas, ed., *Jailbirds: Blicke zum Himmel über den Knast* (Freiburg, 2014)
Nayhauß, Dirk von, and Maggie Riepl, eds, *Der dunkle Ort: 25 Schicksale aus dem DDR-Frauengefängnis Hoheneck* (Berlin-Brandenburg, 2012)
Neufeld, Reimund, and Helmut Koch, eds, *Ich muß zurück ins Rattenloch: Unerhörte Geschichten aus dem Frauenknast* (Oberhausen, 2010)
—, Claudia Franck and Julia Schönstadt, eds, *16 Bars Project: Unterdrückte graue Schatten* (Oberhausen, 2016)
Panier, Karin, ed., *Die schlimmsten Gitter sitzen innen: Geschichten aus dem Frauenknast* (Berlin, 2004)
Peters, Friedrich, *Alles auf blau: Knasttagebuch* (Leipzig, 2014)
Redaktionskollektiv, ed., *Wege durch den Knast* (Berlin, 2016)
Riemann, Erika, *Die Schleife an Stalins Bart. Ein Mädchenstreich, acht Jahre Haft und die Zeit danach* [2002] (Hamburg, 2017)
Schacht, Ulrich, ed., *Hohenecker Protokolle: Aussagen zur Geschichte der politischen Verfolgung von Frauen in der DDR*, 2nd edn (Leipzig, 2009)
Schlicke, Birgit, *Knast-Tagebuch: Erinnerung einer politischen Gefangenen an Stasi-Haft und das Frauenzuchthaus Hoheneck* (Wiesbaden, 2001)
Unrast-Kollektiv Anares Nord, ed., *Freiheit gestreift – Texte gegen den Knast: Überwachen, Strafen, Widerstand* (Münster, 1995)
Vormbaum, Thomas, *Einführung in die moderne Strafrechtsgeschichte*, 3rd edn (Heidelberg, 2016)
Wensierski, Peter, *Schläge im Namen des Herrn: Die verdrängte Geschichte der Heimkinder in der Bundesrepublik* (Munich and Hamburg, 2006)
Wunschik, Tobias, *Knastware für den Klassenfeind: Häftlingsarbeit in der DDR, der Ost-West-Handel und die Staatssicherheit (1970–1989)* (Göttingen, 2014)

Acknowledgements

Sincere thanks are due to the Leverhulme Trust, which supported a critical first year of research on this book. Thanks, too, to the Schroder Foundation and to my colleagues in Medieval and Modern Languages and Linguistics and at Jesus College, Cambridge, for actively enabling an environment where 'difficult' research is supported.

When I started this project the world of the prison was foreign to me, and I needed to address that. In Scotland I was a participant-researcher for drama projects with young men in HMYOI Polmont, and my thanks go to Edinburgh's Traverse Theatre and to the young men we worked with for the insights gained on that project. Later, in the context of the year-long *Inspiring Change* project that brought a range of arts projects to five Scottish prisons, I was fortunate to work with a phenomenal team from Glasgow's Citizens Theatre and with women held in HMP Greenock, as well as with an inspiring group of academics: Kirstin Anderson, Fergus McNeill, Mike Nellis, Katie Overy, Richard Sparks and Lynn Tett. My thanks to all of them, and to Kirsten Sams, whose energy made the entire project happen. In Germany, the Berlin prison theatre company Theater aufBruch let me attend a rehearsal and two of their shows in Tegel prison (*Kohlhaas* in 2010 and *Wallenstein's Death* in 2013), and talk with prison officers and the men involved, another experience for which I am extremely grateful. (Some of that experience is recorded in my article 'Why Should Criminology Care about Literary Fiction? Literature, Life Narratives and Telling Untellable Stories', *Punishment and Society*, XVII/2 (2015), pp. 211–29.) In Cambridge I was fortunate to contribute to the phenomenal 'Learning Together' project led by Ruth Armstrong and Amy Ludlow. Since 2014 I have served on the steering committee (now advisory group) for the National Criminal Justice Arts Alliance, and my thanks go to all my colleagues and friends past and present in that visionary and resilient organization.

For the moral and intellectual support, advice, conversations and references that sustained me as I finished this challenging project, my huge gratitude goes to Cary Parker, Christopher Parker-Colvin, Mark Taplin, Jo Whaley, Preti Taneja, Sander Gilman, Andy Watson OBE, Andrew Wilkie, Thomas Galli, Johannes Feest, Katharina Karcher, Stephanie Galasso,

Naomi Reiss, Nick Courtman, Kathrin Wunderlich and Michael Leaman of Reaktion Books.

Gaining permission to cite and reproduce material in this book was often a uplifting experience, as many of those who generously gave their permission also shared memories and/or sent good wishes for the work. Sincere thanks in particular to Ludwig Lugmeier, Kristian Wachinger, J. Monika Walther, Erol Gurian, Philipp Khabo Koepsell, Marie Bicker, Alexander Boger, Carl Werner Wendland, Monika Thiele, Melanie Oster-Daum and Dirk van Bitteren.

Photo Acknowledgements

The author and publishers wish to thank the relevant organizations and individuals listed below for authorizing reproduction of their work.

Alamy: pp. 28 (Granger – Historical Picture Archive), 69 (World History Archive), 71 (Brigitte Friedrich/Sueddeutsche Zeitung Photo), 91 (dpa picture alliance); Bundesarchiv/German Federal Archives: pp. 33, 50, 181; Getty Images: p. 38 (Gert Kreutschmann/Ullstein bild via Getty Images); Erol Gurian: pp. 15, 210; Stiftung Sächsischer Gedenkstätten: p. 137; Wikimedia Commons: pp. 8 and 223 (GeoTrinity/CC-BY-SA 3.0 Unported), 23 (Sue Gardner/CC BY-SA 4.0 International), 32 (Public Domain), 36 (Arthur Szyk/The Arthur Szyk Society, Burlingame, CA (www.szyk.org)/CC BY-SA 4.0 International), 66 (Public Domain), 89 (US Department of Defense/ Public Domain), 102 (Rüdiger Trautsch/ Schwules Museum, Berlin/CC-BY-SA 3.0 Unported), 112 (Brück & Sohn Kunstverlag/Meißen/CC-BY-SA 3.0 Unported), 121 (United States Information Service, Department of State/Public Domain), 126 (Benutzer Knarf-bz/Public Domain), 131 and 142 (Max Wahrhaftig/CC-BY-SA 3.0 Unported), 134 (Stefan Kühn/CC0 1.0 Universal Public Domain Dedication), 149 (US Army/Public Domain), 154 (Stephencdickson/CC BY-SA 4.0 International), 195 (Fridolin Freudenfett/ CC BY-SA 4.0 International).

Index

Page numbers in *italics* indicate illustrations